EDMUND KEAN

Fire from Heaven

EDMUND KEAN

Fire from Heaven

BY

RAYMUND FITZSIMONS

TAMERLANE: The world, 'twould be too little for thy pride,
Thou would'st scale heaven?
BAJAZET: I would—away!—my soul disdains the
conference.
NICHOLAS ROWE, *Tamerlane.*

THE DIAL PRESS
1976
NEW YORK

*Originally published in Great Britain
by Hamish Hamilton Ltd.*
Copyright © 1976 by Raymund FitzSimons

Manufactured in the United States of America
First American printing 1976

Library of Congress Cataloging in Publication Data

Fitzsimons, Raymund.
    Edmund Kean, fire from heaven.

    Bibliography: p.
    Includes index.
    1. Kean, Edmund, 1787-1833. I. Title.
PN2598.K3F44   792'.028'0924 [B]   76-176
ISBN 0-8037-4533-8

to Mary, with love

CONTENTS

CONTENTS

ILLUSTRATIONS

Between pages 114 *and* 115

AUTHOR'S NOTE

I HAVE attempted to tell the story of Edmund Kean and to re-create, along the way, some of the most exciting moments in the history of the English theatre. If my pages do not bristle with references and footnotes, this is not from lack of research: my sources should be evident from the text and bibliography. But, while dealing fully with Kean's achievement in the theatre, I have been anxious not to impede the flow of the narrative, for I believe that the strange story of this tortured man has an interest far beyond that of the theatre historian.

There are five substantial biographies of Kean, three written in the nineteenth century and two in the twentieth. The three earlier ones are inaccurate on many points. The two later ones—*Edmund Kean*, by Harold Newcomb Hillebrand, published in 1933, and *Kean*, by Giles Playfair, published in 1939—seek to establish the truth about him. My book is a continuation of that search; it contains new facts and new interpretations of events in his life. I do not claim to have discovered the whole truth about him; it is doubtful if this will ever be known.

My chief source has been the Diaries of James Winston. None of the other biographers made use of these manuscripts, which give an intimate account of Kean's behaviour from 1819 to 1827, when he was a great star at Drury Lane. The Diaries were used by Maurice Willson Disher for his fictionalised life of Kean, *Mad Genius*, published in 1950, but mine is the first biography of the actor to be based on them. I am grateful to the Henry E. Huntington Library for permission to quote from the Diaries, and to Alfred L. Nelson and B. Gilbert Cross, of Eastern Michigan University, for showing me their transcripts of all entries relating to Kean. I am especially grateful to Professor Nelson for allowing me to read his doctoral dissertation on James Winston.

My study of Kean led me to believe that much of his eccentric
behaviour could have been caused by his medical condition. I,
therefore, prepared an abstract of all references to his health and
sent this, together with his autopsy report, to Mary Mackenzie
Munro, a distinguished pathologist. I am grateful to her for an
expert evaluation of this data. While she shares my view that Kean
had enough organic disease to account for much of his temperamental trouble, this does not mean that she is necessarily in agreement with the conclusions I put forward.

Every biographer of Kean comes up against the unsolved
question of the date of his birth. I have accepted Professor Hillebrand's assessment of the evidence, which places the probable date
at 4 November 1787. In doing this, I am aware of Mr. Playfair's
subsequent research, which led him to give the date as 17 March
1789. In effect, however, Mr. Playfair's only additional evidence
of any merit is a passport belonging to Kean, issued in Dieppe,
in 1817. In this, Kean gives his age as twenty-eight, which places
his date of birth in 1789. This, in itself, is insufficient to upset
Professor Hillebrand's assessment. Kean was notoriously inaccurate about his age, if, indeed, he knew the truth of it himself.
Varying dates were given by him at different times throughout
his life and my own research has revealed yet another. James
Winston states: 'Kean was born January 19, 1788, from his own
writing given to Smith of British Museum.' This date differs by
only eleven weeks from 4 November 1787 and I have accepted
the earlier date to avoid confusing the question even more.

During the three years I have worked on this book, I have
placed myself in the debt of several people and institutions, in
addition to those already mentioned. I am grateful to Christopher
Murray, of University College Dublin, for showing me the relevant chapters from the manuscript of his forthcoming book,
Robert William Elliston, Manager: a Theatrical Biography to
the Folger Shakespeare Library for permission to quote from
the contracts drawn up between Elliston and Kean; to the Society
for Theatre Research for putting me in touch with sources of
information and, in particular, to George Speaight and Jack
Reading; to Margaret Brander and Ernest Wilkinson, of the

Cumbria County Library, for answering my many queries; to Robert Eddison; to Raymond Mander and Joe Mitchenson; to my wife, Anne, for her help with the research; and to Edwina Fraser for the impeccable typing of my manuscript. Finally, I am grateful to Christopher Calthrop for the interest he has taken throughout the writing of this book and for his generosity in allowing me to call on his help whenever I needed it.

CHAPTER ONE

THE AGING PRODIGY

SAMUEL TAYLOR COLERIDGE said that to see Edmund Kean act was 'like reading Shakespeare by flashes of lightning'. Douglas Jerrold said that his performance as Shylock impressed audiences 'like a chapter of Genesis'. William Hazlitt said that, as Othello, his voice 'struck on the heart like the swelling notes of some divine music, like the sound of years of departed happiness'. Kean was a tragedian of genius and, strangely enough, the tragedy of his own life has the power to arouse the same emotions as those he aroused in his audiences.

Generations of theatre historians have attempted to separate fact from fiction in his life, but the truth remains as bizarre as the legends. The brilliance of his success is heightened by the obscurity of his early life. No information exists which can be used with confidence and certainly no reliance can be placed on the accounts of his childhood given by Kean himself. If his picturesque stories could be believed, he would be as great a Romantic hero as he was a Romantic actor: he always claimed the Duke of Norfolk as his father.

Even the date of his birth is uncertain and, again, Kean is not to be trusted on this point, for he always made himself out to be younger than he was. The weight of the evidence suggests that he was born in London, on 4 November 1787. He was the son of Edmund Kean and Ann Carey. His father was the youngest of three brothers of Irish descent. All the brothers were unmarried and lived with their widowed sister, Mrs. Price. Nothing is known of Aaron, the eldest brother, beyond the fact that he was a drunkard, but Moses, the second brother, enjoyed a reputation in the theatre as a ventriloquist and mimic. Edmund was articled to a firm of surveyors. It was while his firm was building the Royalty Theatre that he first met Ann Carey.

Ann, or Nance, as she preferred to be called, had run away from home, at the age of fifteen, to join a company of strolling players. She was the daughter of George Savile Carey, an entertainer. Nance was not a very good actress, but her sluttish good looks were useful in other directions and when her services as an actress were not in demand, she made a living by street hawking and occasional prostitution. Edmund and Nance slept together and she became pregnant.

When the child was born, Nance put him out to nurse and returned to her roving life. The boy was neglected by his nurse and, by the time he was two years old, his condition had become so pitiful that his uncle, Moses Kean, intervened. The boy's father had become incapable of doing anything for him; like his eldest brother, he was now a hopeless drunkard. The boy was cared for by his aunt, Mrs. Price, until he was four years old, when Moses put him·in the care of Charlotte Tidswell.

Charlotte was Moses' mistress. He was not her first lover; she had previously been the mistress of the Duke of Norfolk. This was the notorious Charles Howard, the eleventh Duke, a gross, drink-sodden creature, who was reputed to have sired almost as many bastards as Charles II. When he had tired of her, he had used his influence to get her a position as supporting actress at the Theatre Royal, Drury Lane. In 1791, when young Edmund Kean went to live with her, she was thirty years old. Aunt Tid, as he called her, was to have a great influence on him, for through her he was first introduced to the world of the theatre.

Drury Lane Theatre was being rebuilt and the company were accommodated at the King's Theatre, in the Haymarket. Charlotte used to take the boy with her and he played behind the stage, while she rehearsed. The company made a fuss of him; he was cuddled and kissed by the actresses. He was an attractive child, slim and pale, with dark eyes and a superb head of black curly hair. It is not surprising that he was soon playing child parts.

His first appearance probably coincided with the first dramatic production at the new Drury Lane Theatre, on Monday, 21 April 1794. This was a great occasion. Richard Brinsley Sheridan, the lessee, had commissioned Henry Holland to tear down old Drury and build in its place a new theatre of unsurpassed splendour. It was generally agreed that Holland had succeeded in his task. Tier upon tier of seats rose to a lofty ceiling; the whole effect was spacious and breathtaking. Unfortunately, in carrying out Sheridan's grandiose ideas, the architect had designed a building that was totally unsuited to its purpose. The gallery was so far away that the actors had to shout at the top of their voices to make themselves heard; from some parts of the auditorium, the audience were unable to see the stage; the seating capacity of 3,611 was much too large and the theatre was rarely ever to be more than half-filled. Even the highly publicised fire precautions—the iron curtain and the reservoir of water—were to prove of little use when the theatre burned to the ground fifteen years later.

As the new theatre was dedicated to the memory of Shakespeare, many people had argued that the opening should have been delayed until the Wednesday, which was the birthday of the poet; but there were pressing reasons why Sheridan could not delay the opening by even a couple of days. The estimated building cost had been £150,000, but, with characteristic extravagance, he had exceeded this by £70,000. He had raised the money by methods that created far more difficulties than they solved and that were eventually to lead to the most spectacular bankruptcy in the history of the English theatre.

Drury Lane opened with a lavish production of *Macbeth*. John Philip Kemble and his sister, Mrs. Siddons, played their famous roles. The scenery and costumes had been specially designed; there were ballets of goblins and spirits; glittering serpents coiled themselves round the bodies of the witches. During the incantation scene in the fourth act, a band of infant goblins scurried on stage and lined up at the mouth of the cave. Kean was the goblin at the end of the row. He knocked against his fellow goblin and the whole line tumbled like a pack of cards. The audience laughed and the effect of the scene was ruined. This unfortunate début did not prevent him from making other occasional appearances at Drury Lane, usually as an imp or a monkey in the pantomimes.

Moses Kean had died in December 1792 and his brother Edmund, who had been deeply attached to him, sank into a depression from which he never recovered. A few months later, he killed himself by jumping from the roof of his home. His son continued to be cared for by Charlotte Tidswell, but, as a regular actress, she was unable to give him all the time he needed. When she was not at home, he ran wild in the streets, without shoes or stockings. She sent him to school, but he often played truant. He was quick-witted and intelligent, but he would not respond to discipline. He was stubborn and self-willed; if he did not get what he wanted, he ran away. Sometimes he would be missing for as long as a week, sleeping in trees and anywhere he could find. Once she found him in a tavern at Vauxhall, singing to the customers in return for food and lodging. He refused to return home and she had to drag him back by a rope round his waist, as though he were a wild beast. Sometimes she had to lash him to the bed to prevent him from escaping and she was even driven to put a dog's collar round his neck, with the inscription, 'Bring this boy to Miss Tidswell, 12 Tavistock Row'.

He was happiest when he was at Drury Lane, being petted by the company and amusing them with his impersonations. In this respect, he was very precocious. Mrs. Charles Kemble recalled hearing a noise in the theatre one night and was told, 'It is only young Kean reciting Richard III in the green-room; he's acting after the manner of Garrick. Will you go and see him? He is really very clever.' Some members of the company encouraged his interest in the theatre. Incledon, the music-master, gave him lessons at odd times, as did D'Egville, the dancing-master. Angelo, the fencing-master, showed him how to handle a sword and the pantomimists taught him the art of tumbling.

But when he was nine years old, his association with Drury Lane came to an end. Nance, who had visited him occasionally in the past, now turned up to reclaim him completely. She did this not from any belated urge to do her duty by the child, but simply because he was now old enough to be of use to her. She took him with her on the road, together with his half-brother and half-sister, Henry and Phoebe, who were her bastards by a man named Darnley. Nance and her ill-begotten family made a living by street hawking and performing in strolling companies. They were, at times, members of Richardson's and Saunders' companies, troupes which visited every fair and market within a hundred miles of London, performing melodramas and pantomimes in competition with dwarfs, mermaids and educated pigs. In these troupes, Kean acted, sang and tumbled a dozen times daily.

Nance soon realised that the boy had talent and she exploited this by launching him as an infant prodigy. At this time, prodigies were enjoying a vogue which was to culminate six years later in the Master Betty craze. These prodigies recited scenes from famous plays. They usually performed in private homes and small entertainment halls, although the more successful ones appeared occasionally at Drury Lane and Covent Garden. From 1798, when he was eleven years old, Kean was mainly in London, earning his living as a prodigy. Nance was his manager and he was using her family name, Carey. A glimpse of him around this time is given by Charles Mayne Young, the actor. Young's father, a surgeon, was giving a dinner party and, as Young came downstairs, he noticed a slatternly woman, with a boy beside her, waiting in the hall. The boy had 'the blackest and most penetrating eyes he had ever beheld in a human head'. At first, he thought they were gipsies, from Bartholomew Fair, come for medical advice, but, after dinner, the boy was brought in to entertain the company. On another occasion at Dr. Young's house, Nance met Mrs. Clarke, a middle-class lady, who had known her father. Mrs. Clarke was not taken with '*Miss* Carey', as she was introduced, describing her as 'a rather graceful figure of a young woman, in exceedingly shabby attire, set off with faded finery, and cheeks highly rouged, though it was mid-day'.

During the time he had been associated with Nance, Kean had come to resent her; he was old enough to realise that she was little more than a prostitute and that her only interest in him was what she could get out of him. This is probably the reason why he began to wish that Charlotte Tidswell was his mother. When he learned of her former relationship with the Duke of Norfolk, he was to conceive the romantic idea that he was one of the Duke's many bastards. This was the story he put about when he became famous. Aunt Tid denied it and so did the Duke himself, but

Kean could never be shaken in his conviction that it was true. He found it infinitely preferable to think of himself as the son of a noble lord and an actress than that of a suicidal drunkard and a money-grasping whore.

His reputation as a prodigy continued to grow and, by 1801, he was advertised as 'The Celebrated Theatrical Child'. His most virtuoso performance was a recitation of the whole of *The Merchant of Venice*. As the degree of admiration given to the performance of child prodigies was in direct ratio to their age, it was not uncommon for them to falsify their date of birth. The varying ages attributed to Kean on the playbills around this time, with the intention of making him out to be younger than he was, have confused theatre historians in their attempts to establish his true age.

His success as a prodigy made him difficult to handle; he was constantly having rows with Nance over money. He believed, with some justice, that he was keeping the whole family. On 18 May 1802, he performed at Covent Garden, reciting in the interval between the tragedy and the farce. This was to be the zenith of his career as a prodigy; no golden contract followed and he returned to the small entertainment halls. He was anxious to break with Nance and he knew that he was becoming too old to continue much longer as a prodigy. Shortly after his appearance at Covent Garden, he ran away from London to try his luck in the provinces.

At this time, the English provincial theatre was in its heyday. In the fourteen years which had elapsed since 1788, when Parliament passed the Act legalising acting in the provinces, many new theatres had been built and companies had flourished. Prior to this, they had suffered much harassment from the law, culminating in the Licensing Act of 1737, which abolished the right of all provincial companies to act for reward and again branded players as rogues and vagabonds. But now the provinces were booming; they commanded most of the theatrical talent of the time. Drury Lane and Covent Garden looked to the provinces for their recruits. Bath, Liverpool and Dublin were important centres.

Engagements there were eagerly sought after, for they were regarded as stepping stones to London.

Early success as a prodigy had spoiled Kean and he was looking for instant fame in the provinces. He expected the managers to give him leading roles right away. He believed that what was good enough for London would be more than good enough for the provinces. But no reputable manager would take him on such terms. To them he was that most pathetic of creatures, an aging prodigy living on his past reputation. None of the leading companies would employ him and he was forced to look for work among the smaller circuits.

The provincial theatre worked on a circuit system. A company adopted a number of towns in their district, which they visited regularly. One town became the headquarters and the circuit was so arranged that towns could be visited during busy periods, such as race meetings and assize weeks. The season in principal towns lasted from two to four months. The chief circuit companies concentrated on large towns, leaving the smaller ones to lesser circuits. One great advantage of the circuit system to an actor was the security it offered him. Salaries were low, but at least they were regular. Some players were on the payroll of a company for twenty years or more. They brought in their children, who started to appear on the stage at the age of three or four. Some of the smaller companies in which Kean played were very much family affairs. Nepotism was common and he soon discovered that it was not always the best actor who got the leading roles.

It was a hard life. Performances began around five o'clock in the evening and lasted five or six hours. Audiences expected not only acting but also singing, dancing, mime and fencing. A performance would comprise a five-act tragedy or comedy, followed by at least one afterpiece, such as a farce or a pantomime. In addition, there were interludes of singing, dancing and recitations. Audiences demanded a frequent change of programme and so the companies had large repertoires, performing more than a hundred plays and afterpieces in a year.

In the provinces, as in London, all classes of society went to the theatre and the separation into box, pit and gallery corresponded to the social division into upper, middle and lower class. Audiences were badly behaved and often violent. They showed their disapproval by pelting the players with oranges and, when especially roused, by breaking up the benches. They demanded humility from the players, who frequently had to beg their forgiveness for some real or imagined lack of respect. The manager often had to appear on the stage to apologise for any shortcomings in the production. At the end of the performance, he was expected to thank the audience for their patronage.

A minor circuit was a good school in which to learn the craft of acting, for the small numbers in the company necessitated the doubling and even trebling of parts. Kean soon had a large repertory and he also became an accomplished fencer and a superb Harlequin. In the spring of 1804, when he was sixteen years old, he was sufficiently competent at his trade to be offered a job by Samuel Jerrold, manager of a small but respected circuit company serving the south-eastern towns in the neighbourhood of Sheerness. Kean was now a slightly built youth, below average height, but well proportioned. He walked lightly on his feet. His face was thin and sallow, his hair black and curly. His expression was sinister and watchful. His eyes were dark and unusually brilliant.

Jerrold started him at a salary of fifteen shillings a week and during his first season he played the whole round of tragedy, comedy, farce, interlude and pantomime. He left at the end of the season, because Jerrold refused to make him his leading tragedian. The tragedian was the chief man in any company and commanded the highest salary. This ranged from twenty-one shillings a week in a small company, such as Jerrold's, to fifty shillings a week in a large one. Jerrold told Kean that he did not consider him to have the necessary experience. During his ten years in the provinces, Kean was to be constantly thwarted by managers who did not take him at his own high valuation. At first they told him that he was too young and later that he was too small. Although he was a little man, he was by no means the pigmy some theatre historians have made him out to be. The report of the autopsy performed on his body recorded his exact measurement, which was five foot six and three-quarter inches. This was not exceptionally small, but shortness was a great disadvantage to an actor who wished to play tragic roles. Garrick was on the small side, but, as a general rule, audiences expected their tragedians to be tall impressive men like John Kemble. Altogether, provincial managers thought Kean better suited to pantomime than to tragedy, for he danced well and turned wonderful handsprings. They preferred his Harlequin to his Hamlet.

In the spring of 1805, Kean left Jerrold and went to London, where he played leads in a small theatre located in Wivell's Billiard Room in Camden Town. There he was spotted by the manager of the Belfast Theatre and in the autumn he was in Belfast, playing second roles in a company which starred Mrs. Siddons. But this opportunity came to nothing and, when the Belfast season ended, he was on the road again, frustrated and impatient. Then, in the summer of the following year, through the influence of Aunt Tid, he was engaged to play small parts at the Haymarket Theatre. This was the third most important theatre in London and it seemed that his big chance had come at last.

At that time, only two theatres in London, the Theatres Royal of Drury Lane and Covent Garden, were permitted to stage, throughout the year, the drama of the spoken word, that is, five-act tragedy or comedy, without the introduction of music. This included all such plays from dramatists as diverse as Shakespeare and Sheridan. These theatres were sometimes called major or patent houses, because they derived their monopoly from royal patents granted by Charles II. Hence the term legitimate drama. In all other theatres in London, no legitimate drama was permitted. The Theatres Royal guarded their prerogative jealously and saw to it that the minor theatres, as they were termed, confined themselves to melodrama, burlesque, pantomime and ballet. The Haymarket was the one exception to this rule. Drury Lane and Covent Garden usually opened in September and closed in early June. During the recess, the leading players set off on highly profitable tours of the provinces, starring in the circuit companies. While the patent houses were closed, a summer season of legitimate drama was permitted at the Haymarket. The players consisted chiefly of lesser lights from the patent houses and talented newcomers from the provinces.

During the summer season of 1806, Kean played at the Haymarket. The competition from his fellow-actors was not very formidable, but his roles were so small that he had little chance to shine. The leading tragedian, Alexander Rae, was a mediocre actor, but while he played Hamlet, Kean played Rosencrantz. Kean resented having to support so inferior an actor and matters were made worse by Rae's condescending attitude towards him. While rehearsing a scene in *The Iron Chest*, a popular melodrama by George Colman, Jnr., Kean could not get the effect Rae wanted. At last, as though despairing of ever making Kean understand his meaning, Rae said wearily, 'Never mind, sir, we'll try it tonight.' An eye-witness reported: 'Kean's brow changed, a look which I have since marked often came over his pale face, and a peculiar motion of his lips as if he were chewing or swallowing, which in Kean was a certain sign of hurt feeling or supposed rage. I do not believe that Kean ever forgot that circumstance.' Nor did he. Eleven years later, when Rae was playing the same part, Kean, then the greatest actor of the day, magnificent in evening dress and attended by his toadies, occupied a front box in the theatre and listened to his every word with mock attention. He never forgave anyone who did him an injury; he brooded on slights, real or imagined. He claimed that he could see a sneer across Salisbury Plain.

He was so anxious to score a success in this brief season at the Haymarket that he acted his small parts in a manner calculated to make them appear more important than they were. In doing this, he made a fool of himself in the eyes of the company, for it was considered pretentious for a player of small parts to attempt to shine. He was expected to conduct himself onstage in a manner befitting his place in the company. While Kean was playing the minor role of Carney in *Ways and Means*, another play by Colman, Jnr., his fellow-actors stood in the wings ridiculing him. 'He's trying to act,' they said. 'The little fellow's making a part of Carney.'

But despite all his efforts, the season on which he had built such hopes proved to be a disappointment. No managers from the Theatres Royal came backstage to offer him a contract; instead, he had to go to Drury Lane and Covent Garden to beg for an interview. John Kemble, now at Covent Garden, saw him for a moment and told him he could do nothing for him. His attitude was so cold that Kean vowed he would rather never play in London than act with Kemble. He became solitary and depressed. It mattered nothing to him that he had been expecting too much, that he was not the only great player who had failed to attract attention during a first appearance in London. Mrs. Siddons had gone back to the provinces for seven years and in the case of George Frederick Cooke it had been twenty-two. But Kean could take no consolation from these examples; he had nothing but contempt for other actors and admitted no talent but his own. He saw events only as they affected himself, and the lesson he had drawn from the Haymarket season was that mediocre actors were succeeding while he continued to fail. Although he was only eighteen, he was already eaten up with envy and frustrated ambition.

He returned to the provinces and joined the Canterbury circuit. This was a more important company than Jerrold's and he got the position on the strength of his London season. He was billed as 'Mr. Kean, late of the Theatre Royal, Haymarket'. The manageress, Mrs. Sarah Baker, was a famous figure in the world of the provincial theatre. In a career of over fifty years in the risky business of theatre management, this illiterate but canny woman had always made a profit. She had started as the mistress of a puppet show, but now she owned theatres in Rochester, Maidstone, Tunbridge Wells, Canterbury, Feversham and Deal. She was so powerful in her own area that she was dubbed 'Governor-General and Sole Autocratix of the Kentish Drama'. Joseph Grimaldi wrote: 'She managed all her affairs herself, and her pecuniary matters were conducted on a principle quite her own. She never put her money out at interest, or employed it in any speculative or profitable manner, but kept it in six or eight large punch bowls, which always stood on the top shelf of a bureau, except when she was disposed to make herself particularly happy, and then she would take them down singly, and after treating herself to a sly look at their contents, would put them up again.'

She was notorious for the stinginess of her productions; even current playbills were made up with cuttings from old ones. She personally took the money at the box office, which was so arranged that all patrons, both high and low, had to pass before her. Grimaldi has described her in action: ' "Now then, pit or box, pit or gallery, box or pit?" was her constant and uninterrupted cry. "Pit, pit!" from half-a-dozen voices, the owners clinging to the little desk to prevent themselves from being carried away by the crowd before they had paid. "Then pay two shillings—pass on Tom-fool!" was the old lady's invariable address to everybody on busy nights, without the slightest reference to their quality or condition.'

She confined herself to the financial aspects of her enterprises, leaving the stage management to a gentleman known as 'Bony' Long, a tall thin man remarkable for having five fingers and no thumbs on each hand. Kean appears to have suffered from what he called Mr. Long's 'unaccountable objection to small men, which aversion he carries to so great an excess that I firmly believe had Mr. Garrick offered himself as Candidate to Mr. Long's Management, he even *He* would have been rejected'. In Mrs. Baker's company, Kean played second or third parts, such as Gratiano in *The Merchant of Venice* and Lennox in *Macbeth*. 'Mr. Long,' he complained, 'kept me in the background as much as possible and frequently gave those characters which undoubtedly were mine to fellows who certainly would have adorned the handles of a plough but were never intended for the stage; but these met with Mr. Long's approbation because they were taller than me.'

It may be true that 'Bony' Long did not give Kean the chances he deserved, but it is also probable that the actor was indulging a neurotic suspicion that people were conspiring against him to prevent him from succeeding. He could never take disappointments in his stride, but moaned constantly about them. He could never admit that what was happening to him was no more than the usual lot of a circuit player; indeed, during his years in the provinces, he was to have an easier time than most. But he could never compare himself with other provincial players. So far as he was concerned, they belonged to the provinces, they would live and die there; but he was an exile, who had played at the greatest London theatres. His place was with a major company, not with these provincial ranters.

He remained in Mrs. Baker's company for a year, from September 1806 to September 1807, when he accepted an offer from Samuel Jerrold, who was now willing to give him a chance as leading man. Jerrold's was a less important company than Mrs. Baker's, but Kean would rather be leading man in a poor company than play second in a good one. He opened at Sheerness in Nathaniel Lee's drama, *Alexander the Great* and immediately met with an objection to his height. While he was being drawn across the stage in a triumphal car, the occupant of one of the stage boxes shouted, 'Alexander the Great, indeed! It should be Alexander the Little.' The laughter of the audience was suddenly checked as Kean fixed them with a terrible look and said, 'Yes—with a GREAT SOUL.' From that moment on, they gave him a respectful hearing. During this second engagement with the Sheerness circuit, he built up a following and then he suddenly left the district. Perhaps things were not going his way as much as he would have liked, although he himself always said that he had incurred the displeasure of a Very Important Person, who had set a press-gang after him. He had been forced to go into hiding, and eventually escaped, hidden aboard the Chatham boat.

Be that as it may, he turned up in Gloucester in the spring of 1808, as a member of William Beverley's company. This was not a good move, for he was only a supporting player on a salary of ten shillings and sixpence a week. Beverley, the manager, was the principal actor. He had made his reputation as a comedian, but, since forming his own company, he played all the leading tragic roles. His productions that season were not attracting the people of Gloucester and, in an attempt to bring in the audiences, he mounted a spectacular presentation of the pantomime, *Mother Goose*. It was the invariable practice of provincial managers, when all else failed, to put on a pantomime, for they knew that people who were reluctant to turn out for Othello and Desdemona would jam the theatre for Harlequin and Columbine. This must have been especially true when Othello was played by actors of the calibre of Beverley.

In *Mother Goose*, Columbine was played by an Irish girl named Mary Chambers. By the summer, Kean and Mary were engaged to be married. There was quite a disparity in their ages: he was only twenty years old, while she was twenty-eight. Mary had only recently become an actress. At the beginning of the year, she had come from Waterford to Cheltenham as a governess, but she was stage-struck and she had left her post to join Beverley's company. She had no great talent as an actress, but she was pretty and she danced and sang well. She was quickly disenchanted with the theatrical world. She was a prim person, reared in the gentility of the lower middle class, and her feelings were outraged by the coarser aspects of the life—the *droit de seigneur* attitude of the manager; the actors taking advantage of their roles to run their hands over her body; the drunkenness, the obscene language, the whole closed bohemian world of a circuit company—none of this was to her liking. All she wanted now was a cosy little home and a husband in a secure job, no matter how humdrum. This was her ambition when she met Kean.

In the summer, the company moved to Stroud and here Beverley allowed Kean to play leads. But his performances did not attract large audiences; in fact, the receipts were so poor that Beverley decided to engage the services of a star. The star system, by which players who had gained a London reputation acted a few nights or weeks with a provincial company, started in the seventeen-eighties and since then, it had snowballed. As the demand for stars increased, their prices rose accordingly; soon they were refusing salaries and demanding instead a half-share of the profits. On a profit-sharing basis, John Kemble or Mrs. Siddons could earn around fifteen hundred pounds a month in the provinces. The star system was to have a ruinous effect on the provincial theatre, because audiences ceased to be satisfied with the efforts of the stock company, and the more stars that were brought in on exorbitant terms the more they demanded. Already small companies such as Beverley's were compelled to use stars and, at Stroud, Beverley engaged Master William Betty for a few nights.

Four years previously, at the age of thirteen, Master Betty had taken London by storm. During the season of 1804–1805 he had appeared at both Drury Lane and Covent Garden in some of the tragic roles of Shakespeare. He was a slightly-built lad, with clean-cut features and brown hair falling in ringlets on his shoulders. Audiences were enchanted by him. His performances were no more than those of a clever boy, but he was hailed as the wonder of the age, and the 'Betty craze' began. He was presented to George III and Queen Charlotte. The Prince of Wales entertained him at Carlton House. Ducal carriages bore him to and from the theatre. Prints of him were displayed in shop windows. James Northcote painted a portrait of him which showed Shakespeare standing at a respectful distance in the background. The receipts for the twenty-eight nights he performed at Drury Lane amounted to £17,210, a nightly average of £614. His own profit from these evenings was £2,782, not counting his benefits, which realised more than £2,000. The following season he appeared again at Drury Lane and Covent Garden, but the curiosity of the public had generally abated and audiences were by no means as large as before. His London career was at an end, but he continued to reap a golden harvest in the provinces.

Kean had followed Betty's career with envy, for during his own years as a prodigy he had come nowhere near achieving such fame and fortune. He had often expressed his bitterness that the mechanical performances of Betty were highly praised, while his own, which were so passionate and imaginative, were largely ignored. Now Betty came to Stroud and took over the parts Kean had been playing. To Kean's paranoid mind it seemed that Beverley had brought Betty to Stroud with the deliberate intention of stealing his parts and so, as he had always done when things did not suit him, he ran away. He was missing for two days before he returned, dirty and dishevelled. He declared that he had lived in the fields, eating nothing but turnips and carrots, and would do so again rather than play second to such an impostor as Master Betty. Beverley chose to ignore this breach of discipline and Kean remained with the company until July, when it was disbanded. In the same month he married Mary Chambers.

The Betty episode crystallised Kean's thoughts about his own future. It was after this that he formed his great ambition to become the leading actor of the English stage. He was conscious of his own powers and he resolved that he would be no temporary craze like Master Betty. No matter what it cost him he would become the greatest tragic actor in England. He poured out his ambition to Mary; he told her that this was the road to the security and respectability she craved. Was not John Philip Kemble the most respected of men? When an actor reached that stature, he was no longer regarded as a vagabond. He told her how she could help him: she had been a governess and could educate him, so that he would be fitted for the position that would be his. The future he painted appealed to Mary's imagination, but she was practical enough to know that the chances of it happening were remote. She knew that this was the dream of every young actor in the provinces. She promised to teach him all she could, but her interest in his education was to be chiefly motivated by the hope that it would help him to find employment outside the theatre.

He was ashamed of his lack of education and regretted all the times he had played truant from school. Ever since leaving Nance he had tried to educate himself. His reading was wide but unconnected, and included botany, history, and translations of Anglo-Saxon epics. He had bought Latin and Greek dictionaries, but he was never to make much progress with either language, and eventually he used the dictionaries chiefly for culling the classical quotations with which he was so fond of embellishing his speech and correspondence. After his triumph, when he tried to pass himself off as a gentleman, he used to say that he had been educated at Eton.

Later that summer, Kean and Mary moved to the Cheltenham circuit, which was managed by John Boles Watson. By the time the company moved from Cheltenham to Warwick, Kean was playing leads. In October, they moved to Birmingham and, as this was an important theatre, Watson brought in other players to improve the quality of his company. As a result, Kean was no longer given leading roles. In his disappointment, he turned to drink. Mary was perturbed that he could be so easily depressed by his first setback. It convinced her that the theatre was not the best place for him and that he would be better suited to a less precarious career. By the end of the year she was more concerned than ever about security, because she found herself pregnant.

Although brandy helped Kean to forget his troubles, it did not relax him, but made him excitable and truculent, quick to take offence and always ready to pick a quarrel. His drinking was morbid and compulsive. He would sometimes stay in a tavern three days and nights at a stretch, drinking all the time, with brief intervals for sleep. But when the dissipation had run its course, the habit of work would re-assert itself. Mary recalled: 'He used to walk about for hours, walking miles and miles alone, with his hands in his pockets, thinking intensely on his characters. No one could get a word from him. He studied and slaved beyond any actor I ever knew.'

In Birmingham, his heavy drinking led him into debt, and he was compelled to ask Watson for a rise in salary. Like all the other provincial managers who had employed Kean, Watson admired his Harlequin more than his tragic roles, and he told him that he would raise his salary from twenty-one to thirty shillings a week if he were willing to play Harlequin in addition to his other parts. This was an exhausting commitment for an actor, but Kean agreed to it. After his long night's work was over, he would fling his greatcoat over his patchwork costume and, bathed in perspiration, the paint still on his face, go straight to the tavern. There he would sit drinking until the early hours, brooding on his failure.

It was certainly a galling time for him. While other actors played the leading tragic roles, he starred in the pantomimes and farces. One night, in Birmingham, when Kean was acting in a pantomime based on the story of Alonzo the Brave and the Fair Imogene, William Charles Macready, then a schoolboy aged fifteen, sat in a box with his sister. Mrs. Watson, the manager's wife, a large ungainly woman, played the beautiful Imogene. Years later, Macready recalled: 'As if in studied contrast to this enormous "hill of flesh", a little mean-looking man, in a shabby green satin dress (I remember him well), appeared as the hero, Alonzo the Brave. It was so ridiculous that the only impression I carried away was that the hero and the heroine were the worst in the piece. How little did I know, or could guess, that under that shabby green satin dress was hidden one of the most extraordinary theatrical geniuses that have ever illustrated the dramatic poetry of England. When some years afterwards, public enthusiasm was excited to the highest pitch by the appearance at Drury Lane of an actor by the name of Kean, my astonishment may easily be conceived in discovering that the little insignificant Alonzo the Brave was the grandly impassioned personator of Othello, Richard and Shylock.'

In June 1809, after eight months in Birmingham, Kean receive an offer from Andrew Cherry, manager of the Swansea circuit, to play leads at twenty-five shillings a week. Cherry, an Irishman by birth, had been a member of the Drury Lane company until 1807, when he took over the lease of the newly built theatre at Swansea. His circuit extended from Caermarthen and Haverfordwest in south Wales to Waterford in Ireland. His company was not so good as the Birmingham one, but Kean's desire for quick recognition got the better of him and he accepted the offer.

He could not leave for Swansea right away, because he had debts in Birmingham totalling fifteen pounds. He wrote to Cherry for an advance and the manager sent him two pounds. He used most of this to pay his landlady and, ignoring his other debts, Mary and he sneaked out of Birmingham. They could not afford to take a coach to Swansea. They travelled the hundred and eighty miles on foot, covering ten to twelve miles a day and sleeping rough in fields and barns. It was fortunate for them that they travelled in summer, but, even so, the journey was a nightmare experience for Mary, who was now six months pregnant. By the time they reached Bristol all their money was gone and they still had eighty miles in front of them. Kean wrote again to Cherry and five days later he received another two pounds. During the intervening days, they survived by singing and dancing in the Bristol taverns. At last they reached Swansea and, as soon as they arrived, Cherry asked Kean to open that night as Rolla in Sheridan's *Pizarro*. Mrs. Cherry played Elvira and the pregnant Mary played the Virgin of the Sun.

Kean's first few months in Cherry's company were difficult ones financially, for out of his wage of twenty-five shillings he was repaying the advance of four pounds at the rate of four shillings a week. Years later, usually after a good supper, when the brandy bottle was circulating, he would tell his cronies that never in his life had he been so hungry than one night when playing Lear in Cherry's company. The pangs of his empty stomach were so acute that they gave a wildness to the mad king's eye which no effort of the imagination could have produced. But his acting, whether on a full stomach or an empty one, was not appreciated by the Swansea audiences. He was convinced that he would never be properly valued until he had a fair trial in London, but he knew there was little hope of a London manager coming to Swansea. The Theatres Royal of Drury Lane and Covent Garden rarely looked beyond Bristol, Liverpool, Bath, York and Dublin for their recruits. He had written to all these companies for an engagement but none of them wanted him.

His feeling of rejection was intensified later that summer, when, after the Bath season closed, Cherry asked Henry Bengough to star in the company. For Kean this was the Master Betty business all over again, but this time he dared not run away, for he was about to become a father and could not afford to lose the money. Bengough was a second-rate actor; a big man, with a loud voice and a swashbuckling manner, who shouted everyone else off the stage; but the audiences preferred him to Kean.

On 13 September, Mary gave birth to a son, who, in recognition of the patrician blood that flowed in his veins, was christened Howard, the family name of the Dukes of Norfolk. After the birth of Howard, Mary did little to encourage her husband in his ambition. It was not only that she wanted security for her child, but she had begun to fear what success might do to so unstable a man. Her intuition told her that it would not be the best thing for him. But the birth of his son had made Kean more anxious than ever to succeed. He spoke of the great things he would do for his family when he was rich and famous. He told her that she would mix with the highest society in the land, for was he not the son of the Duke of Norfolk? He made her uneasy when he raved on about carriages, servants and fine houses. She could not understand this strange man, who worked so hard for so little reward; she was frightened by the daemon that lived within him.

CHAPTER TWO

THE CLIMAX OF MISERY

WHEN the Swansea season closed at the end of September, Henry Bengough left the company and Kean resumed the leading roles. The company moved on, first to Caermarthen and then to Haverfordwest. The following year, in April 1810, they crossed the sea to Waterford, in Ireland. Waterford was Mary's home town and she was looking forward to showing off her husband and baby to all her relatives and friends. It was in Waterford that Kean met Thomas Colley Grattan, one of the few true friends he was ever to make from that world of polite society he admired so much. Grattan has described the circumstances of their first meeting.

He was, at the time, a young subaltern in a regiment stationed at Waterford. One evening, he was strolling along the Mall with a brother officer and they paused to read the playbills outside the theatre. *Hamlet* was the main attraction that night. They agreed that the first four acts of the tragedy were a bore, but decided to go in for half-an-hour at the beginning of the fifth act, for the celebrated sword fight between Hamlet and Laertes. They were themselves enthusiastic fencers and thought it would be amusing to see what sort of mess the strolling players would make of the duel. They bought their tickets, and telling the door-keeper to let them know when the fifth act began, they passed the time in a nearby billiard room. When the door-keeper sought them out to announce the beginning of the fifth act, they left their game and took their seats in an almost empty theatre.

Grattan wrote: 'The young man who played Laertes was extremely handsome and very tall; and a pair of high-heeled boots added so much to his natural stature, that the little pale thin man, who represented Hamlet, appeared a mere pigmy beside him. Laertes commenced (after slurring, 'for better for worse', through the usual salute), to push *carte* and *tierce*, which might, as far as the scientific use of the small-sword was concerned, have been as correctly termed cart and horse.

'My companion, who had by no means a poor opinion of his own skill, and who was rather unmerciful towards the awkwardness of others, laughed outright, and in a manner sufficient to disconcert even an adroit performer. He proposed to me to leave the place, calling out theatrically, 'Hold! enough!'—and I might have agreed, had I not thought I perceived in the Hamlet a quiet gracefulness of manner, while he parried the cut-and-thrust attacks of his adversary, as well as a quick glance of haughty resentment at the uncivil laugh by which they were noticed. When he began to return the lunges, *secundum artem*, we were quite taken by surprise to see the carriage and action of a practised swordsman; and as he went through the whole performance, we were satisfied that we had, in the phrase of Osrick aforesaid, made "A hit—a very palpable hit."

'We immediately inquired of the woman who filled the nearly sinecure place of money-taker, as to the gentleman whose "excellence for his weapon" had so pleasantly surprised us. She told us that his name was Kean, that he was an actor of first-rate talent, chief tragic hero (for they were *all* honourable men) of the company; and also the principal singer, stage-manager, and getter-up of pantomimes, and one of the best Harlequins in Wales or the west of England.'

Grattan became friendly with Kean, and rarely a day passed without them taking up the foils. The actor was a welcome visitor at the barracks, for many of the officers were also anxious to test his skill as a swordsman. He was flattered by their interest in him. He saw to it that he was always on his best behaviour and the officers remarked on his quiet and unassuming manners. This was how Kean struck people when he was sober; it was another story when he was drunk. His connection with Grattan's regiment probably inspired the tale he gave out after his triumph at Drury Lane, that he had been an officer in the army.

His standing with the garrison paid dividends at his benefit performance. Benefits were of great importance to all players; they depended as much on these as on their salary. They were allowed one or two a year, single or shared, according to their importance in the company. After the running costs were met, all the receipts were given to the beneficiaries. In the larger companies, a benefit night for a popular player might bring in as much as two or three hundred pounds, but often, in the smaller ones, the receipts barely covered the expenses and the player received very little and sometimes nothing at all. A poor benefit could be a catastrophe for a player, who more often than not, was depending on it to make ends meet. Kean's benefit was patronised by the officers and their families. They, together with Mary's numerous relatives, made up a good audience and he received the splendid sum of forty pounds.

He certainly earned his money. The main piece of the evening was Hannah More's popular tragedy, *Percy*, in which he played the hero. After this, he gave a demonstration of tight-rope walking, sparred with a professional pugilist, took the leading part in a musical interlude, and, finally, played Chimpanzee the Monkey in the melodramatic pantomime, *Perouse*. After the performance, he went straight to the tavern, still dressed in his monkey skins. When he eventually came home, drunk and exhausted, he went to bed in his costume. The stench of the undressed skins was too much for Mary. She had often shared her bed with a sodden Harlequin, but on this occasion she was driven to spend the rest of the night on the sofa.

Kean remained in Cherry's company for two years, in the course of which he made a second circuit of Swansea, Caermarthen, Haverfordwest and Waterford. On 18 January 1811, at Waterford, Mary gave birth to a second son. He was christened Charles, after his supposed grandfather, the eleventh Duke. Now that there were two children to support, Mary put even more pressure on Kean to give up the theatre and find a secure job. He had continued to offer his services to the better companies, but none of them wanted him. The most recent refusal had come from Frederick Jones, manager of the Dublin Theatre, turning down his offer to 'do everything' for two pounds a week. Mary saw every rejection as another reason for him to quit the theatre.

That summer his affairs reached a crisis. He had demanded a rise in salary and Cherry had refused it. In a rancorous mood, Kean acted hastily: he left the company before he had secured another post and so threw himself and his family on the world without a penny. In July 1811, they crossed from Ireland to Whitehaven, a port on the north-west coast of England. For the next six months, their route lay through Dumfries, Annan, Carlisle, Penrith, Appleby, Richmond and York. They travelled on foot, pushing a handcart containing their possessions, with the two babies secured on the top. At each town Kean would hire a room at an inn, and Mary and he would give a programme of recitations, songs, dances, and scenes from plays. At Whitehaven, Annan and Dumfries their performance was a failure, but they did well at Carlisle, for the assizes were on and the town was busy. Penrith and Appleby brought in very little, and by the time they reached Richmond, in Yorkshire, they were in a pitiful state. 'In Richmond,' Mary recalled, 'we suffered privations of more than common. My Husband took a Room at the principal Inn & gave recitations singing & a gentleman who kept a large establishment for the Education of Young gentlemen was very kind & the young gentlemen called next day with their pocket money & left it with the Land-lady addressed to Mr. Kean the sum amounting I think to eleven shillings & sixpence. There is something in the generosity of youth.' They had become little more than beggars.

In York, they starved. There was now no need for Mary to beg him to look for other work: he tramped the streets asking for employment of any kind. He even thought of enlisting as a soldier. They were again saved by kindness. A Mrs. Nokes, the wife of a dancing master, heard of their distress and visited Mary. On leaving, she passed a folded piece of paper into her hand. To her astonishment, Mary found that she had been given a five-pound note. Kean regarded this gift as divine intervention on his behalf and he used the money to take his family by coach directly to London. There he intended to hammer with both fists on the doors of Drury Lane and Covent Garden.

five pounds. He threw himself upon the charity of Aunt Tid, but she would only allow them to stay for a few days. She had disapproved of his marriage and she wanted nothing to do with Mary. He turned next to Aunt Price, but she was not pleased to see them either and grudgingly consented to a stay of one week. He tried to get an interview with the managers of Drury Lane and Covent Garden, but neither of them would see him. He went from one minor theatre to another asking for work, but again no one wanted him. Then he heard that Richard Hughes, at Sadler's Wells, was looking for a clever actor for his circuit in the West Country.

Hughes had begun his career as a strolling player and now managed theatres in Plymouth, Exeter, Weymouth, Truro, Penzance, Dartmouth, and Guernsey in the Channel Islands. In 1791, he had bought a quarter share in Sadler's Wells, the most important minor theatre in London. He remained chiefly in the metropolis, leaving his provincial affairs to his son. Kean was reluctant to return to the provinces, but he realised that he had no choice. He applied to Hughes at Sadler's Wells and was engaged to play tragedy, comedy, farce and pantomime on the West Country circuit at a wage of two guineas a week. He was instructed to join the company at Weymouth, but having spent all his money on the journey to London, he had to write to Hughes for a loan. The letter, with its Latin and Greek embellishments and grandiose reference to expensive baggage and a servant, is a brave composition, remembering the hardships and disappointments he had recently endured.

Dear Sir,
Having travelled lately some Hundred Miles with a large family and most expensive baggage, I am left in London in a situation which many of our brother professionals are acquainted with. *Non est mihi argentum.* It is my wish therefore to depart by tomorrow's coach for Weymouth, but I frankly confess I at present have not the means; if, sir, you would oblige me with the sum of ten pounds, Mr. Finch or Miss Tidswell will become Answerable for my immediate appearance

at Weymouth, and Mr. Hughes might proceed to the reduction of ten shillings per week till the debt is discharged. As I am fully sensible this is a great obligation from a stranger, it is my wish to pay any interest on the money you may please to demand, and as Mr. Hughes, Jnr. will have the means in his own hands, there can be no *doubt* of the payment, and I shall bear the recollection of your kindness Πάρ' ὄκον τὸν Βίον. I should not ask so great a favour, but My Aunt, whose purse is ever open to my necessities, is at the moment as bare in pocket as Myself, and another Relation from whom I have been in the habit of receiving Supplies is not in London. I can only say, sir, however exorbitant the request may appear to a stranger, there is no Manager who *knows me* would refuse it; it is my intention, should fortune favour my designs, to make the Situation you have offered me a permanency, and as I have ever shown unremitting attention to my professional duties, I despair not of joining your approbation to the public's and of making it pleasant to all parties. The money I write for is for immediate service, and if you would commit it to the charge of the bearer —My Servant—it would be brought very safe to Me, and tomorrow we would depart for Weymouth.

> I am, Sir,
>
> With the greatest Respect, Yours,
>
> E. KEAN

Hughes advanced Kean a sum sufficient for his travelling expenses and not a penny more. The actor and his family left London for Weymouth, arriving there at the beginning of January 1812. The season was almost finished and, by the middle of the month, the company had moved to Exeter. The theatre at Exeter was a fairly important one. The inhabitants of this quiet cathedral town had seen all the great stars from London and they prided themselves on their critical judgement. This was the best audience Kean had had since Birmingham and here he was to bring his art to full maturity. He played Richard III, Othello, Macbeth and other leading roles. At the conclusion of his engagement with Hughes, he had formed practically all the repertory on which he was to base his reputation in London.

A point that has puzzled many theatre historians is why it was that the performances that were to electrify London two years later made so little impression in the provinces. Grattan has answered this by claiming that Kean did not play so well in the provinces as he did in London, that he needed the stimulus of Drury Lane and a metropolitan audience to bring his talent into full play. But Kean himself always declared that he had played equally well in the provinces. After his triumph, he told Douglas Kinnaird: 'I have often acted the third act of *Othello* in the same manner as now calls down such thunders, when the whole house laughed. After that can you think that I care much for public taste?'

While his performances at Exeter were appreciated by some connoisseurs of the drama, they did not attract large audiences. Most people preferred him as Harlequin, and Hughes asked him to play this role more often than any other. How greatly in demand he was as Harlequin may be judged by the fact that, on his recovery from an illness, Hughes placarded his return not as Othello or Macbeth, but with the promise that 'Mr. Kean will Resume the character of Harlequin this Evening'. Kean hated this character and only played it because the manager compelled him to do so. 'I never feel degraded,' he said, 'but when I have the motley jacket on my back.'

In the spring the company moved to Weymouth and here Kean had to stand down again in favour of Master Betty. After two years at Cambridge University, the former prodigy was attempting a come-back. The attempt was to prove a failure, but, at first, his past reputation was sufficient to ensure full houses. When Betty came to star at Weymouth, in April 1812, bills had already been distributed announcing Kean as Alexander in *Alexander the Great*. Now his name was crossed out and that of Betty written in. Kean felt this deeply. What had happened at Stroud four years ago was happening again. With the arrival of Master Betty, the wheel had come full circle: he was getting nowhere.

His confidence was undermined not only by Betty but also by Mary. Her chief concern was the welfare of their two children, and she wanted to see him settled in a regular job, perhaps as a clerk in some office. She was no longer giving him the encouragement he needed, but adding to his own growing doubts on his ability to succeed as an actor. She was not the best of wives to him in this respect, nor, it would seem, in another. There is reason to believe that she was not a satisfactory partner sexually. She was eight years older than Kean and her interest in that side of their marriage had declined with the birth of their children. He had begun to turn to other women. He did not form any lasting relationships; his need was solely an animal one and he satisfied it with tavern wenches and prostitutes. Mary found this hard to bear. She wrote to her girlhood friend, Miss Margaret Roberts: 'To forget sorrow he first took to Drinking—every dissipation follow'd of course. His Nights were spent with a Set of wretches a Disgrace to Human nature. One step led on to another, till ruin, inevitable ruin was the end.'

Kean was terribly short of money. Mary was no longer acting. The worry and exhaustion of the past year had drained her so much that she was incapable of playing even the smallest parts. This meant that only one wage was coming in, and Kean, like most married actors, counted on a joint wage to make ends meet. On the other hand, he was getting two guineas a week, the highest wage he had ever received. He could have managed on this had he lived temperately, but too much money went on drink and prostitutes. At Weymouth, his financial affairs reached a crisis. Mary and the children were ill and he needed money to pay the doctor's bills. On 20 April, he took a benefit, playing Luke in *Riches*, an adaptation of Massinger's *City Madam*. He had chosen the part carefully; the character of the villainous Luke suited him perfectly and he hoped it would prove a popular attraction. To his dismay, he not only failed to make a penny from his benefit but he also lost money on it. These were miserable days for Mary. In a letter to Margaret Roberts, she wrote: 'I was so ill no one expected I should ever get better—the two boys dying in measles and whooping cough, Edmund entirely ruining

his health with Drink. I saw nothing but misery before me ...
As I expected we had but 6 pounds in the House for our Benefit—
we were out of pocket. ... If you have any bits of silk Muslin you
can send it or any old thing. Little Howard is very delicate, the
Measles has weakened him much. Mr. Kean's aunt has been trying
to prevent his living with me—oh!: you know not half what I am
suffering.'

Kean was concerned for his wife and children; he was tortured
by the thought of how much he was making them suffer in the
pursuit of his ambition. He was only twenty-four years old, but
already he had spent ten years in the provinces, and it seemed to
him that he was doomed to remain there for the rest of his life. He
tried to earn extra money by giving lessons in elocution, dancing,
and fencing, but whatever he earned his own appetites came first.
In August, the company were in Totnes and, on the sixth of the
month, he again had a benefit. In the hope of attracting a large
audience, he arranged a varied entertainment. The main item was
The Merchant of Venice, with himself as Shylock. After this he
danced in a *pas de deux*. Next came a serious pantomime, *The
Savages*, in which he played Kojah, the Noble Savage. In the
course of this pantomime, he took part in a 'Savage *Pas de Trois*';
demonstrated the 'Otaheitan method of using the Bow and
Arrow'; engaged in 'Several Extraordinary Combats with
Bamboos, Battle Axe, Shield and Sword'; delineated 'Savage
Distraction' and danced a 'Savage Dance of Peace'—all being
exact representations as described by 'that wonderful Navigator,
Captain Cook'.

The financial result of all this effort was negligible and by the
following month his position had become so desperate that on
23 September he wrote to Samuel Arnold, manager of Drury
Lane, begging for the chance to play small parts. He wrote: 'I find
the fame gained by acting Richard & Hamlet in the Country is
not so *estimable* or *profitable*, as the Richmond or Tressel, Laertes
or Horatio, in London: to be settled in the Metropolis in a *third* or
fourth rate Situation, & on a salary sufficient to support my family
with respectability wou'd be the summit of my ambition.'
Arnold did not offer him a position of any kind and, in October,

he moved with Hughes' company to Weymouth, where Mrs. Jordan was engaged as the star for a short season. As she was the greatest comic actress of the day, the emphasis at Weymouth was on comedy. Kean was her leading man, but he was not at ease in comedy and she was displeased with him. It seemed to him that nothing could go right on Hughes' circuit. He had ceased to care about the standard of his acting. He was now drunk most of the time, both on and off the stage.

In April 1813, the company moved to Guernsey in the Channel Islands for a four-month season. They opened on Easter Monday, 19 April, at the Theatre Royal, St. Peter Port, the chief town on the island. Kean's family joined him in Guernsey shortly afterwards and he greeted his wife with the words, 'My dear Mary, what do you think? I can get brandy here for eighteen pence a bottle: I can drink it instead of beer.' In Guernsey his performances were erratic. The audiences soon realised that this was because he was either drunk or recovering from the effects of drink. During the day, he was often seen drunk around the island. Sometimes his head had to be held under a pump to clear his brain sufficiently to get through a part and sometimes he was too drunk to appear at all. On one occasion, when Hughes came forward to announce the 'unavoidable absence' of Kean, someone in the audience shouted, 'Search the public houses.'

Hughes warned him that if he continued to carry on in this way, he would have to leave the company. The final break came over a performance of William Dimond's play, *The Royal Oak*, in which Kean was announced to play Charles I. At the time the play was scheduled to begin, Kean remained in the tavern, sending Hughes the message that King Charles had been beheaded on his way to the theatre. Hughes, though unfamiliar with the part, had no alternative but to stumble through it himself. Halfway through the performance, Kean, completely drunk, occupied a box in the theatre and encouraged Hughes by continually calling out, 'Well done, my boy, well done.' This was the end; Hughes kicked him out of the company. In August, when the others returned to the mainland, Kean and his family were left behind on the island.

He was penniless and in debt. To raise money, he arranged a family recital at the Assembly Rooms in St. Peter Port, and even the three-year-old Howard did a turn. Because of the pitiable condition of the family, the governor of the island, Sir John Doyle, put the recital under his patronage. This ensured a good audience and Kean made six pounds, which was sufficient to pay his debts and the boat fares back to the mainland.

Early in September, Kean was back in Exeter, but he stayed only long enough to settle Mary and the children in lodgings before setting off for London in an attempt to find work. This was a difficult time for Mary. The little money he had given her was soon gone and to raise some more she was forced to exhibit Howard in a programme of recitations, even though the child was unwell at the time. On 5 September, she wrote to her friend, Margaret Roberts: 'He is gone to London. Disease on disease has ruin'd my Health—I cannot act, none will engage one incapable of supporting a line of business. What can I do. I have written to my Dear Sister—and my Dear Margaret will you advise me. Heartbroken I write to you. You have been my *Sister*, my FRIEND, I never had a thought concealed from you. Wild in ideas—my imagination warm in my favourite project—now pining in Misery—I can boast of nothing but a Heart & character unsullied—nothing to blush for, but my Misery. I write to you, Dear Margaret, for advice, shall I say for assistance. Could you send me the smallest trifle. Do not I beg of you be offended. If I could get to Ireland, could I, think you, get my bread in any way whatever. I wish to preserve my children off the Stage. Howard is wonderfully clever, but could I make them good clerks, they might, if they grow up with the Dispositions they have at present help me in my old age. Could I, think you, keep a little School? I want nothing but a bare subsistance—my tears blind me—you cannot read this.'

Kean returned from London. His search for work had been a failure. He accepted an offer to play four nights at Teignmouth, a watering place fifteen miles south of Exeter. There his encounter with Dr. Joseph Drury was to set in motion the train of events that was to bring him glory and wealth, and eventually to destroy him.

Since retiring as headmaster of Harrow School, Dr. Drury had more time than ever to cultivate his artistic interests, the chief of which was a passion for the Drama. He had influential friends, who were connected with the Patent Theatres, and these included several members of the Drury Lane committee. The previous year he had seen Kean act at Exteer and had been impressed. At Teignmouth he introduced himself to Kean and complimented him on his acting. He told him that he was to dine shortly with Pascoe Grenfell, a member of the Drury Lane committee, and that he would bring Kean's name to Grenfell's attention; but he warned him not to place too much hope on the outcome, telling him 'not to let it impede any present engagement, for it is but uncertain though I have hopes of its success'.

At the close of the Teignmouth engagement, Kean accepted an offer from Henry Lee, manager of a small circuit centred on Taunton, to join his company at a salary of thirty shillings a week. He had no sooner done this than he received a letter from Aunt Tid, dated 27 September, telling him that Robert William Elliston, lessee of the Olympic Theatre in London, wished to offer him the post of 'Acting Manager'. Elliston had recently acquired the Olympic in Wych Street and was preparing to re-open it at the beginning of November. Kean would receive a salary of three guineas a week and have the choice of parts he wished to play. Kean was compelled to consider this offer, even though he knew that its acceptance would put an end to his ambition to act the great tragic roles in London, legitimate drama there being the prerogative of the two patent houses. The Olympic, like all minor theatres, was restricted to farces, burlesques, operettas, pantomimes, melodramas and ballet. The patent houses rarely looked to the minor theatres for their recruits. It was all very well for Elliston to offer him the choice of parts, but he knew that these could not include Richard, Othello and Macbeth. He suspected that Elliston, like all the other managers, wanted him chiefly for his Harlequin and that this would be the part that he would be forced to play over and over again. But hopes of better days had vanished. All his efforts to get into Drury Lane or Covent Garden had been fruitless. He had little faith in any attempt Dr. Drury might make on his behalf. Drury had hedged his offer of help with too many qualifications to arouse hope even in the most optimistic of men, let alone Kean, who had become accustomed to disappointment. Kean's immediate concern was the condition of his family. While he had been in London, his children had come close to starving and now Howard was ill with whooping cough. Mary was almost out of her mind with worry; for her the hardships and poverty of the strolling life had become unendurable. She begged him to accept the offer. He knew that for a time at least he must find a permanent home for his family. Although poorly paid, there was a certain amount of security in Elliston's offer. He could not afford to turn it down, for he knew that he might never get a better one; and so he accepted it. Mary had the grace to understand the sacrifice he was making. She told her sister, Susan: 'Out of a situation & in great Distress—very reluctantly he accepted it, knowing he could never get into either of the great Theatres after mumming there.'

His letter of acceptance was written to Elliston, on 2 October, from Barnstaple, where the company were playing.

Sir/I have this moment rec'd your proposals for the Wych Street Theatre, id est Little Drury, & much lament your letter not finding me, as a neglect of answering, must have appeared negligent or abrupt which failing I do not rank in the Catalogue of my follies.

the terms Miss Tidswell, by your authority mentions to me is the Superintendence of the Stage business, the whole of the principle Line of *business*!!!! & an equal division of the House, on the night of my benefit, with three guineas per week allotted as salary.

these terms I own do not bring my expectations to a level with the respectability of the establishment, but I place so firm a confidence in your reported liberality, that on the proof of my humble abilities & assiduity towards the general promotion of the business you will be inclined to increase it, *that I accept your present proposals*, simply requesting you to name the extent of the Services expected from me & what time you expect me in London (be kind enough to allow me as much as possible, as I am making out the time very profitably) I stay here three weeks shall be glad to hear from you immediately

Yours obediently

E. KEAN

Elliston's reply, dated 8 October, was ambiguous and unsatisfactory. He agreed to engage Kean for general business, was uncertain when the Olympic would open and asked him to let him know where he could be found in a month's time. This letter made Kean uneasy. These proposals were not the same as those expressed through Aunt Tid. To be engaged *generally* in the business was totally opposite to *principally*. The letter was so vague that he had no idea where he stood with Elliston.

In the meantime Dr. Drury had met Pascoe Grenfell and urged him to bring Kean's name to the attention of the Drury Lane committee. He knew that it was an opportune time to do this, for the committee were on the look-out for a new tragedian to save the theatre from bankruptcy. Four years previously, on 24 February 1809, Drury Lane Theatre had been destroyed by fire. The reservoir of water and the iron curtain, so proudly displayed on the opening night, had proved useless and the great theatre burned to the ground. The blaze had lit all London and was seen for miles. From the Piazza Coffee House, in Covent Garden, Sheridan sat in a window, drinking a bottle of wine and watching the fire. When some friends complimented him on his self-possession, he replied, 'May not a man be allowed to drink a glass of wine by his own fireside?' He had controlled Drury Lane for thirty extravagant years, during which his talent as a dramatist was more than matched by his genius in playing off one creditor against the other. An audit taken after the fire disclosed the enormity of his mismanagement. The debts of the theatre totalled almost half-a-million pounds. The situation was so serious that for a time it was doubted whether Drury Lane would ever be rebuilt. The direction of the theatre's affairs was taken over by

Samuel Whitbread, a wealthy brewer and a member of Parliament. Sheridan was forced to resign and all claims against the theatre were settled at twenty-five per cent. New stock was issued and a committee of nineteen major stockholders was elected to run the theatre under the chairmanship of Whitbread. Samuel Arnold, from the Lyceum Theatre, was appointed stage manager. He was under the control of the committee, which included the Earl of Essex, Lord Holland, Lord Byron, Hon. Douglas Kinnaird, Peter Moore and Pascoe Grenfell. All except Arnold were amateurs.

A new theatre, designed by Benjamin Wyatt, was built at a cost of over £150,000, and this is the Drury Lane which stands to-day. The portico in front and the colonnade at the side have been added since, and the interior has been remodelled several times, but substantially the theatre remains as it was when it was opened on 10 October 1812. This was a gala occasion. A brilliant audience strolled to their seats down the great vestibule and through the imposing rotunda. Few lessons had been learnt from the faults of the old auditorium. The lines of sight had been improved, but the seating capacity was still around 3,060 and the gallery was too far from the stage. A poetic address by Lord Byron was read by Elliston and a performance of *Hamlet* followed. This inaugurated a highly successful season. The receipts on the opening night reached a record total of £842 and for the first fortnight averaged nearly £600. At the end of the season the committee congratulated themselves, for it seemed that at last Drury Lane had entered upon an era of prosperity. But when the next season began, in the autumn of 1813, the average receipts for the first fortnight were little more than £250. Whatever play was selected, whatever actors engaged, they all failed to attract attention. The committee realised that if this trend were to continue, the theatre, already burdened with a heavy mortgage, must go bankrupt. They decided on a policy of rigorous economy. The acting strength was reduced and salaries cut. Savings were made in scenery, costumes and stage machinery. This only made matters worse, for it resulted in such parsimonious productions that the public stayed away in even greater numbers than before.

The committee did not yet realise that the chief cause of Drury Lane's troubles lay in its system of management. A great theatre could not be run successfully by a group of gentleman amateurs. A practical man of the theatre was needed, like Thomas Harris, of Covent Garden, who combined sound business sense with a flair for public taste. Harris had controlled Covent Garden for forty years and during this time he had consistently made a higher profit than Drury Lane. Only during the previous year, with the novelty of a new theatre, had Drury Lane cut into profits, but now he was in the lead again. The average receipts at Covent Garden were £400 a night, £150 more than Drury Lane. Eventually all this was to become obvious to the members of the committee themselves, but at the time they thrashed about seeking a recipe for success. It seemed to them that the most probable cause of failure was a weakness on the tragic side of the company. In John Liston and Joseph Munden, they had first-rate comic actors, but no comparable tragedian, while Covent Garden had not only John Philip Kemble but also Charles Mayne Young. They convinced themselves that a good tragedian would go a long way towards solving their problems. They began an intensive search through the provinces, looking for talent. Their need was known to Dr. Drury and this is why Pascoe Grenfell listened so readily to his recommendation of Kean.

On 3 October, the day after Kean's letter of acceptance to Elliston, Grenfell passed on Drury's recommendation to Samuel Whitbread, chairman of the committee. Whitbread wrote to Drury, telling him that Kean would be given a trial. When Drury told Kean what was happening, the actor's worries about Elliston's vagueness vanished completely, and, as his hopes of playing the great tragic roles in London began to revive, everything relating to Elliston seemed more and more abhorrent. But October went by with no word from Drury Lane. These were anxious days for Kean, waiting for the letter that never came. To make matters worse, Howard was still very ill from the effects of whooping cough and did not begin to recover until the end of the month. As October drew to a close, Kean could restrain himself no longer. On the 29th, from Barnstaple, he wrote to Dr. Drury.

Sir/the state of suspense I have been in on account of my poor little boy, who has just recovered from a most alarming illness prevented me from the pleasure of addressing you before with a heart fill'd with anxiety, I now request the Issue of your kind application to the Proprietors of the Drury Lane Theatre, if Sir, soliciting your advice wou'd not be deemed intrusive I wou'd learn whether a personal application to Mr. Whitbread aided by the powerful influence of Dr. Drury's recommendation wou'd not be more serviceable than distant correspondence, I have offers from Mr. Elliston, for a new theatre in Wich Street, his proposals are by no means so advantageous, & the nature of the entertainments I am afraid, detrimental to the reputation of a Dramatic actor, it is however in reserve in case of the failure, of the more desirable point. I leave Barnstaple for Dorchester on Wednesday or Thursday next (where I play six nights) I need not say how proud I shall feel by the favour of a line from you—in the meantime Sir allow me to thank you for all the flattering marks of attention I have rec'd from you which must be ever foremost in my remembrance & with sincere respect

I sign myself
Yours Obediently,
E. KEAN

Drury's reply was not encouraging. He told Kean that he had heard nothing from Drury Lane, but promised that in case of failure there he would use his influence to secure a place for Kean at the Haymarket Theatre. Kean's appeal, however, did spur Drury on to make another effort. He wrote to Whitbread, who replied asking when Kean could be in London for a trial. On 7 November Drury wrote to Kean, telling him the good news. By a cruel stroke of luck, this letter was delayed for six days and did not reach Kean at Dorchester until the 13th. In the meantime, Howard had suffered a relapse, and Kean believed it imperative to be in a position where he could afford the best medical attention for his child. As the last letter from Drury had been so doubtful, he had written to Elliston telling that when the Dorchester engagement ended he would be happy to be at his disposal. Then, on the 13th, Drury's letter arrived, telling him to go to Drury Lane for a trial. By this time he had already closed with Elliston. The delayed letter was the first link in what Kean was to call 'a chain of evil consequences'.

More than five weeks had gone by since Grenfell had passed on Drury's recommendation of Kean to Whitbread. During this time the committee had done very little about the matter, but now it seemed as though they could not move fast enough. Instead of bringing Kean to London, they sent their manager, Samuel Arnold, to see him act at Dorchester. Arnold arrived in Dorchester on 15 November. All that day Howard's condition had worsened and on the evening Kean reluctantly left his child's sick bed for the theatre, where he was to play Octavian in *The Mountaineers* and Kojah in the pantomime, *The Savages*. The events of that marvellous night were to be recounted frequently by Kean.

'When the curtain drew up,' he would begin, 'I saw a wretched house. A few people in the pit and gallery, and three persons in the boxes, showed the quantity of attraction that we possessed. In the stage-box, however, there was a gentleman who appeared to understand acting. He was very attentive to the performance. Seeing this, I was determined to play my best. The strange man did not applaud; but his looks told me that he was pleased. After the play I went to the dress-room [this was under the stage] to change my dress for the "Savage", so that I could hear every word that was said overhead. I heard a gentleman (who I supposed was the gentleman of the stage-box) ask Lee the name of the performer who played the principal character. "Oh!" answered Lee, "his name is Kean—a wonderful clever fellow; a great little man. He's going to London. He has got an engagement from Mr. Whitbread; —a great man, Sir." "Indeed!" replied the gentleman, "I am glad to hear it. He is certainly very clever; but he is very small." "His mind is large: no matter for his height," returned Lee to this. By this time, I was dressed for the "Savage", and I therefore mounted up to the stage. The gentleman bowed to me, and complimented me slightly upon my play, observing, "Your manager says that you are engaged for London?" "I am offered a trial," said I, "and if I succeed, I understand that I am to be engaged." "Well," said the gentleman, "will you breakfast with me in the morning? I am at the ————— hotel. I shall be glad to speak to you. My name is Arnold; I am the—*Manager of Drury Lane theatre.*" I staggered as if I had been shot. My acting in the "Savage" was done for. However, I stumbled through the part, and—here I am.'

At the interview with Arnold the following morning, the manager praised Kean's acting and said he had no doubt of his success in London. He admired his 'fine Italian face' and only regretted that he was not 'half a head taller'. He advised him 'in the language almost of a Parent' not to risk a trial in London under the handicap of a large salary, as those who did rarely came up to the expectations of a capricious audience. Finally, he offered him an engagement for three seasons, on an advancing scale of eight, nine and ten pounds a week, regardless of whether his début was a success or not. The character in which he wished to make his first appearance would be left to his own choice, and that he might have a fair trial, he would be allowed to play six parts before a verdict was pronounced upon him.

Surely this was the hour of Kean's triumph. After the long years of obscurity, the darkness was lifting at last and the future seemed brilliant. No more poverty, for eight pounds a week was a fortune to the poor actor. No more Harlequin, but instead the chance to play his interpretations of the tragic roles of Shakespeare, which he had perfected over the years. Some thoughts of his negotiations with Elliston must have crossed his mind, but he said nothing about them to Arnold. Here he acted with a certain measure of duplicity, but, in the circumstances, who can blame him? Had he explained the situation to Arnold, the manager might have helped him to break his engagement with Elliston, but, on the other hand, he might not. Learning that Kean had already closed with Elliston, he might have broken off his own negotiations. No one knew better than Kean that the whole life of a provincial actor could be spent in a fruitless effort to get a trial at one of the two great London theatres. He knew that the offer Arnold was making him was not likely to be repeated. He had no intention of resigning his chance of glory for the position of general factotum in a minor theatre. Had Drury's letter not been delayed, he would never have written to Elliston. In any case, Elliston had not replied and Kean did not know whether he was engaged at the Olympic or not. So he settled with Arnold without mentioning his previous commitment to Elliston. As events turned out, this proved to be a grave error of judgement.

Arnold had barely left Dorchester than Kean received a letter from Elliston, dated 15 November, telling him that the Olympic Theatre would open in Christmas week and that he looked forward to seeing him before then. To this, Kean replied: 'Since last I wrote to you, I have received a very liberal offer from the proprietors of Drury Lane Theatre. It gives me unspeakable regret that the proposals did not reach me before I had commenced negotiating with you; but I hope, sir, you will take a high and liberal view of the question when I beg to decline the invitation of Little Drury. Another time I shall be happy to treat with you.' Hoping that this was the end of the Elliston affair, Kean turned his mind to the pleasant contemplation of his future career at Drury Lane.

His happiness is reflected in a letter he wrote to Dr. Drury, on 21 November, a letter abounding in cheerfulness, gratitude and Latin quotations. He wrote: 'I have again and again read your instructive letter, and have each time received additional pleasure from the perusal. Be assured, sir, I shall treasure the admonitions it contains *memoria in aeterna*; the *verbum* from you is alone sufficient to create a *sapienta* in the object that may have been insensible before . . . You have, sir, opened a path of happiness to me, so sudden, so unexpected, that I can scarcely think it but a dream. *Ita ad hoc aetatis a pueritia fui, ut omnes labores periculo consueta habeam.* You have dispelled those clouds and difficulties, and the event I trust, shall render me deserving of such exalted friendship.'

On the following day, Howard died; he was four years old. The profundity of Kean's grief is evident in the letter he wrote to Dr.

Drury, informing him of his loss. Unlike his previous letter, it is brief and unadorned. He wrote: 'The joy I felt three days since at my flattering prospects of future prosperity, is now obliterated by the unexpected loss of my child. Howard, sir, died on Monday morning last. You may conceive my feelings and pardon the brevity of my letter."

During Howard's illness, Kean appears to have remained sober, but now, in his grief, he turned again to the bottle. As always, the drink did not soothe him, but drove him wild. He refused to believe that Howard was dead and kept trying to wake him. He was no help to Mary in her sorrow. They buried the child in a style they could ill afford, for no matter how poor they were, Mary always tried to keep up a genteel appearance. The coffin was handsome and four girls in white walked in front, strewing flowers. At the graveside Kean was almost insane. To add to his distress, he had that morning received a letter from Elliston, filled with 'Hauteur and Upbraidings', calling him a deserter and declaring that he would claim his man.

Kean replied to this letter in obsequious terms, stating the advantages he must forgo by complying with Elliston's demands and appealing to his liberal feelings. In the midst of all this grief and trouble, he had to continue with the Dorchester engagement, otherwise he would lose his benefit, and he needed the money for the doctor and the undertaker. As it happened, his benefit cleared barely sufficient to pay these bills, and in order to get to London he had to borrow five pounds from Lee. Early in December, he arrived there and took lodgings at 21 Cecil Street, near the Strand.

One of the first things he learned was that a Mr. Russell, late of Drury Lane, had been employed for some time as acting manager at the Olympic Theatre. This piece of information, together with the fact that he had received no further word from Elliston, gave him reason to hope that he was no longer wanted at the Olympic. He presented himself at Drury Lane, where he was interviewed by the committee. He was dressed in shabby mourning, which heightened his natural pallor, and taken altogether, his appearance struck them most unfavourably. He told them he would make his début as Shylock, but the committee, seeing nothing but failure ahead, suggested that perhaps it would be better if he made his first appearance in a character of secondary importance. Kean stood firm. He reminded them that a choice of characters had been guaranteed him and demanded that this promise be fulfilled. *Aut Caesar aut nullus*, he quoted to them. The committee yielded and he withdrew. After Kean had left the room, Arnold was criticised by the committee for lack of judgement in saddling them with this little coxcomb of an actor, who not only spoke of his rights but dared to mouth Latin at them.

Kean drew his first salary of eight pounds from the Drury Lane treasury. He now had the money to bring his wife and child from Dorchester. As Mary took a last look at Howard's grave, her 'Heart strings cracked.' She was tortured by guilt for having exhibited the child at Exeter so shortly before his final illness. 'Oh, Dear Susan,' she wrote to her sister, 'tell me I have no sin to answer for in exposing his innocence, his angel form, to gain a dinner for his parent—the thought sometimes harrows up my soul.'

When Kean next went to Drury Lane, Arnold received him coldly, saying, 'Young man, you have acted a strange part in engaging with me when you were already bound to Mr. Elliston.' The worst had happened. Elliston had informed the committee that Kean was engaged to him. When the committee learned this, they were deeply offended. Not only had Kean been disrespectful but he had also had the audacity to try to deceive them. They believed that they had been put upon by a trickster from the provinces, who had entered into a contract he was unable to fulfil. Kean tried to explain to Arnold, but the manager would not listen. He told Kean that he must settle the matter himself with Elliston and produce a written release before he could consider himself a member of the Drury Lane company. Until that time, the treasury had been ordered not to pay his salary.

In trying to get the better of Robert William Elliston, Kean had made a powerful enemy. His future career was to be bound up with this strange man, and he was to find that in all his dealings with him he always came off the worse. At the time of this first dispute, Elliston was thirty-nine years old. As a boy, he had been intended for the Church, but amateur theatricals had given him a taste for acting and when he was sixteen he ran away to Bath, playing there and on the York circuit. He made his London début at the Haymarket in 1796, and soon became one of the most popular actors of the day. But he disliked being employed by other men and decided to make theatre management his main interest.

In March, 1813, he had taken over the Olympic Theatre. This was situated at the west end of Wych Street, one of the dirtiest and most disreputable thoroughfares in London, the haunt of thieves, informers and prostitutes. He had immediately changed the name of the theatre to Little Drury Lane. The major theatre had objected strongly to this implied association with a minor one and, as a result, his licence was withdrawn and he was forced to close. By promising that the Olympic would be known solely by its old name, he had managed to get another licence and he was re-opening the theatre in Christmas week. It was for this coming season that he wanted the services of Kean, and Robert William Elliston usually got what he wanted.

He was a middle-sized man, whose round face seemed always on the verge of laughter. He was extremely loquacious and his lips continued to move even when he was not speaking. He was a man of pleasure, devoted to drink, women and gambling. He was also a convincing liar. At the time of his dispute with Kean, he was the manager of two metropolitan theatres, the Olympic and the Surrey; he also managed the Theatre Royal, Birmingham. In addition, he acted at Drury Lane three nights a week. The players he engaged for his two London theatres were made to divide their labours between both, often on the same night. The Surrey and the Olympic lay far apart, on opposite sides of the Thames, and it was a common sight, on Blackfriars Bridge at night, to see a group of half-clad players, with painted faces, racing past in cold winds or pelting rain, their expressions strained and anxious from fear that they would be late. Elliston was an erratic person and green-rooms buzzed with the latest story of his odd behaviour. But beneath the eccentricity was a hard-headed business man, charming to those he would conciliate and ruthless to those he wished to punish or subdue.

On 6 December Kean wrote to Elliston: 'the fate of my family is in your hands. Are you determined to crush the object that never injured you ... Through your means I am deprived of my situation in Drury Lane Theatre, unless I produce a document from you that I am not a member of the New Olympic. How can you reconcile this more than Turkish barbarity? ... You have become a thorn in the side of my young fortune. I shall conclude by simply requesting you to inform me whether I am to become a member of the Theatre Royal, Drury Lane, or again, penniless, hopeless and despised, am I to be cast again in the provinces, the rejected of this great city, which should afford a home to industry of every kind. With my family at my back will I return, for the walls of Wych Street I will never enter.' Elliston replied: 'To any man with the smallest gift of intellect and the dimmest sense of honour, it must appear that on the 11th of November, and previous to that time, you deemed yourself engaged to me, and that subsequently a more attractive offer having been made, you held it convenient to consider a pledge as idle as words muttered in a dream. All my engagements are made and fulfilled with honour on my part, and I expect an equal punctuality from others.'

Kean hung about Drury Lane every day, hoping to hear from Arnold of a settlement, but the manager consistently refused to see him. As the players passed to morning rehearsals, they looked curiously at the little man huddled in a shabby great-coat with capes. They regarded him as one who had come to usurp their rights, and they openly ridiculed him, saying, 'The little man with the great capes is here again. Poor little fellow: he'll be smothered in his capes. He wants to come out: What will the stage come to? Who will come next?' They told him to return to the provinces, for among such actors as surrounded him in London, he would have no chance. Rae, with whom he had played for a season at the Haymarket, passed him without a word. Munden advised him 'to spend his evenings in front, trying to improve himself by witnessing the performances of good actors'. He was generally spoken of as 'Arnold's hard bargain'.

Kean wrote to Whitbread, imploring his help. The chairman

replied that if Kean had talent, he would be able to show it on his appearance, if not he must return to the provinces; but concerning his misunderstanding with Arnold, he knew nothing. Kean wrote to Drury, who told him to 'bear all; bear all, only come out'. Every day he went to Drury Lane, enduring in a proud silence all the humiliations heaped upon him. If by chance he caught a glimpse of Arnold, the manager gave him a look which crushed every hope. At length, a meeting was arranged between Arnold, Elliston and Kean. At the outset, Arnold stated that Kean stood most unfavourably in his opinion and that 'the most profound submission' was to be expected from him. Then Elliston, arrogant and voluble, shouted down every attempt Kean made to explain his position. Even Arnold found it difficult to get a word in. The meeting ended badly for Kean, with Arnold telling him that the Drury Lane committee considered him to be a member of the company, but admitting that Elliston had a prior claim. Until Elliston released him, Kean could not play at Drury Lane, and the committee would bring legal action against him if he played in any other theatre. This placed Kean in a terrible dilemma. If he could not play at Drury Lane and Drury Lane would not let him play elsewhere, then he was a ruined man. For a fortnight he had to endure this agony. His mind was almost unhinged. He suspected that powerful enemies were working against him. He told Mary: 'If I should succeed now, I think it would drive me mad.'

Then, just before Christmas, Elliston sent for him. To Kean's astonishment, he was received in a most friendly manner. Elliston told him that he had decided to relinquish his claim on his services, and all that he would extract from him was a promise to play at his Birmingham theatre during the Drury Lane vacation. As this was a compliment rather than a condition, Kean could not agree quickly enough. Unknown to Kean, Elliston had been forced by the Drury Lane committee to alter his position. As a salaried member of their company, they had been able to exert pressure on him to release Kean from his commitment. The financial state of the theatre had become so desperate that they were willing to try Kean, or, indeed, any tragedian who had an outside chance of success. But they were still determined to punish him for his behaviour towards them. That evening Elliston and Arnold met at Drury Lane, and, after Elliston had left, Kean was called into the manager's office. He was told that an actor, Mr. Barnard, was to be sent from Drury Lane to the Olympic as his substitute at a salary of two pounds a week, but that he himself must bear the cost. This was a harsh decision, for it brought Kean's wage down to six pounds a week. And he had not yet done all his penance, for Arnold told him that there would be no pay for him the following day unless he could produce a written release from Elliston.

The next day Kean ran all over London in search of Elliston. He tried his theatres, his home and various haunts, but he was no-where to be found. He caught up with him at three o'clock in the afternoon, and after much procrastination, Elliston wrote out the necessary document. Anxious to draw his money before the treasury closed, Kean hurried to Drury Lane and sent in his name to Arnold. He was told that the manager was busy, and 'for nearly one hour', he told Dr. Drury, 'I waited in the passage with *the rest of the Menials* of the Theatre, had the mortification of seeing them all conducted to his presence before myself & when summon'd at last to appear, was with the continued brow of Severity informed, that I had no claim upon the treasury, my engagement had all to begin again, *I shall not forget the day of the month.*' It was Christmas Eve.

'Sad & melancholy ever is my theme to be at this happy season, while thousands are revelling in Luxury,' Mary wrote to her sister. 'I with many other forlorn ones, shed the tears of Misery— *no hope now—no, no resource*—cold, cold in the Earth is that jewel that was my only consolation. . . . we are now at the very Climax of Misery—happiness I have never known, nor do I now feel that sorrow for the loss of it—*I should, a few weeks ago* . . . I would give worlds, my Dear Sister, to see you *once more.* . . . I have no one to speak of him, his father can't name him.'

On Friday, 31 December, Kean went again to the treasury, only to be told that his engagement was not yet in order. He had the additional mortification of learning that Huddart had been brought from Dublin to play Shylock, the very character in which he had planned to make his début. And so the old year ended. On 7 January 1814, he again presented himself at the treasury and again there was no money for him. He and his family had now lived in London for more than five weeks on his first wage of eight pounds. Aunt Tid did nothing to help them, she could not even bring herself to visit Mary. Kean and his wife had to sell most of their possessions and sometimes they starved in order to have sufficient food for their child. They would have found it even harder to survive but for the generosity of the Misses Williams, in whose house they had taken lodgings. When the landladies became aware of their predicament, they did not ask for rent. One of them told Mary: 'There is something about Mr. Kean, ma'am, which tells us he will be a great man.'

There is no doubt that at this great crisis in his life, Kean behaved with dignity. This time he had not run away, as he usually did when things went wrong. He also seems to have remained sober. He was sustained throughout by the conviction that the position of leading tragedian at Drury Lane belonged to him by right; he was a king claiming his throne. And his tenacity was about to be rewarded. Drury Lane was still losing ground to Covent Garden. The theatre was facing bankruptcy. In desperation, actor after actor was thrown into the breach—Huddart as Shylock, Rae as Jaffier, Sowerby as Othello—but all of them failed. At last the committee decided to give Kean his chance. They did not expect him to succeed, but at least he could do no worse than the others. It was announced that he would make his first appearance at Drury Lane, on Wednesday, 26 January, as Shylock in *The Merchant of Venice*.

CHAPTER THREE

THE SAVIOUR OF DRURY LANE

To appreciate the memorable events of 26 January 1814, it is necessary to look at the state of tragic acting on the English stage at the time of Kean's début. Poetic drama flourished as the dominant form, as it had done from the days of the Elizabethans. Since then, the approach to tragic acting had been heroic, for the tragic role was considered to be the expression of the finest qualities in mankind. At the time of the Restoration, this ideal remained the same, but with Thomas Betterton the style of acting became more formal and declamatory. Betterton heightened the speaking of verse and widened the gap between it and familiar speech. His style was carried on by Barton Booth and then by James Quin, in whom all the characteristics of the classical school —the solemn gaze, the measured strut, the sing-song chant—were seen to perfection. Then, on 19 October 1741, David Garrick made his début at Goodman's Fields Theatre and swept away, for ever it seemed, all this artificiality.

Garrick's acting remained heroic, but it was more varied. He revived the discarded technique of transition, by which the expression of one emotion gave way rapidly to that of another. His acting had such force that beside him Quin and his school seemed languid and monotonous. Like Kean, Garrick lacked the height expected in the tradition of the tragic drama, but he overcame this disadvantage by his powerful acting. Under his influence, acting became more naturalistic, but this was not to last, for, in 1783, John Philip Kemble made his London début at Drury Lane and re-established the classical style.

Kemble had all the physical attributes that the public expected to find in a leading tragedian. He was tall and well-built, with strongly marked Roman features and a commanding presence. Since Garrick, acting had become increasingly subjective; actors seized on certain aspects of a character, ignoring whatever did not fit in with their conception. Kemble was the first to attempt a consistently developing characterisation. He never took the obvious view of a part, as Garrick had done; his interpretations were the result of long study. His Macbeth and Hamlet were particularly admired. He was at his best in the roles of characters gravely pre-occupied with themselves, such as King John, Brutus and, above all, Coriolanus.

Although he was capable of as much emotional transition as Garrick, he chose to use it more sparingly. The coldness of his acting was broken only occasionally by bursts of emotion, sometimes no more than once in a performance. He believed that these bursts were all the more effective for their rarity. Every line he spoke contributed to the development of the character. It has been suggested that his slow and clear enunciation was the result of the asthma from which he suffered so chronically; that in evolving his theory of tragic acting, he was making a virtue of necessity. In all physical actions, he aimed at a superlative grace. Whatever he did on stage—sitting, standing, walking, kneeling—he did gracefully. In his efforts to attain this, he often sacrificed the energy of his acting. Unfortunately, many of his disciples, especially Charles Mayne Young, exaggerated the faults of his style and, as a result, tragic acting became stiff and artificial.

During his time at Drury Lane, Kemble revived many of Shakespeare's plays and, when he moved to Covent Garden in 1801 he continued his work of presenting Shakespeare as perfectly as possible. Since the Restoration, Shakespeare had been presented in a mangled form. His adaptors, intent on 'improving him', had curtailed acts, eliminated characters, transposed scenes, changed plots and written in new lines. Kemble restored the original texts, but this is not to say that audiences saw the plays in their entirety: this was not to happen until the twentieth century. Having restored the text, he then cut it, bearing in mind the length of time allotted for the performance, the tastes of his audience and the powers of particular players in his company. As far as possible, the leading role remained untouched, so the more that was chopped away the more attention was directed towards the star, and this was usually Kemble himself.

This was strictly practical, as the audiences of the time were more interested in the star than in the play. The interpretation of a part was entirely the actor's own responsibility; there was no director to supervise his movements and inflections. With Shakespeare's plays being so frequently repeated, one of the great pleasures of theatre-going was the opportunity of comparing different actors' interpretations of major roles. Certain crucial moments in each play were closely observed. These were the actor's 'points', and he was judged on the number of successful points he made. Some of these points had become hallowed by tradition, handed down from generation to generation. Any deviation from them was not to be undertaken lightly and could often result in disapproval.

The major theatres, with their nightly change of programme, had always relied heavily on Shakespeare, but there was another reason why the first quarter of the nineteenth century was so rich in revivals of his plays and those of other Elizabethan dramatists. There was a lack of contemporary plays. Although the age was rich in poets, among them Wordsworth, Coleridge, Shelley, Keats, and Byron, and poetry was the dominant form in drama, they wrote very little for the stage. There were two reasons for this: on the whole their poetry was not suited to drama and also the interest in Shakespeare weighed heavily on them. Their own poetic natures and the excellence of Shakespeare inhibited them when they tried to write for the theatre.

At the time, dramatic criticism was flourishing in the hands of a group of masters that included Coleridge, Lamb, Hunt and Hazlitt. These critics deplored the fact that Shakespeare, as presented in the major theatres, was tailored to the demands of the star system and the tastes of the audience. They concluded that contemporary productions of Shakespeare constituted a travesty of his genius. Coleridge and Hazlitt both made out a case for preferring to read Shakespeare's plays rather than witnessing their performance on the stage, yet Hazlitt continued to visit the theatre, hoping to discover there an actor who could match the ideal performances that were taking place in the theatre of his mind. He did not find this ideal in Kemble, who, through formal attitudes and measured cadences, coldly delineated the mental processes of Shakespeare's characters. He believed that an actor must evoke in his audience an imaginative and sympathetic response to characters who shared the same humanity as themselves, and the degree to which he could invoke this response would be the measure of his greatness.

Leigh Hunt never tired of seeing Shakespeare's plays on the stage, even though his judgement told him that the performances were inadequate. He, too, believed that it was the style of acting as much as the mangled texts which was inhibiting the genius of Shakespeare. He argued that while tragedy needed a loftiness of language and manner not used by people in real life, this did not necessarily mean the artificiality of Kemble. He agreed that the conventions of the drama must be preserved, but saw no reason why these conventions need prevent an actor from becoming more naturalistic. He admitted that the perfect conjunction of artifice and nature could possibly be found only in a genius, but, if such a one existed, he would be the ideal actor. Hunt's views, together with those of Hazlitt, show that early nineteenth-century taste was shifting from the classical to the romantic, outdating Kemble and preparing the way for Kean.

When Kean made his début at Drury Lane, Kemble was approaching the end of his career. For thirty-one years he had been acknowledged as the leading tragedian of the English stage, and, during this time, the classical style of acting had become universally accepted. During his long reign, no one had come anywhere near to displacing him. In 1801, he had been briefly challenged by George Frederick Cooke, a vigorous, naturalistic actor, who carried his audiences along by the violence of his passions and the rapidity of his transitions. But Cooke had no staying powers. He was usually drunk when he played, and it was said that the drunker he was the better he acted. He did not diminish the reputation of Kemble, who continued to reign as the undisputed monarch of the English stage. But now, at Drury Lane, on 26 January 1814, another challenger was about to take the field.

*

The day of Kean's début was cold and miserable. A heavy fall of snow two days previously was thawing slowly, covering the streets with deep slush, and a drizzling rain had set in, which was to continue all day. Only one rehearsal had been allotted him and this was called for twelve o'clock on the day of the performance. Until then he had never gone through a scene with any of the players who were to act with him that night. The stage manager was George Raymond, generally known as 'Bustling' Raymond, and neither he nor any of the players gave Kean a word of encouragement. The atmosphere was one of defeat, for they were certain he would fail, like all the other provincial tragedians who had come and gone in the past few weeks.

That night Kean set out for Drury Lane. He could not afford a carriage, and trudged through the slush, carrying a bundle containing his stage costume. At the theatre, he was offered a dressing-room to himself, for on that night at least he was the star, but he refused this because of the attitude of the committee towards him, and he changed below the stage with the supporting actors. They were startled when they saw him lay out a black wig and beard. The news spread quickly backstage that the strange little man from Exeter had rejected the traditional red wig worn by every Shylock since the days of Shakespeare himself. Even Charles Macklin, who, seventy-three years previously, had been the first to interpret the part as a tragic instead of a comic one, had retained the red wig. This was the first of the many surprising events that were to happen at Drury Lane that night.

There were few people in the theatre. The boxes were completely empty and the pit and gallery barely half full. The weather had inclined people to stay at home rather than sit on the cheerless benches at Drury Lane to witness the failure of yet another provincial tragedian. The actors expected no more to come until half-price, for obviously the only attraction of the evening was the afterpiece, with the comedian, Jack Bannister, playing in a farce entitled *The Apprentice*. The curtain rose and *The Merchant of Venice* began.

Alexander Rae, as Bassanio, listlessly expounded his love for Portia. The prompter told the call-boy to summon Kean, but the boy found him already waiting in the wings. When he made his entrance as Shylock, and stood listening gravely to Bassanio's request for money, a ripple of expectancy ran through the thin audience. They sensed that this was no ordinary actor. Dr. Drury told him later: 'I could scarcely draw my breath when you came upon the stage. But directly you took your position, and leaned upon your cane, I knew that all was right.'

Bassanio said, 'Be assured you may take his bond,' and Shylock's sardonic reply, 'I *will* be assured I may,' drew the first applause of the evening. Then his mood changed, as with the garrulity of age, he told the story of Jacob and his flock. By the time he had finished, everyone in the vast cold theatre had been warmed into responsive life. When he addressed Antonio, the contempt in his voice drew further applause.

> Hath a *dog* money? is it possible
> A *cur* can lend three thousand ducats . . .

The expressions playing rapidly over his thin, pallid face wore, in turn, sinister, vigilant, ascetic and revengeful. His arms and hands were in constant play; his whole body was eloquent. No one in the audience had seen anything like this.

By the end of the second act, the theatre had filled up a little. A new comic opera, *A Farmer's Wife*, advertised for first production that night at Covent Garden, had been withdrawn at the last minute, and some of those disappointed crossed over to see the new tragedian at Drury Lane. But even with these additions, the theatre was far from full. The newcomers were in time to see the remarkable playing of Kean in the first scene of the third act, between Shylock, Solanio and Salarino. Shylock said: 'He hath disgraced me and hindered me half-a-million; laughed at my losses, mocked at my gains, scorned my nation, thwarted my bargains, cooled my friends, heated mine enemies . . .' He hurried through the catalogue of wrongs Antonio had done him, accentuating each one in a high-pitched voice, but when he reached the climax—'and what's his reason? I am a Jew'—he came down by a sudden transition to a gentle suffering tone on the words, '*I am a Jew.*' The natural simplicity he gave to the words touched the heart of the audience. Then he continued, with passionate recrimination in his voice, 'If you prick us, do we not bleed? if you tickle us, do we not laugh? . . .' The audience were on their feet, greeting each savage interrogation with roars of approval.

The players seated in the green room were startled by the din. They rushed to the wings in time to see Shylock raging like a lion in the dialogue with Tubal. Dr. John Doran, the theatre historian, wrote: '[His] anguish at his daughter's flight, his wrath at the two Christians who make sport of his anguish; his hatred of all Christians, generally, and of Antonio in particular; and then his alternations of rage, grief, and ecstasy, as Tubal relates the losses incurred in the search of that naughty Jessica, her extravagances, and then the ill-luck that has fallen upon Antonio;—in all this, there was such originality, such terrible force, such assurance of a new and mighty master,—that the house burst forth into a very whirlwind of approbation.' William Oxberry, who played the role of Launcelot Gobbo, wrote: 'How the devil so few of them kicked up such a row was marvellous.'

In the trial scene in the fourth act, Kean consolidated his triumph. When urged by Portia to accept Bassanio's offer of three times the sum owed in place of a pound of Antonio's flesh, he replaced the traditional severity of Shylock's reply, 'An oath, an oath, I have an oath in heaven,' with the bantering tone of a man who knows that things are going his way. Again, his reply to Portia's entreaty to procure a surgeon for charity's sake, 'I cannot find it; 'tis not in the bond,' was accompanied by a delightful chuckle instead of the sneer given by Macklin and other actors. Doran wrote: 'His calm appearance at first, his confident appeal to justice; his deafness, when appeal is made to him for mercy; his steady joyousness, when the young lawyer recognises the validity of the bond; his burst of exultation, when his right is confessed; his fiendish eagerness, when whetting the knife:—and then, the sudden collapse of disappointment and terror, with the words, 'Is *that*—the *LAW*?'—in all was made manifest, that a noble successor to the noblest of the actors of old had arisen. Then, his trembling anxiety to recover what he had before refused; his sordid abjectness, as he finds himself foiled, at every turn; his subdued fury; and, at the last (and it was always the crowning glory of his acting in this play) the withering sneer, hardly concealing the crushed heart, with which he replied to the jibes of Gratiano, as he left the court,—all raised a new sensation in an audience, who acknowledged it in a perfect tumult of acclamation. As he passed to his dressing-room, Raymond saluted him with the confession, that he had made a hit; Pope, more generous, avowed that he had saved the house from ruin.'

With the trial scene, Kean's part was over and by the time the play finished, he had already left the theatre. He hurried home to tell Mary of his triumph and he burst in upon her, shouting exultantly, 'Mary, you shall ride in your carriage, and Charlie shall go to Eton.'

Only two newspapers, the *Morning Post* and the *Morning Chronicle*, had sent their dramatic critics to Kean's début. The *Morning Post* praised his expressive face, his intelligence and mastery of his art. The critic for the *Morning Chronicle* was William Hazlitt. He was thirty-five years old and he had worked for the newspaper since the spring of the previous year. He had started as Parliamentary correspondent, but in October the editor, James Perry, had appointed him dramatic critic. Perry had no idea that in Hazlitt he had a genius on his staff and he sighed at the length of the dramatic criticisms that landed daily on his desk. He had been asked by the Drury Lane committee to report kindly on Kean's début, and he had instructed Hazlitt accordingly. Hazlitt recalled: 'I had been told to give as favourable an account as I could: I gave a true one. I am not one of those who, when they see the sun breaking from behind a cloud, stop to ask others whether it is the moon. Mr. Kean's appearance was the first gleam of genius breaking athwart the gloom of the Stage.'

It was a remarkable stroke of destiny that Kean's début coincided so closely with that of Hazlitt as a critic, for in Hazlitt he was to have a chronicler worthy of his performances. But if this was fortunate for Kean, it was equally so for Hazlitt. For years he had brooded on the characters of Shakespeare until they had become part of his blood and spirit, but he was beginning to doubt that he would ever see them fully realised on the stage of a theatre. He was to find in Kean not only an understanding of Shakespeare that matched his own, but the power to give expression to it, visible and tangible, on the boards of Drury Lane. To this, Hazlitt was to respond ardently, and his accounts of Kean's performances are written with a passion unequalled in the history of dramatic criticism. With Kean's début as Shylock, Hazlitt embarked on a voyage of discovery that he would not have believed possible this side of the grave. 'Before the night was ended,' he wrote, 'I had hailed in such poor words as I could muster at the moment, the advent, I might almost say the portent, of Edmund Kean.'

While the Drury Lane committee were pleased with Kean's reception, two favourable reviews and the applause of a small audience did not completely allay their uncertainty as to how the great majority of playgoers would react to him. Kemble had made the classical style of acting fashionable and many people might not care for Kean's rapidity and energy. The committee had not enough confidence in him to alter their schedule and his next performance did not take place until 1 February, almost a week later. This was his real test. The audience was double that of his début and included many connoisseurs of the drama. With the exception of *The Times*, all the newspapers were represented. Hazlitt had come again to see whether Kean could sustain his previous performance, and he was not disappointed. He wrote in the *Morning Chronicle*: 'His style of acting is, if we may use the expression, more significant, more pregnant with meaning, more varied and alive in every part, than any we have almost ever witnessed. The character never stands still; there is no vacant pause in the action; the eye is never silent.'

Leigh Hunt's *Examiner* was equally enthusiastic. Thomas Barnes was covering the theatre in place of Hunt, who was in prison for a libel on the Prince Regent. Like Hunt, Barnes was totally opposed to the artificiality of Kemble and his school. He wrote of Kean: 'There was an animating soul distinguishable in all he said and did, which at once gave a high interest to his performance, and excited those emotions, which are always felt at the presence of genius—that is, at the union of great powers with a fine sensibility. It was this that gave fire to his eye, energy to his tones, and such a variety and expressiveness to all his gestures, that one might almost say "his body thought".'

On 3 February Kean gave his third performance as Shylock. The prestigious *Times*, which would never have condescended to report on a completely unknown actor, was now sufficiently interested to send their critic. He wrote: 'We have seldom seen a much better Shylock. If he be inferior to Kemble in those peculiarities which distinguish that great actor, and to Cooke, in the force which he, above most performers, must give to particular passages, he need have no fear of a successful competition with any other man on the stage who attempts the sordid and malignant Jew.' This was praise indeed, for *The Times* had always favoured the classical style of Kemble. In the eyes of the committee, this review, above all others, set the seal of approval on Kean. They began to hope that in him they had at last found the tragedian they were seeking. It was too early to know this for certain, but now Kean was about to give another demonstration of his powers. He was preparing to show what he could do with Richard III.

He had planned his campaign with care. He had chosen Shylock for his début, because the loose costume and stoop of age disguised his shortness. The deformity of Richard, the crook-backed king, would do the same. Shylock had gained him the attention of the public, but it was a comparatively small part. Richard, on the other hand, was longer and more arduous, but it was also a show-piece. If he could succeed in it, he would consolidate his reputation before playing Hamlet, Othello and Macbeth, roles in which his lack of height could not be hidden. Richard III, like Shylock, was not a direct challenge to Kemble, for this had never been con-sidered one of his greatest roles. As Richard, Kean would be challenging comparison with Garrick and Cooke. This was the character in which Garrick had taken London by storm, and Cooke was considered by many to be unrivalled in the part.

Kean acted Richard III in Colley Cibber's adaptation, the version which had held the stage since 1700. To the original play, Cibber had added parts of *Richard II*, *Henry IV*, *Henry V* and

Henry VI. From all these he had fashioned a well-constructed thriller and a dazzling piece of theatre. He had made Richard more villainous by removing the self-questioning of Shakespeare's character and substituting an unrelenting determination to seize the throne. Two of Richard's most effective lines—'Off with his head; so much for Buckingham,' and 'Richard's himself again,' —were written by Cibber. His Richard was not so subtle as Shakespeare's, but he was a fascinating monster, evil and charming.

On Saturday, 12 February 1814, Kean appeared as Richard III at Drury Lane. The theatre was crowded, and, if there were few among the audience who had seen Garrick, there were many who remembered Cooke. At his first entrance, Kean bustled across the stage, every movement of his body alert and quick. The audience, accustomed to the heroic strut of tragedians, were startled. He seemed completely unaware of them; conscious of nothing but his own reflections. His opening soliloquy was not declaimed, but spoken in natural tones. The line, 'But I that am not shaped for sportive tricks,' was given with a mixture of ironical contempt and self-approval. His courtship of Lady Anne was a wonderful exhibition of hypocrisy. Hazlitt wrote: 'An enchanting smile played upon his lips, while a courteous humility bowed his head.' 'His attitude in leaning against the side of the stage before he comes forward in this scene, was one of the most gracious and striking we remember to have seen. It would have done for Titian to paint.' 'He seemed like the first tempter, to approach his prey, certain of the event, and as if success had smoothed his way before him.'

When Buckingham asked him what should be done if Hastings did not join their conspiracy, the offhandedness of his reply: 'Chop off his head,' conveyed how little he cared for anyone who stood in his way. As he listened to the taunting of the young Duke of York, his acting was a masterpiece of controlled anger. When his nephew, Prince Edward, said, 'I fear no uncles dead,' and Richard turned and answered, 'Nor any, sir, that live, I hope,' the action was performed and the words uttered with the quickness of a snake. Then his air of listening to the entreaties of the Lord

Mayor that he should be king; the scarcely subdued triumph in his eyes as he refused the throne; his acceding to the pleas of his confederates; and, after they had all departed, his burst of exultation, 'Why, now my golden dream is out!'—in all this, he held the audience spellbound. Later that night, he was to tell Mary of the power that had possessed him throughout the performance. 'I could not feel the stage under me,' he said.

When he was preparing to fight against Richmond, and Stanley told him that his friends were all ready in the north, his retort,

> The north! why, what do they i' the north,
> When they should serve their sovereign in the west?

was shrill and taunting. The instant he heard of the capture of his old confederate, Buckingham, he said 'Off with his head,' then added, with contemptuous levity, 'so much for Buckingham.'

The closing scenes of the play were even more brilliant. The manner in which he stood apart on the night before the battle, completely abstracted, drawing patterns in the sand with the point of his sword, and his sudden recovery of himself with 'a goodnight, my friends,' followed by his abrupt withdrawal to his tent, drew a prolonged round of applause. The *Morning Post* described this as 'one of the finest pieces of acting we have ever beheld, or perhaps that the stage has ever known'. His awakening from his nightmare with the groan, 'Give me another horse,' sent a shudder of terror through the audience. He staggered forward, leaning on his sword, sank on one knee, then started back, as if he wished to rise. His free hand, held high in the air, shook violently, even to the fingertips. Still shaking with fright, he advanced on his knees to the front of the stage. Then, with the words, 'Conscience, avaunt!' he thrust his fears behind him, and rising to his feet, he brandished his sword above his head and shouted triumphantly, 'Richard's himself again.'

Even these wonderful moments paled before the radiance of the death scene. Although disarmed and mortally wounded, he continued to thrust at Richmond with his fists, his glances half extinguished but still furious. Hazlitt wrote: 'He fought like one drunk with wounds, and the attitude in which he stands with his hands stretched out, after his sword is taken from him, had a preternatural and terrific grandeur, as if his will could not be disarmed, and the very phantoms of despair had the power to kill.' When, at last, he stopped fighting, the eyes that searched the audience were already those of another world. The audience sat in silence, awed by the sublimity of the scene.

Most of the critics were enthusiastic about his performance, while Barnes, in the *Examiner*, was lyrical. Of the death scene, he wrote: 'We have felt our eyes gush on reading a passage of exquisite poetry, we have been ready to leap at the sight of a noble picture, but we never felt stronger emotion, more overpowering sensations than those kindled by the novel sublimity of the catastrophe.' Hazlitt, in the *Morning Chronicle*, was more restrained. In the first place, he deplored the presentation of Shakespeare in Cibber's 'miserable medley'. Then, although he considered Kean's performance 'brilliant and original', it was 'not absolutely perfect'. It must be remembered that Hazlitt was judging Kean by a standard of perfection no mortal actor could possibly attain. The ideal performances of Shakespeare were taking place in the theatre of his mind, and it was against this ideal that he was always to measure Kean.

Of Kean's performance as Richard, he wrote: 'To be perfect, it should have a little more solidity, depth, sustained and impassioned feeling, with somewhat less brilliancy, with fewer glancing lights, pointed transitions, and pantomimic evolutions ... If Mr. Kean does not completely succeed in concentrating all the lines of character, as drawn by Shakespeare, he gives an animation, vigour and relief to the part, which we have never seen surpassed. He is more refined than Cooke; more bold, varied, and original than Kemble, in the same character ... He gave to all the busy scenes of the play the greatest animation and effect. He filled every part of the stage ... on the whole the performance was the most perfect of anything that has been witnessed since the days of Garrick.' He thought Kean's greatest faults were hoarseness and lack of dignity, but what were these when set against his dazzling achievement. 'In one who *dares* so much,' he wrote, 'there is little indeed to blame.'

The exertions of his performance had so weakened Kean that he was compelled to rest for a week. When he resumed the part of Richard on Saturday, 19 February, the audience included some of the most famous men and women of the day, among them Lord Byron.

'By Jove, he is a soul!' Byron wrote. 'Life—nature—truth without exaggeration or diminution. Kemble's Hamlet is perfect; but Hamlet is not nature. Richard is a man; and Kean is Richard.' Hazlitt was there again, hoping to see the perfect performance, and finding that Kean still fell short of this. 'But why do we try this actor by an ideal theory,' he wrote. 'Who is there that will stand the same test?' Hazlitt was beginning to realise that he was watching over the unfolding of a genius, that from one who '*dares* so much', what might not be expected. Could ideal performances of Shakespeare's plays take place only in the theatre of the mind, or —the thought staggered his imagination—did this actor have the power to reveal the great tragic heroes—Lear, Macbeth, Othello and Hamlet—as they had never before been seen on earth?

With *Richard III*, the Drury Lane committee were in the unusual position of having a smash hit on their hands. On 19 February the receipts were £544, on the 24th £592, on the 28th £608, and on 3 March £655. The free list was suspended. As there were no reserved seats in the pit or gallery, people fought their way into the theatre, and even inside there was a struggle to gain a seat on the benches. Kean had become a personality. His mysterious background was a constant source of gossip. It was said that he had been educated at Eton, that he had been an officer in the army and that he was the bastard son of the Duke of Norfolk. The story that Kean was a Norfolk came to the ears of the Duke himself. This happened one night during this first season at Drury Lane, when Kean was playing Richard III. Lord Essex, going out of his box into the lobby, ran into the Duke and asked, 'Why don't you acknowledge your son?' The Duke was startled by the question and retorted, 'What son?' 'Why, Kean,' said Lord Essex. 'It is reported generally that he is your son and that Miss Tidswell is his mother.' 'I assure you,' the Duke replied, 'that I should be very proud to acknowledge him, but this is the first intimation I have received on the subject.'

Together with Napoleon Buonaparte, Kean was the chief topic of conversation in the drawing rooms and clubs of London. When Joseph Farington, the painter, dined at the Royal Academy Club, on 2 March, the talk there was of 'the extraordinary talents of Edmund Kean, a new actor in Tragedy, and of His being perfectly *original* in His manner of representing characters.—They said that Wroughton, an Old Actor, spoke of Him as having much of what Garrick possessed.' Five days later, Farington heard a different opinion from the artists, William Westall and John Aytoun. 'They spoke of *Kean* the new Actor, & said that he was puffed beyond His claim, probably to fill the Drury Lane Theatre which was reduced almost to Bankruptcy.' Kean had become a controversial figure. Some said that he was another Garrick, others that he was a passing fancy like Master Betty. Kemble had made artificiality the fashion on the stage and some found Kean's naturalistic style strange and confusing. They argued that Kemble was by far the better actor, and even Kean's supporters had to admit that so far he had done little to disprove this.

No one knew better than Kean that to challenge comparison with Kemble he must show not only brilliance in character roles such as Richard and Shylock, but also intellectual depth and universality. Therefore, he chose Hamlet as his next part. This was the supreme test. Success in this part was essential if he were to be acknowledged as the complete tragedian. Also in choosing Hamlet, he was challenging Kemble in one of his greatest roles.

On Saturday, 12 March, Kean appeared as Hamlet at Drury Lane. For hours before the play began, there had been a struggle at the doors. The orchestra could not be heard above the din of the audience. Even when the curtain rose on the first scene the noise continued, but silence fell as the royal court of Denmark assembled and Hamlet entered. When Kean first appeared, a wave of disappointment swept over the audience. His smallness, which had been hidden by the long gown of Shylock and the deformity of Richard, could not be concealed in the black costume of Hamlet. The contrast with Kemble was startlingly apparent. But from the moment Hamlet encountered his father's Ghost, the audience forgot about his height and were attentive only to his performance. Where Kemble had struck a conventional sculptured attitude, Kean sank on one knee, and when addressing the spectre, 'I'll call thee Hamlet, King, Father, Royal Dane,' his voice vibrated tenderly on the word 'Father'. The Ghost beckoned and Hamlet followed, sword in hand. Kemble had trailed his sword behind him, but Kean did more than this. He kept his sword pointed at Marcellus and Horatio, as if to prevent them from following him. The audience were thrilled by the originality of these conceptions.

When he took Rosencrantz and Guildenstern under each arm, on the pretence of confiding in them, the action brought out perfectly how indistinguishable these two were. During the play scene, while the poisoner was making his short speech from the stage, he inched forward from the feet of Ophelia to the King, moving like a serpent nearer and nearer; then at the moment of the murder on the stage, he uncoiled himself and screamed his challenge in the King's ear, 'He poisons him i' th' garden for's estate.' Hazlitt wrote: 'Its extreme boldness "bordered on the verge of all we hate", and the effect it produced was a test of the extraordinary powers of this extraordinary actor.'

In the closet scene, his comparison of the portraits of his father and uncle, 'Look here upon this picture, and on this,' seemed suggested by an accidental thought. Some of the audience were a little uneasy that he did not display any of the theatrical tricks they had come to expect in this scene. Barnes observed that, unlike Kemble, he did not 'shake his mother out of her chair, nor wave his handkerchief with a dignified whirl, nor spread his arms like a heron crucified on a barn-door, when he cries "Is it the king?" ' The most striking moment of all was the parting with Ophelia. From Garrick onwards, the scene had been played violently, but Hamlet's distracted speech to Ophelia was spoken quietly by Kean. After commanding her to go to a nunnery, he hurried from the stage, then overcome by tenderness and regret, he came back, pressed her hand to his lips and rushed off again. Hazlitt wrote: 'It had an electrical effect on the house. It was the finest commentary that was ever made on Shakespeare.'

On the whole, the critics were pleased with his performance. *The Times*, after criticising his voice, lack of dignity and over-emphasis of sarcasm, stated: 'He is clearly a person of excellent good sense and of a powerful discrimination.' The *Morning Post* was delighted with him and believed that whatever faults he had rose 'from want of physical means, not from any error of judgment, or deficiency of feeling'. The *Champion* thought his performance 'the finest example of the art of acting that has ever been seen on the modern stage'. This chorus of praise was led by Hazlitt in the *Morning Chronicle* and Barnes in the *Examiner*.

Hazlitt wrote: 'High as Mr. Kean stood in our opinion before, we have no hesitation in saying, that he stands higher in it (and, we think, will in that of the public), from the powers displayed in this last effort.' He did not think that Kean was altogether right in his 'general delineation' of the character. 'It was too strong and pointed,' he wrote. 'There was often a severity, approaching to virulence, in the common observations and answers. There is nothing of this in Hamlet . . . A pensive air of sadness should sit unwillingly upon his brow, but no appearance of fixed and sullen gloom.' He thought that in some scenes Kean displayed 'more energy than was requisite; and in others where it would have been appropriate, did not rise equal to the exigency of the situation'. But he was well pleased with Kean. He wrote: 'To point out the defects in Mr. Kean's performance in the part is a less grateful but a much shorter task than to enumerate the many striking beauties which he gave to it, both by the power of his action and by the true feeling of nature.'

Barnes, unlike Hazlitt, was unqualified in his admiration. He thought that Kean's acting was too good for the public 'whose taste has been vitiated by the long established affectations of the school of Kemble'. He used the occasion to make a savage attack on Kemble. He wrote: 'In his representations of Hamlet, Mr. Kemble shewed an ignorance of the character which would have been scarcely pardonable in the first stroller picked up at a country fair. Hamlet, whose sensibility is so keenly alive that every trifle administers fresh pangs to its distress, was converted by Mr. Kemble into a dry scholastic personage, uttering wise saws with a sneer, and delivering his ironies with a spruce air and smart tone such as is used by forward girls and boys on their introduction into the world, when they wish to excite attention to their abortive bon mots and unfledged sarcasms.' He proclaimed that Kean as Hamlet had caused the downfall of the classical school.

After Kean's Hamlet, there was a polarisation of opinion between the classical and romantic schools of acting, as embodied in Kemble and Kean. The partisanship of critics such as Barnes was responsible for this, because they could not praise one without attacking the other. On 30 March, Joseph Farington had company for dinner and Kean was a subject of conversation. John Taylor, the journalist said, 'He is a *Humbug*: His acting is often false, & without anything like classical taste. He is a *Pot-House* Actor.' Robert Smirke, the painter, said, 'He knew that every effort was made when He first appeared, to render Him popular; the Theatre was almost filled by persons admitted by *Orders*.' Farington told Taylor that Wilson, having once seen Kean, said, '"I wd not give Sixpence to see Him again."' Someone reported that Thomas Morton, the dramatist and an acknowledged judge of acting, had been met by Pascoe Grenfell, when returning from seeing Kean as Hamlet. 'Well,' said Grenfell, 'You have seen Hamlet.' 'No,' Morton replied. 'I have not seen Hamlet.'

After his début as Hamlet, Kean entered upon a weekly routine of plays, Monday, Thursday and Saturday, performing in *The Merchant of Venice*, *Richard III and Hamlet*. The receipts were good whenever he appeared, but *Richard III* was the most popular and was to remain so during his entire career. At Covent Garden, Thomas Harris did all he could to attract the crowds away from Drury Lane. Kemble appeared in all his greatest roles, Brutus, Wolsey, Cato, Hamlet and Coriolanus. At first, Kemble had been indifferent to Kean's success, believing it to be a passing craze, but, since Kean's performance as Hamlet, he had come to realise that a formidable rival had entered the field. He came secretly to Drury Lane one night to see Kean act Richard. He later remarked: 'Our styles of acting are so totally different, that you must not expect me to like Mr. Kean; but one thing I must say in his favour—he is at all times terribly in earnest.'

As a counter-attraction to Kean's Richard III, Harris announced Charles Mayne Young in the same part. Young's style of acting was classical; cold, declamatory and dignified. It was said of him that he plunged a dagger into his breast with the same elegance and lack of emotion as he handed a chair to a lady. He acknowledged himself as a disciple of Kemble; and the resemblance in style was so great that when they were on the stage together it was difficult for the audience to know which one had spoken. His Richard came nowhere near to challenging the blazing performance of Kean and the play was soon withdrawn. It was a poor season for Covent Garden, because Harris had no one to match the pulling power of Kean.

At Farington's, on 7 April, Kean was spoken of again. Sir Thomas Lawrence, the portrait painter, said 'that whether his conception of a character was just or not, He could act up to that conception with more truth and effect than *Young* could do when acting agreeably to *His own* conception'. At Farington's, on 13 April, Sir George Beaumont was present. For many years he had enjoyed a great reputation as a patron of the arts and an arbiter of taste. His opinions were always listened to with the greatest respect. He told the company that he had not yet seen Kean, because of the difficulty of getting seats, but he said, 'He already could, from what he had heard of Kean, judge to a pretty good certainty who would and who would not like Him. The admirers, or at least the admirers & *friends* of Kemble would not like Him, He had found this to be the case, in several instances. Others who remembered *Garrick*, spoke highly of *Him*, & Sir George seemed to mean that those who felt *nature* strongly approved Kean, while those who were devoted to the art of the Kemble School disapproved him.' Prince Hoare, the dramatist, suggested very sensibly that people might be gratified both by Kemble and Kean, but no one, certainly not Sir George, seems to have paid any attention to him.

Some idea of the great crowds that came to see Kean during his first season at Drury Lane is given in an account by Joe Cowen, the actor. Cowen and his friend, Robert Keeley, the comedian, hearing of Kean's success, decided to go to a performance of *Hamlet*. At four o'clock in the afternoon they joined the crowd already assembled at the pit entrance of Drury Lane. This crowd had increased by thousands before the doors opened at half-past five. Cowen wrote: 'Half crushed to death, we found ourselves, after a desperate effort, at the back of the passage which surrounds the pit, from whence I could, by straining to my utmost height, catch a glimpse of the corner of the green curtain nearest to the top, but little Bob hadn't even that satisfaction. There, at any rate, we could not see Kean, nor live to see anything else at the end of a few hours' squeeze such as we were then enduring, and we agreed to pay the extra three-and-sixpence and go into the boxes; but as to obtaining a pass check, it was impossible. We had nearly as much trouble to get out as we had to get in, and were content to lose our three-and-sixpence apiece, and pay fourteen shillings more for the privilege of standing on a back seat of the upper tier of boxes at the corner next the stage, an excellent point of sight for a perspective view of the crown of a man's hat, or a bald spot on the head of a lady who, seated in the pit, had been obliged to take off her bonnet whether she liked it or not.

'Bruised in body,' he continued, 'and sorely afflicted in spirit and pocket, we were just in the mood not to be easily pleased with anything or anybody. When Kean came on I was astonished. I was prepared to see a small man; but, diminished by the unusual distance and his black dress, and a mental comparison with Kemble's princely person, he appeared a perfect pigmy; his voice unlike any I had ever heard before, perhaps from its very strangeness, was most objectionable, and I turned to Keeley and at once pronounced him *a most decided humbug*; and if I could have got out then, I should have said so to everybody, because I honestly thought so; and if afterwards I had been convinced of his enormous genius, I might, like Taylor, the oculist and editor of the *Sun* newspaper, have persisted in my denunciation, rather than confess my incapacity at the first glance to comprehend the sublimity of Shakespeare and Nature being upon such familiar terms. But I was obliged to remain, and compelled to be silent; so invoking patience, and placing my hand on a young lady's shoulder for support, I quietly gazed on through three tedious scenes—for all the actors seemed worse than usual—till it came to the dialogue with the ghost, and at the line

I'll call thee Hamlet—king—father,

I was converted. I resigned the support of the lady, and employed both hands in paying the usual tribute to godlike talent. Father is not a pretty word to look at, but it is beautiful to hear when lisped by little children, or spoken by Edmund Kean in *Hamlet*.'

Everyone was talking about Kean. The effect his Richard III had on Benjamin West was so strong that it kept the painter awake all night. West said: 'I never saw such expression in any human face before.' Mrs. Siddons said: 'His eyes are marvellous, having a sort of fascination, like that attributed to the snake.' Garrick's widow, a sprightly old lady of eighty, went to Drury Lane every night Kean performed. She asked him to call on her and, when he arrived, she placed him in her husband's chair, telling him that she had never allowed anyone else to sit in it and that only he was worthy of the honour. Before he left, she gave him Garrick's stage jewels. Even Coleridge overcame his reluctance to witness contemporary productions of Shakespeare and went to see Kean at Drury Lane. He found the experience strange and unsatisfactory. He wrote: 'KEAN is original; but he copies from himself. His rapid descents from the hyper-tragic to the infracolloquial, though sometimes productive of great effect, are often unreasonable. To see him act, is like reading Shakespeare by flashes of lightning.'

Byron had come to love the theatre more and more that season since he had discovered the acting of Kean. He recognised his kinship with the actor, who played Shakespeare's heroes as he himself would have created them. In his *Ode to Napoleon Buonaparte*, he introduced Kean's action as Richard, on the night before the battle, when he abstractedly drew patterns in the sand with the point of his sword.

Or trace with thine all idle hand,
In loitering mood upon the sand,
That Earth is now as free.

Napoleon had been deposed and, on 30 March, the Allies had entered Paris. The ode was published on 16 April and all the newspapers discussed it. The reference to Kean was commented on and Byron was asked why he did not write a poem on Kean's Richard. In reply, Byron quoted the lines in the first canto of *The Corsair*, published the previous January, as illustrative of Kean's performance:

There was a laughing devil in his sneer,
That raised emotions of both rage and fear;
And where his frown of hatred darkly fell,
Hope withering fled, and Mercy sigh'd farewell!

By 23 April, when he was again a guest at Farington's, Sir George Beaumont had seen Kean as Richard III and 'was decidedly of opinion that no actor since Garrick exhibited so much genuine *feeling of nature*. At times, sd. He, He appears to be Richard himself. He never, said He, can have dignity or grace, His person is too diminutive, but He is a true natural actor, and wholly free from the measured and artificial practise of the Kemble school.' At Farington's, on 3 May, the intrepid John Taylor told Sir George that he differed from him entirely in his opinion of Kean. Taylor said, 'Kean has art in His acting in attempting to give touches of nature, but it is low vulgar art, without dignity or elevated conception of character.' Sir George did not agree.

The announcement that Kean would play Othello on 5 May aroused great interest, and on the first night the vast auditorium of Drury Lane was filled to capacity. Kean's dressing-room was crowded with admirers, who formed a semi-circle around him, while he contemplated his new costume in a cheval glass and practised attitudes. When someone attempted to address him, Frederick Reynolds, the dramatist, raised his hand and whispered,

'Hush! do not disturb him.' Everyone in the room was surprised that Kean was to play Othello with a brown complexion instead of the conventional black. Kean argued that a Moor need not be jet black, but what was more important to him was that the lighter make-up ensured that none of his facial expressions would be lost.

From beginning to end the audience were dazzled by his performance, whirled along relentlessly by the hurry and violence of the scenes. Hazlitt, who had suspected that Kean had not yet shown all his powers, was now proved to be right. Kean showed the manliness, nobility and tenderness of the open-hearted Moor; the frenzy of his suspicions and the transcendent power of his rage. His performance was a marvellous display of passion, pathos and suffering. He played the first two acts quietly, almost negligently, saving himself for the great exertions that were to come. The tremulous melody he gave to the passage beginning 'If it were now to die,' in which he spoke of his love for Desdemona, prefigured the inexpressible beauty of his Farewell in the third act.

In the third scene in the third act, the intensity of his passion crackled into flame with the words he spoke after Desdemona had left the stage,

> Perdition catch my soul
> But I do love thee! and when I love thee not
> Chaos is come again.

As he listened to the insinuations of Iago concerning Desdemona and Cassio, he seemed to Hazlitt to present 'the very face, the marble aspect of Dante's Count Ugolino. On his fixed eyelids "horror sat plumed".' When Iago said, 'O, beware my lord of jealousy,' Othello's body contracted spasmodically as though he had been stabbed. When Iago told him that he hoped he had not disturbed his peace of mind and he replied, 'Not a jot, not a jot,' Hazlitt observed that 'the look, the action, the expression of voice' with which he accompanied the exclamation was 'perfectly heart-rending', while, a moment later, his words on seeing his wife, 'I do not think but Desdemona's honest,' were 'the glorious triumph of exceeding love; a thought flashing conviction on his mind and irradiating his countenance with joy like sudden sunshine.'

Othello's jealousy, like poison in the system, ebbed and flowed. He re-entered murmuring, 'Ha! Ha! false to me!' He raised his head as Iago addressed him, saw in him the immediate cause of his anguish, and ordered him sharply to go. His burst of anger faded, and his arms dropped to his sides in a gesture of utter exhaustion. He began the passage, 'What sense had I in her stolen hours of lust.' The words were spoken so mildly that the audience were startled by the frenxy in his cry, 'I found not Cassio's kisses on her lips.' To Hazlitt, this 'laid open the very tumult and agony of the soul'. It had such an effect on the audience that for a while after its delivery, they sat motionless. In this immense silence Kean spoke the apostrophe beginning

> Oh now, for ever,
> Farewell the tranquil mind! farewell content!

ending with the words, 'Othello's occupation's gone.' As he lingered fondly on each particular circumstance which had made his occupation dear to him, Leigh Hunt observed that 'his voice occasionally uttered little tones of endearment, his head shook and his visage quivered'. Crabb Robinson wrote: 'I could hardly keep from crying, it was pure feeling.' To Hazlitt, Kean's voice 'struck on the heart like the swelling notes of some divine music, like the sound of years of departed happiness'.

The Farewell was immediately followed by a powerful display of rage as Othello seized Iago by the throat, saying,

> Villain, be sure thou prove my love a whore;
> Be sure of it; give me the ocular proof.

His nostrils were distended, the veins stood out on his forehead, his eyes were dilated and his breathing obstructed. Then all his passions were yielded up in his terrible vow of revenge, 'O, blood, blood, blood!'

In the great passages with Desdemona in the fourth act, love and hate fought for mastery of Othello's soul. Not even Kean's greatest admirers were prepared for his representation of 'a mind

perplexed in the extreme'. In this connection, George Henry
Lewes remarked on a peculiarity in Kean's acting that he had
never seen so thoroughly realised in any other actor, namely the
expression of 'subsiding emotion'. Lewes wrote: 'Although fond,
far too fond of abrupt transitions—passing from vehemence to
familiarity, and mingling strong lights and shadows with Cara-
vaggio force of unreality—nevertheless his instinct taught him
what few actors are taught—that a strong emotion, after dis-
charging itself in one massive current, continues for a time expressing itself in feebler currents. The waves are not stilled when
the storm has passed away. There remains the ground-swell
troubling the deeps. In watching Kean's quivering muscles and
altered tones you felt the subsidence of passion. The voice might
be calm, but there was a tremor in it; the face might be quiet, but
there were vanishing traces of the recent agitation.' Thus, in the
midst of Othello's raging, the speaking of the line, 'Ah, Desdemona!—away! away! away!' had in it, according to Procter,
Kean's first biographer, 'all that belongs to love, to grief, to pity'.
The words sank 'by gradual gradations, from reproof into
compassion, from compassion into a faint and indistinct sound,
which itself gradually expired, like the sound of a melancholy
echo'. And again, when he trembled and halted through the lines
beginning, 'Had it pleas'd heaven to try me with affliction,' Hunt
wrote: 'His louder bitterness and his rage were always fine, but
such passages as these were still finer. You might fancy you saw
the water quivering in his eyes.'

Then came the wonders of the final act. The violence with
which he killed Desdemona; the aching sadness in his reflection,
'My wife! my wife! what wife?—I have no wife'; the stillness of
his despair when he discovered he had been duped and the utterance of the line, 'O fool! fool! fool!' He did not shout as Kemble
did, neither did he rave nor tear his hair as Garrick had done. He
repeated the words quickly, almost inarticulately, with a half-
smile of amazement at his own incredible stupidity. He began his
final speech to his officers. When he asked them to speak of him at
'one that lov'd not wisely, but too well', it seemed to Hazlitt that
his 'lips might be said less to utter words than to distil drops of

blood gushing from his heart'. He began to tell them the story of the 'malignant and turban'd Turk', whom he had slain in Aleppo, and, as he did, he felt for his hidden dagger. His eyes flickered from face to face to see if any of them suspected what he was about to do. When he came to the line, 'And smote him—thus,' he thrust the dagger into his heart. A shudder swept over him, he crossed to the bed, and, in attempting to kiss Desdemona's face, he fell across her, dead.

As Othello, Kean achieved his greatest and most lasting triumph. Hazlitt called it 'the finest piece of acting in the world', an achievement which placed Kean 'far beyond the touch of Time'. For Hazlitt, the miracle had happened. He had witnessed a performance of Othello that was worthy of the genius of Shakespeare. He was thankful to have seen the actor 'who bore on his brow the mark of the fire from Heaven'.

It was announced that on the second night of *Othello* Kean would play Iago and thereafter alternate the roles. He usually alternated with Pope and occasionally with Rae or Elliston. Byron and Tom Moore were present at Kean's début as Iago. They did not view the performance from Byron's private box, preferring to sit in the pit, where they were near enough to the stage not to miss any of the actor's expressions. Iago's glance of triumph at the dead bodies of Othello and Desdemona was unforgettable. The next day Byron wrote to Moore: 'Was not Kean perfection? particularly the last look.' The performance was praised on all sides. *The Times* called Kean's Iago 'a masterly performance'. Barnes, in the *Examiner*, was struck by 'the most complete absorption of the man in the character', and found it difficult to persuade himself that Kean was 'merely a young man who had put on a soldier's coat to play the villain for an hour or two'. In the *Morning Chronicle*, Hazlitt wrote: 'Perhaps the accomplished hypocrite was never so finely, so adroitly portrayed —a gay light-hearted monster, a careless, cordial, comfortable villain.' Kean continued playing the characters of Othello and Iago alternately, among his other parts, until the end of the season. He acted these two parts most often, always to large houses, although the nights he was Othello brought slightly higher receipts. The *Merchant of Venice* and *Hamlet* were played occasionally. *Richard III* was played more frequently, because it brought in the most money.

Kean was now the greatest fashion in London. Hazlitt, recalling this sensational first season, wrote: 'If you had not been to see the little man twenty times in Richard, and did not deny his being hoarse in the last act, or admire him for being so, you were looked on as a lukewarm devotee, or half an infidel.' Moore wrote perceptively: 'Poor Mr. Kean is now in the honeymoon of criticism. Next to the pleasure of writing a man down, your critics enjoy the vanity of writing him up; but when *once* up and fixed there, he is a mark for their arrows ever after.'

On 19 May Sir George Beaumont sang the praises of Kean as Othello to the company assembled in Joseph Farington's drawing room. He said 'there was at times a fire in his acting that was electric; & that His smile was bewitching. He rejoiced that such a man had appeared on the stage to bring it back to truth and nature. He admitted that there were particular characters, Coriolanus for instance, to which Kemble's stile of acting was suited, but he must say that Kemble did not touch his feeling.' Kemble himself said of Kean's Othello: 'If the justness of its conception had been equal to the brilliance of execution it would have been perfect; but the whole thing is a mistake; the fact being that Othello was a slow man.' The older actor was jealous of the younger one. His niece, Fanny Kemble, recalled: 'I have lived among those whose theatrical creed would not permit them to acknowledge Kean as a great actor.'

The Drury Lane committee, reluctant to bring such a good season to an end, extended it until 16 July, when the final performance was *Richard III*. Kean had played 68 nights. The total receipts on these nights were £32,940. The total receipts for the entire season of 235 nights were £68,329. The nightly average for Kean was £484. The nightly average for the rest of the season was £212. The season's receipts without Kean would have been £49,820. Therefore, his value to the theatre was £18,509. This sum is all the more astonishing when it is remembered that the season was already three months gone when he made his début. No wonder there was cheering at the shareholders' end of season meeting when these figures were announced. In his speech, Whitbread praised Arnold for acquiring 'that incomparable performer Mr. Kean . . . the most shining actor that has appeared in the theatrical hemisphere for many years . . . one of those prodigies that occur only once or twice in a century'. The manager must have smiled wryly as he recalled that this same actor had been referred to at the beginning of the year as 'Arnold's hard bargain'.

When these figures were generally known, it was rumoured that the committee had bribed Hazlitt with the sum of £1,500 to ensure that Kean was reviewed favourably in the *Morning Chronicle*. The rumour was false, but it does show the extent to which people believed that Hazlitt's articles had made Kean's reputation and in so doing had saved Drury Lane from bank-ruptcy. And, after all, who can blame them? The truth was hardly credible. Six months ago Kean had been an unknown provincial actor, literally starving in London. Now he was acclaimed as the greatest tragedian on the English stage and the matchless inter-preter of Shakespeare.

CHAPTER FOUR

MAD WITH APPLAUSE

DURING this time, Kean and Mary continued to live in Cecil Street, with the Misses Williams, who had been so kind to them in the anxious days before his début. The change in their fortunes had been so sudden and so miraculous that neither of them could take it in. Mary had forgotten all the doubts she had had about his future in the theatre; he was now a great star and she was proud of him. Every day the street was thronged with the carriages of callers; wealthy and influential people crowded into the sitting-room to pay their respects. Nance Carey turned up, accompanied by her two children, Phoebe and Henry Darnley, who, despite repeated snubs, insisted on calling Kean 'dear brother'. Kean allowed Nance a pension of fifty pounds a year, which he was to pay with unfailing regularity until the day of his death.

There was no shortage of money now. He had saved the theatre from bankruptcy and the committee fell over themselves to show their gratitude. On 14 March, following his success as Hamlet, his salary was raised to £20 a week flat. In addition to the increased salary, they made him a present of £500. Lord Essex and several other members of the committee each gave him a share in the theatre. Samuel Whitbread took Kean's infant son on his knee and pressed a draft of £50 into his hand. In an anonymous memoir published after Kean's death, a friend wrote: 'I called upon Mrs. Kean when his benefit was announced. I do not exaggerate when I say, that money was lying about the room in all directions; the present Mr. C. Kean, then a fine little boy with rich curling hair, was playing with some score of guineas (then a rare coin) on the floor; bank notes were in heaps on the mantel-piece, table and sofa; and poor Mrs. K. was quite bewildered with plans of the house and applications. I remember three ladies being introduced, who approached Mrs. K. as if she were a divinity. Little Charles had deserted his guineas, and mounted himself on a large wooden horse with stirrups. "What a sweet child," they whispered, and eyed him as if he had been a young prince.—I think the receipts of that benefit amounted to £1150.'

Invitations flowed in from members of the committee. Kean and Mary dined with Lord Essex, the Honourable Douglas Kinnaird and Samuel Whitbread. Lady Elizabeth Whitbread was much taken by Mary's naivety and took an interest in her welfare. Mary responded with delight to the friendly attentions of the aristocracy, but Kean was ill at ease in their company. While he was flattered that they sought him out, nothing in his rough and tumble past had prepared him to meet such people and he was morbidly aware of his lack of social graces. 'Kean is a simple man,' John Cam Hobhouse recorded in his diary. 'Kinnaird told me that he sent his wife to Pascoe Grenfell, his patron, to ask him if he thought there would be any presumption of impropriety in his now keeping a horse.' When asked to spend Easter with the Grenfells, Kean was in agony over what clothes to wear.

Everyone of note wanted to meet him. On 19 May, after seeing him play Othello, Byron, accompanied by Tom Moore and John Cam Hobhouse, went to the green room to congratulate him. Hobhouse recorded: 'Kean came in in a pepper-and-salt suit, a very short man, but strongly made and wide-shouldered, hollow, sallow face, thick black hair. Lord Byron was introduced to him, and from some compliment from him, said he was proud of his Lordship's approbation. Douglas Kinnaird introduced me. I asked him after his health, which, he said, was tolerable, but that he sometimes found his voice fail him. He had a sweet accent and manner. He soon withdrew.' Byron gave Kean a gold snuff box, with a boar hunt worked in mosaic on the lid. The boar had been the crest of Richard III and Kean now adopted it as his own. He dined frequently with Byron and accompanied him into his private box at the theatre. Byron was the only aristocrat with whom he felt at ease. He liked the informal suppers at Byron's home, where Tom Moore was a regular guest. They would talk and drink into the early hours, and Kean, who loved singing, would harmonise with the composer of *Irish Melodies*. But on other social occasions with the aristocracy he was more constrained. On 12 June he was guest of honour at a dinner given at Holland House. Lady Holland, the great hostess, was delighted to have secured Kean to include in her circle, which contained all the lions of the day. Conversing with the other guests was an ordeal for Kean. Among the topics discussed was the inadequate representation of nobles and clergy in the Cortes of Spain. Hobhouse noticed that Kean 'knitted his brows . . . when he couldn't exactly make out what was said . . . ate most pertinaciously with his knife, and was a little too frequent with ladyships and lordships, as was natural in him'.

At the close of the Drury Lane season, Kean and Mary went to Ireland, where he was to play a short season in Dublin. All the provincial managers now wanted him and he had received offers to star at £50 a night. The provinces were to prove a lucrative source of income for him and, from the start, he was determined to exploit the situation for all it was worth. On the very same day he travelled to Dublin, he played Richard at Cheltenham in the afternoon and again at Gloucester in the evening. The committee were perturbed when they heard of these plans and they urged him to spare himself for the sake of his health. He had become their most valuable property and they were concerned that he might not be fit enough to play during the coming season.

On 25 July, Kean opened at the Theatre Royal, Dublin, and played to crowded audiences until 31 August. Three years ago, the manager, Frederick Jones, had rejected his offer to 'do everything' for two pounds a week, but now he was happy that he had secured his services for an equal division of the profits. Kean had brought with him Alexander Pope, of the Drury Lane company, as his chief supporting actor and boozing companion. After every performance, the two of them drank their way through the taverns of Dublin.

Mary had gone on to Waterford, to dazzle all her relations and friends. Her sister, Susan, had written to Margaret Roberts: 'She will be as rich as a Jew. She tells me I must get 30 or 40 pounds worth of clothes—the richest and the best *all from you*, and when she comes she will pay, as well as all other debts.' This was indeed a triumphant return for Mary; only two years previously she had been begging the same Miss Roberts for scraps of clothing. Where she had been an object of pity, she was now Lady Bountiful, with an ever-open purse of gold. She promised her family that they would never want for anything and her sister, Susan, would come and live with her in London.

Before returning to London, Kean redeemed his promise to Elliston by playing a short season at Birmingham. He had intended leaving Birmingham on the morning following his final performance, but, when the time came to depart, he was still in the tavern, where he had been drinking all night. It was noon before he mounted the coach, roaring drunk, with a pistol in each hand to protect himself from highwaymen.

His second season at Drury Lane began on 3 October 1814, with *Richard III*, and continued with repetitions of his other successes. The public were still enthusiastic and he played to good houses. His first new offering, *Macbeth*, was given on 5 November. Like *Hamlet*, this was a direct challenge to Kemble. In this instance, however, Kemble's supporters were convinced that Kean was bound to fail. For a generation the play had belonged to Kemble and his sister, Mrs. Siddons. He was strong and effective in the part and she was the greatest Lady Macbeth the stage had ever seen. Mrs. Bartley, who played opposite Kean, was certainly no Mrs. Siddons, not that this worried him, as he was the last man to care for equal partnerships. Banquo was played by Pope and Macduff by Rae. The version used was the quasi-operatic one that had been popular since the Restoration. *Macbeth* was generally produced as a kind of spectacular pantomime, and this production, with its chorus of witches and flying ballet of hobgoblins, was no exception. The opening performance was crowded, even the lobbies were packed with those satisfied merely to hear Kean's voice.

But his portrayal of Macbeth was not entirely successful. Hazlitt, now writing in the *Champion*, thought him 'too agile and mercurial', not at all like a man who had 'encountered the weird Sisters'. He believed that Kean had confused Macbeth with

Richard III, a common error with actors, because both characters had murdered for power. But to Hazlitt, such a confusion belittled the genius of Shakespeare, none of whose characters were identical. He concluded that either Kean had not studied the part sufficiently, or had failed to get to the heart of it. Procter found Kean's incessant activity less impressive than the tragic repose of Kemble. He wrote: '[Kemble] was not fretful at every turn, but wore the settled aspect of a man acquainted with his doom; of one admitted to superhuman mysteries, and who bore the stamp of fate upon his soul. Kean, on the other hand, relied upon his vigour, his point, and upon the terrible effects which he knew he could produce in certain passages of the play. And thus it was that Kemble left a more complete and permanent impression upon the memory; while Kean struck the imagination, in parts, in a manner that has never been exceeded.' One of these parts was the banquet scene in the third act. Kemble had bullied the spectre, but Kean retired from it with averted eyes and in fear. He scored over Kemble again in the fifth act, when, hearing of the approach of Malcolm's army, he rushed on the stage and shouted in a voice of command, 'Hang out our banners on the outward walls.' Suddenly he paused, lowering his double-handed sword until the point rested on the ground. Leaning on it, he whispered, 'The cry is still, "They come".' He seemed to become grey with fear. But immediately afterwards, in the lines which followed his learning of his wife's death, 'She should have died hereafter,' he was dull and ineffective. Here, in his building up to a climax of despair, Kemble had been at his finest.

All the critics agreed that Kean's greatest effect was in the scene that followed the murder of Duncan. He crept on fearfully, his frame convulsing as his eyes rested on Lady Macbeth. *The Times* stated that 'his remorse and terror' were among 'the most masterly performances that the English stage has ever witnessed'. As a 'lesson in common humanity', Hazlitt found the scene 'heart-rending'. He wrote: 'The hesitation, the bewildered look, the coming to himself when he sees his hands bloody; the manner in which his voice clung to his throat, and choked his utterance; his agony and tears, the force of nature overcome by passion—

beggared description. It was a scene which no one who saw it can ever efface from his recollections.' So Kemble's supporters could not claim that Kean had failed completely as Macbeth. The public generally were pleased with his performance, and during the season, he played Macbeth twenty-four times.

Covent Garden had suffered from Kean's competition during the previous season, but now Thomas Harris, the manager, had an attraction to rival him. She was Eliza O'Neill, an Irish actress, who made her London début in *Romeo and Juliet*, at Covent Garden, on 6 October 1814, three days after Kean began his second Drury Lane season. When Eliza O'Neill, as Juliet, ran on to the stage, her youth and beauty made the audience gasp with admiration. Although she was twenty-three years old, she looked no more than fifteen. She was the ideal Juliet. Macready wrote: 'It was not altogether the matchless beauty of form and face, but the spirit of perfect innocence and purity that seemed to glisten in her speaking eyes, and breathe from her chiselled lips.' Like Kean, she had rejected all the artificialities of the Kemble school. Her lines were spoken with a simplicity that seemed spontaneous. No such Juliet had ever been seen on the English stage. When the curtain fell and the stage manager came forward to announce a different play for the following evening, the audience shouted for *Romeo and Juliet*.

The play was to be repeated many times during the season and O'Neill's Juliet became as popular as Kean's Richard. The Drury Lane committee met this competition with the usual strategy of duplication. The rival theatres were always stealing each other's ideas. The nights the leading actors or actresses played at Drury Lane, Covent Garden would put on theirs. When it was known that a certain play was to be put on by one theatre, the other often rushed the same play into rehearsal to put it on first. So now Drury Lane announced their production of *Romeo and Juliet*, with Kean as Romeo and Mrs. Bartley as Juliet. Romeo was the least successful of Kean's Shakespearian roles. In the love passages he was dull and heavy. He stood like a statue beneath Juliet's balcony, as though determined not to surrender to the tenderness of the scene, Hazlitt wrote: 'Mr. Kean's imagination appears not to have the principles of joy, or hope, or love in it. He seems chiefly sensible to pain, or to the passions that spring from it, and to the terrible energies of mind or body, which are necessary to grapple with, or to avert it.' Kean had shown at moments in other plays that he was capable of expressing love, but as Hazlitt pointed out: 'if he ever conveys the sublimer pathos of thought and feeling, it is after the storm of passion, to which he has been worked up, has subsided. The tide of feeling then at times rolls deep, majestic and awful, like the surging sea after a tempest, now lifted to Heaven, now laying bare the bosom of the deep.' Thus, at such moments of 'subsiding emotion' came the inexpressible tenderness of his parting from Ophelia and the love and compassion in his speaking of the line, 'Ah, Desdemona!—away! away! away!' The same process gave rise to his finest moment as Romeo, which occurred during the interview with Friar Laurence, when, in the midst of his grief at being banished from Juliet, his voice suddenly faltered and choked with sobs when he spoke her name. Hazlitt wrote: 'Those persons must be made of sterner stuff than ourselves, who are proof against Mr. Kean's acting, both in this scene, and in his dying convulsion at the close of the play.' Apart from these moments, Kean failed as Romeo.

He had taken the part on the insistence of the committee and against his better judgement. He knew that he was not the great lover. Moreover, in *Romeo and Juliet*, too much interest, for his liking, centred on the heroine. This was especially true of this production, for the audience came not only to see Kean but to compare Mrs. Bartley's Juliet with Eliza O'Neill's. Mrs. Bartley, who acted in the declamatory style, came off badly in the comparison. The committee, anxious to exploit the interest in rival Juliets, replaced Mrs. Bartley with Miss Kelly for the fourth performance. Again the audience came to make the comparison and found her nowhere so good as O'Neill. After nine performances the play was withdrawn, and Kean never played Romeo again.

His next new offering, *Town and Country*, by Thomas Morton, was even less successful, and this second consecutive failure increased his suspicions about the competence of the committee.

In his next new role he returned to Shakespeare, opening on 9 March 1815, in *Richard II*, with Elliston as Bolingbroke and Pope as John of Gaunt. The version used, with 'Considerable Alterations and Additions', was by Richard Wroughton, a member of the Drury Lane company. As Richard II Kean was not challenging any rival, for the play was rarely acted. His conception of Richard II was not that of a weakling but of a man of courage, and he played the part with all the fire and vigour he had shown as Richard III. Those who did not know the play—and this included the greater part of the audience and most of the critics—were delighted with his performance and many declared it to be his finest part. But Hazlitt, now working for the *Examiner*, knew that Kean's conception was totally wrong. He wrote: 'Mr. Kean made it a character of *passion*, that is, of feeling combined with energy; whereas it is a character of *pathos*, that is to say of feeling combined with weakness.'

Hazlitt had now seen Kean sufficient times to attempt an evaluation of his acting. He believed 'the general fault' was 'that it is always energetic or nothing'. He wrote: 'He is always on full stretch—never relaxed. He expresses all the violence, the extravagance, and fierceness of the passions, but not their misgivings, their helplessness, and sinkings into despair.' A second visit to *Othello* confirmed this opinion. He wrote: 'Mr. Kean is in general all passion, all energy, all relentless will. He wants imagination, that faculty which contemplates events, and broods over feelings with a certain calmness and grandeur; his feelings almost always hurry on to action, and hardly ever repose upon themselves. He is too often in the highest key of passion, too uniformly on the verge of extravagance, too constantly on the rack.' It must be remembered that Hazlitt was continuing to judge Kean by a standard of excellence that he never applied to any other actor.

He had observed that in every character Kean had played there had been 'either a dazzling repetition of master-strokes of art and nature, or if at any time (from a want of physical adaptation, or sometimes of just conception of the character) the interest has flagged for a considerable interval, the deficiency has always been redeemed by some collected and overpowering display of energy or pathos, which electrified at the moment, and left a lasting impression on the mind afterwards'. Some instances of these 'electrical shocks', as he termed them, were Shylock's scene with Tubal, the death of Richard III, the parting with Ophelia, Othello's farewell, the scene that followed the murder of Duncan, and Romeo's interview with Friar Laurence. Hazlitt concluded that Kean's acting had 'no equal truth or purity of style' and that his excellence in a part was in proportion to the number of 'electrical shocks' in it.

Richard II proved to be quite popular and was given sixteen performances during the season, but the next two plays in which Kean appeared, *Ina*, by Mrs. Wilmot, and *The Wheel of Fortune*, by Richard Cumberland, were complete failures. The latter had been specially written for Kemble. The leading part of Penruddock, a misanthrope, was more suited to his dry formal style than to Kean's passion and energy. The critics agreed that Kemble had done it better and that Kean had failed in his challenge. For his benefit on 24 May, Kean chose *The Revenge*, a tragedy by Edward Young, first produced in 1721. This again was a direct challenge to Kemble, for the hero, Zanga, was one of his favourite roles. The plot of *The Revenge* is a transposition of that of *Othello*. Zanga is a Moor captured in battle by Don Alonzo. He is treated more as a friend than an enemy, but his one desire is for revenge. He accomplishes this by using the rivalry between Alonzo and Carlos for the love of Leonora. He poisons Alonzo's mind as Iago poisons Othello's. The malignancy and vindictiveness of the role appealed to Kean and he had acted it frequently in the provinces. Hazlitt thought him perfectly suited to the part. He had always maintained that Kean lacked repose and dignity, but neither of these was required in playing the violent Zanga. He wrote: 'He had all the wild impetuousity of barbarous revenge, the glowing energy of the untamed children of the sun, whose blood drinks up the radiance of fiercer skies. He was like a man stung with rage, and bursting with stifled passions. His hurried motions had the restlessness of the panther's: his wily caution, his cruel eye, his quivering visage, his violent gestures, his hollow pauses, his abrupt transitions, were all in character.'

The theatre was crammed and among the crowd in the pit passage, unable to get into the auditorium, stood a man who had seen Kean play Zanga at Weymouth. Hearing a great clamour of applause, he asked if Kean had just spoken the words, '*Then lose her!*' He had never forgotten the feeling those words had produced in him the first night he heard them. But Kean's greatest moment came in the fifth act, when he disclosed to Alonzo what he had done to him. '*Know then—' T WAS I!*' Procter wrote: 'Here the effect was appalling, beyond anything that we ever witnessed. Rae, who played Alonzo, seemed to wither and shrink into half his size. It is a positive fact, that he appeared less than Kean, in this overpowering scene; although he was considerably the larger man. As we ourselves contemplated the dark and exulting Moor standing over his victim, with his flashing eyes and arms thrown upwards (as though he would lay open his very heart to view), we thought that we never beheld anything so like the "archangel ruined". We were recalling to mind the line descriptive of the "sail-broad vans" of the great spirit of Milton, when our neighbour in the pit exclaimed to his companion, "By God! he looks the devil".'

The afterpiece was *The Tobacconist*, adapted by Garrick from Ben Jonson's comedy, *The Alchemist*. Kean played Abel Drugger, Garrick's famous comedy role. He was good in the part, although he was not a natural comic. The following day he received a note from Mrs. Garrick, which read, 'Dear Sir, You can't play Abel Drugger.' He replied, 'Dear Madam, I know it.' But he was to keep the part in his repertory for more than ten years. On 20 June he appeared again in a comedy, when he played the part of Leon in Beaumont and Fletcher's *Rule a Wife and Have a Wife*, but this was not a success. On 4 July he played Octavian in *The Mountaineers*, in aid of the Theatrical Fund. This was to have been repeated on 6 July, but Samuel Whitbread, chairman of the Drury Lane committee, died that day and the theatre was closed. The following night Kean, as Octavian, gave his last performance of the season.

His second season at Drury Lane had been only moderately successful. His nightly average was £350 compared to £484 of the previous season. To the characters he had played in the first season he had added ten, but only five of these—Macbeth, Richard II, Zanga, Abel Drugger and Octavian—had been successful. He had repeated his old parts—Shylock, Richard III, Hamlet, Othello and Iago—and, generally, these remained the more popular, certainly Richard, which continued to bring in the most money. Although he had played almost twice as many nights, the total receipts were only £67,296 compared to £68,329 of the previous season. Covent Garden, on the other hand, had brought in £90,000. There were two reasons why Covent Garden had gone into the lead again. The Drury Lane committee were continuing their disastrous policy of economising on production costs. Covent Garden productions were far more lavish. The most spectacular production of the season at Drury Lane had been *Macbeth*, but this had only fifteen principal Singing Witches compared with nearly fifty in Harris's production of the play less than six weeks later. Moreover, Harris not only had Eliza O'Neill but also Kemble and Young, while Drury Lane had only Kean. Not even he could carry a whole theatre, yet this is what the Drury Lane committee seemed to expect of him.

The aristocracy continued to invite him to their houses and Kean accepted the invitations, because he believed that it was his duty to do so. He was under the impression that the position of leading tragedian entitled him to mix on equal terms with the upper classes. He believed too that, in his case, as the natural son of the Duke of Norfolk, he had a double right. He was too blinded by pride to realise that the aristocracy sought him out simply because he was reckoned to be a catch for their dinner parties, a 'lion' to be exhibited in their social menageries. He had deluded himself into believing that they accepted him as one of themselves, and so he continued to visit their houses, even though this meant enduring hours of agonised embarrassment. He was happy enough when the eyes of the great were upon him, but when the conversation turned to other topics, he became sullen and silent. Crabb Robinson, who was invited to meet him at the home of Serjeant Rough, the eminent lawyer, observed: 'I should say to *see* him, not to hear him; for he scarcely spoke. I should hardly have known him. He has certainly a fine eye, but his features were relaxed, as if he had undergone great fatigue. When he smiles, his look is rather constrained than natural.' Kean had little knowledge of the subjects discussed at these dinner tables and he was constantly afraid of showing his ignorance. Even when the conversation turned on acting he was equally uneasy, for this was not a subject he could discuss intellectually. His uneasiness led him to brag, with many a Greek and Latin quotation, of his classical education and his connection with the Norfolk family, not realising that the distinguished company found these claims ridiculous and tedious. They were prepared to tolerate the low-born genius, but they despised the little guttersnipe with the pretensions to be a gentleman. By the end of 1814, some of them were finding him a little too awkward for their liking. As Whitbread put it, 'We don't invite him because it seems so painful to him.'

Mary was troubled by Kean's attitude towards high society. She loved all these wonderful people—the Whitbreads, the Grenfells and the great Lord Essex. Unlike Kean, she did not resent their patronising manner, because it would never have occurred to her that she was in any way their equal; it was sufficient for her just to be in the same room as them. But this was not enough for Kean: they must either accept him as one of themselves or not at all.

It was a very different Kean when the company was congenial. William Charles Macready has described an evening around this time, when he and his father were joined for supper by Kean, 'accompanied, or rather attended by Pope'. Macready wrote: 'I need not say with what intense scrutiny I regarded him as we shook hands on our mutual introduction. The mild and modest expression of his Italian features, and his unassuming manner, which I might perhaps justly describe as partaking in some degree of shyness, took me by surprise, and I remarked with special interest the indifference with which he endured the fulsome flatteries of Pope. He was very sparing of words during, and for some time after, supper; but about one o'clock, when the glass had circulated pretty freely, he became animated, fluent and communicative. His anecdotes were communicated with a lively sense of the ridiculous; in the melodies he sang there was a touching grace, and his powers of mimicry were most humourously or happily exerted in an admirable imitation of Braham; and in a story of Incledon acting Steady the Quaker at Rochester without any rehearsal—where, in singing the favourite air, "When the lads of the village so merrily, O," he heard himself, to his dismay and consternation, accompanied by a single bassoon,—the music of his voice, his perplexity at each recurring sound of the bassoon, his undertone maledictions on the self-satisfied musician, the peculiarity of his habits, all were hit off with a humour and an exactness that equalled the best display Mathews ever made, and almost convulsed us with laughter. It was a memorable evening, the first and last I ever spent in private with this extraordinary man.'

This was the side of Kean that appealed most to men such as Byron, Tom Moore and Thomas Colley Grattan—the best of companions, the bawdy raconteur, telling how he replied to the earnest enquiry as to whether he felt his characters on stage by saying that he only did so when acting with a pretty woman. Congenial as Kean found such company, there was another circle where he was even more at home, and that was the world of the tavern. For him the real pleasure of success lay more in the adulation of a crowd of drink-swilling toadies than in the considered praise of Hazlitt and Byron. He was more pleased that his success had given him the entrée into the beds of small-part actresses than into the great houses of Lord Essex and Lady Holland. If, in the taverns, they flattered him for the money or favours they hoped to get from him, at least they did not embarrass him with polite usages and intellectual discussions; and if he had to pay for their praise and affection, he could well afford it. His tendency towards dissipation, apparent before his début, was now allowed full rein. Prior to his success, poverty and driving ambition had imposed a discipline upon him, but now he was completely unrestrained. After all the years of privation, the greatest rewards of his success were having as much to drink and as many women as he wanted. In the anxious days before his début, when it seemed that Drury Lane must surely reject him, he had told Mary, 'If I should succeed now, I think it would drive me mad.' Certainly, after his success, he was never again to achieve an equilibrium.

Kean had hoped that his depravity would remain a secret from the world at large, but, towards the end of 1814, all manner of scurrilous stories about him were circulating around London. There was no lack of jealous players at Drury Lane only too anxious to bring these stories to the ears of the committee. In January 1815 John Herman Merivale, the dramatist, wrote to Dr. Drury asking how best Kean could be rescued from 'the imminent dangers which beset him'. He continued: 'Evil reports have been crowding in upon us from day to day almost ever since our return to town in November.' He told Drury that he had written to Kean 'hinting in a manner as adroitly combined of flattery and remonstrance as I could well imagine, at the want of proper confidence in his own genius, and ambition of better things, which gave a handle to his enemies and paralysed his own exertions'. This letter having made 'a suitable effect', he had written again at greater length telling Kean 'that the worst of his enemies beyond all comparison were those who, for the invidious purpose of degrading him to their own level, made him sacrifice his time and health, talents and reputation, to them, and then went about the town, publishing his disgrace to *their* glory'. Not receiving a reply to this letter, he had called at Kean's house. Only Mary was at home and, when he asked her how Kean had taken the letter, she replied that 'nothing but shame could have prevented him from answering it'. After reading it he had exclaimed, ' "This is all my fault, d——d fool that I am!" '

Mary had sobbed bitterly as she told Merivale that this had been a fortnight of agony for her, 'beset as he is by these infamous scoundrels who swindle him out of his money and keep him for days together at the ale-house'. A fortnight ago he had left town, without her knowledge, and wrote from Woolwich saying 'that it was his resolution never to see her or his child again—that she may take all the money but he would find freedom in a foreign country'. She went to Woolwich and found him in a tavern 'surrounded by all his most pernicious associates'. She begged him to come home with her, but it was no use, and she was forced to return to London without him. A day or so later he came back 'in a state of contrition at least equal to his former madness'.

The Drury Lane committee rallied round. Whitbread, Grenfell and Lord Essex called at the house, all anxious to give him good advice. Mary told Merivale that all this attention had confounded Kean, 'as he had deceived himself into a previous opinion that his eccentricities were known only to himself and those immediately about him'. He was ashamed that his fine friends knew of his other life and he assured them he would mend his ways. When Merivale next called, he found Kean at home and never had he seen 'the gentleman and man of genius more fully combined'. He told Dr. Drury: 'He is but an infant in experience, and till you taught him, he never learned to stand upright. No wonder his foot slipped; and oppressed as he is . . . he requires every possible assistance to recover his former footing.'

So the members of the committee set about recovering the fallen Kean. They advised him that it was the duty of the leading tragedian to behave with dignity offstage; that the interpreter of the great tragic characters of Shakespeare should not dishonour those parts by behaving as a libertine; that an actor should seek fame, not notoriety. They reminded him that Kemble offstage faded into the respectability of the middle classes, that conscious of the uncertainty of an actor's social position, he did not court attention, but was content to be regarded as eminently respectable while belonging to a profession that was not generally respected. This, the committee told Kean, was how he himself ought to behave and he promised to do as they said.

But despite his promises, there were numerous instances of backsliding during the spring and summer of 1815, and his dissolute behaviour was again the subject of common gossip. Mary believed that her security and comfort were threatened by these stories. No one appreciated more than she did the changes her husband's success had made in her life. After the years of poverty, she now had all the money she could spend. She also had her sister, Susan, to help her spend it and together they passed their days pleasantly in shopping expeditions. As Kean had pro-mised on the night of his début, she rode in her own carriage. She enjoyed playing hostess, especially when the guests were people of quality. She knew from bitter experience that she could not stop him from having other women, but she did expect him to exercise discretion and not give rise to scandal.

She suspected Aunt Tid of influencing him against his best interests with the deliberate intention of injuring her. She poured out her fears to various members of the committee, including Lord Essex, Grenfell and Whitbread. Lord Essex replied: 'When you have lived as long as I have, you will find out, my dear Madam, that half the world is made up of *envy*, *hatred* and *malice*. I have heard many idle stories about my friend Kean; and being interested, as I am, in his welfare, and the prosperity of both of you, I always endeavoured to disprove what I knew originated in falsehood and malevolence . . . I do not know anything of Miss Tidswell myself, and am sorry she should wish to be an enemy of those who, I am sure, will always act with gratitude towards her. Kean cannot do better than follow the advice, *upon all occasions*, of two such excellent men as Mr. Whitbread and Mr. Grenfell; and I am also certain, that your mind and heart towards him has the right bias, which ought to regulate it. Depend upon it, I never will believe idle stories. I wish you both happiness and comfort, which, I am sure is in store for you, and, which it is impossible either of you should be so unwise as to sacrifice . . . '

As Lord Essex saw the situation, the immediate problem with Kean was keeping him sufficiently sober to carry out his commit-ments at Drury Lane. In May 1815, when Byron was appointed to the committee, he was amused to find how much time was spent discussing ways of making Kean abstain from alcohol. He told Moore: 'Essex has endeavoured to persuade Kean not to get drunk; the consequence of which is, that he has never been sober since.'

Kean was beginning to resent these intrusions of the committee into his life. He was aware that their paternalism was a mask for their own self-interest. He had not forgotten that a year ago the same committee had been reluctant to give him his chance and had brought him forward only as a forlorn attempt to save the theatre from bankruptcy. He now realised what incompetent managers these aristocrats were and, in the world of the theatre, he had the satisfaction of being able to despise them as much as he believed that they despised him in the world of high society.

If Drury Lane had been run along the same lines as Covent Garden, with a professional manager like Thomas Harris, things would have been very different for Kean. The committee were relying on him to reproduce the magic success of his first season; they placed so much dependence on him that they had allowed the comedic and operatic sides of the company to run down. No professional manager would have concentrated on one tragedian to the detriment of every other member of his company. Covent Garden was strong in all departments, but at Drury Lane a weak and incompetent management were relying solely on an unstable actor, in whom the symptoms of megalomania were beginning to manifest themselves.

Kean had already begun to exercise his own authority over the committee. He had done this by playing at provincial theatres while the Drury Lane season was still in progress. In December he had been severely rebuked by the committee for playing two nights at Brighton without their permission, and again in February, when he played two nights at Woolwich. In these acts of rebellion, he was feeling his own powers. He believed that he was too valuable for them to risk disciplining him and he was proved right. In March his salary was increased to twenty-five pounds and he was given a lump sum of five hundred pounds. He was also granted leave of absence to play Glasgow during Passion week at one hundred pounds a night and to play Newcastle for four nights at the same salary. The committee gave way to Kean because they had no choice. Although he had not repeated the spectacular success of the first season, they kept hoping with each new play that he must surely do so. Threadbare as this policy was, it was the only one they had.

With the death of Samuel Whitbread, in July, 1815, many theatregoers had hoped that a professional manager would be appointed at Drury Lane. Instead the general committee had set up a subcommittee to run the theatre. The five members were Lord Essex, Lord Byron, the Honourable George Lamb, the Honourable Douglas Kinnaird and Peter Moore, M.P.: all gentlemen amateurs. Around this time, Kean founded the Wolves Club, as a protest against amateurism in theatre management. The members were chiefly professional men of the theatre and no gentlemen were admitted. The club met regularly, under the presidency of Kean, at the Coal Hole Tavern in Fountain Court. Within a few weeks of its foundation, the club had acquired an unsavoury reputation. Its declared aims were philanthropic, but, in effect, the meetings were no more than debauched boozing sessions, with argument, song and copulation with prostitutes and actresses.

Mary saw the Wolves Club as another threat to the security of her family, but Kean promised her that he would behave discreetly in all things. In October, he delighted her by moving from Cecil Street to Clarges Street, Piccadilly, where he rented a large house from Lady Rycroft. Clarges Street was in the heart of the most fashionable quarter of Regency London and no actor before him had dared to move so far west. To please Mary, he began a regular series of dinner parties. His guests remarked on how little he drank and how well he behaved, considering all the stories they had heard about him. But, as soon as his guests had departed, he would order his horse and gallop down Piccadilly, through the Haymarket, across Trafalgar Square and down the Strand, back to the taverns and the brothels, the toadies and the whores.

Kean's third Drury Lane season opened, on 16 October 1815, with *Richard III*. This was followed by *Othello*, *Richard II*, *Hamlet*, *Macbeth* and *The Revenge*. The public were tiring of these old productions, and the average receipts were slightly under £250. His first new offering, given on 6 November, was no more successful. This was *Tamerlane*, a tragedy by the Augustan dramatist, Nicholas Rowe, in which Kean played the part of Bajazet, a captive chieftain. This part, like that of Zanga, called for little more than displays of violence, and he played the part ferociously. Crabb Robinson wrote: 'He rushed on the stage at his first appearance as a wild beast may be supposed to enter a new den to which his keepers had transferred him.' Kean's finest moment in the play occurred when Tamerlane remarked,

> The world, 'twould be too little for thy pride,
> Thou would'st scale heaven?

and Bajazet replied, with transcendent scorn,

> I would—away!—my soul disdains the conference.

Tamerlane was withdrawn after seven consecutive performances and Kean's next new play was even less successful, being given only two performances. This was *The Honeymoon*, by John Tobin, in which he played the comedy role of Duke Aranza. The next play did better. This was *The Beggar's Bush*, Douglas Kinnaird's adaptation of Beaumont and Fletcher's *Merchant of Bruges*. During the next three seasons, the subcommittee's search for a successful vehicle for Kean was to result in the revival of other comparatively unknown Elizabethan plays by Massinger, Marlowe and Jonson. In *The Beggar's Bush* Kean played the hero, Florez. He gave great feeling to the scene where he was distracted between his losses and his love for Gertrude. Hazlitt wrote: 'We have seen him do much the same thing before. There is a very fine pulsation in the veins of his forehead on these occasions, an expression of nature which we do not remember in any other actor.' The play was given eighteen performances. The receipts averaged no more than £300, but this was Kean's best average of the season to date.

So far, the subcommittee had failed to find a play for Kean that brought in the crowds. Then, with their next production, they struck gold. This was a revival of *A New Way to Pay Old Debts*, a satiric comedy by Philip Massinger, which opened on 12 January 1816, with Kean in the role of Sir Giles Overreach. The part is one of unrelieved villainy. Overreach is an upstart, who has amassed a fortune by dishonest means. He plans to marry his daughter against her will to an aristocrat. When his plans are frustrated and his villainy unmasked, he goes mad from his own rage. Kean always needed a touch of malignancy to inspire him most, and as Overreach he was given a splendid chance to display his intense power of communicating terror and evil. There were, however, moments in the play which he endowed with great beauty and feeling, as when he was asked,

> Are you not moved with the sad imprecations
> And curses for all families, made wretched
> By your sinister practices?

and he replied,

> Yes, as rocks are,
> When foamy billows split themselves against
> Their flinty ribs; or as the moon is moved
> When wolves, with hunger pined, howl at her brightness.

Doran wrote: 'I still seem to hear the words and the voice as I pen this passage, now composed, now grand as the foamy billows; so flute-like on the word "moon", creating a scene with the sound; and anon sharp, harsh, fierce in the last line, with a look upward from those matchless eyes, that rendered the troop visible, and their howl perceptible to the ear;—the whole serenity of the man, and the solidity of his temper, being illustrated less by the assurance in the succeeding words than by the exquisite music in the tone with which he uttered the word "brightness".'

It was generally agreed, however, that Kean achieved his greatest effect in the last act of the play, when Overreach goes mad. This was probably the most powerful exhibition of human passion that has ever been witnessed upon the English stage. When Kean as Overreach unleashed the storm of his bitterness, his ravings were so frenzied that many in the audience thought he must surely be possessed by the devil. His features were livid. Scream after scream came from his throat and reverberated through the theatre. Women in the audience became hysterical and had to be removed. Byron was seized by a convulsive fit. The effect of Kean's acting was not confined to the audience, but was communicated to the other players on the stage. Mrs. Glover, an experienced actress, was so overcome that she had to be supported to a chair. Munden stood transfixed, his eyes riveted on Kean's convulsed and blackened face. 'My God!' he said afterwards. 'Is it possible?'

Hazlitt could not find a single fault in Kean's performance. 'He is a truly great actor,' he stated simply. With Overreach Kean again became the talk of the town. Not since his Richard III had he achieved such a triumph. The subcommittee were elated as they watched the money roll in On the second night the receipts were £528. By the sixth night they had increased to £584. There were crowds outside the theatre fighting to get in. It was the great days of the first season all over again. It was commented upon that every time Kean as Overreach had to say the word 'lord' he did so with a mixture of servility and contempt which seemed at variance with the part he was portraying. Few guessed that he was expressing his hatred of all the aristocrats who were bedevilling his life both inside and outside the theatre. When he returned home after his first performance and Mary asked him what Lord Essex had thought of it, he replied, 'Damn Lord Essex, *the pit ROSE at me.*'

It seemed to Kean's supporters that his performance as Overreach must surely be the death-blow to Kemble and his school. How, they asked, could the heroic strut and sing-song declamation continue to exist beside the passion and truth of Kean's acting? As though to prove the point for them Kemble challenged Kean in the role. On 26 April, he appeared as Sir Giles Overreach at Covent Garden. No actor was less suited to the part. Hazlitt wrote: 'Sir Giles *hath a devil*; Mr. Kemble has none. Sir Giles is in a passion; Mr. Kemble is not. Sir Giles has no regard for appearances; Mr. Kemble has. It has been said of the Venus de Medici, "So stands the statue that enchants the world"; the same might have been said of Mr. Kemble. He is the very still-life and statuary of the stage; a perfect figure of a man; a petrifaction of sentiment, that heaves no sigh and sheds no tear; an icicle upon the bust of tragedy.' Kemble had failed completely in his challenge. To his dismay, he had heard hissing from the audience. He realised that the spirit of the times was against him. He had been thirty-three years on the London stage and had often thought of retiring. This reception made him decide that the time had come to leave the stage and he resolved that the next season would be his last.

The triumph of *A New Way to Pay Old Debts* led the subcommittee to believe that in the plays of Massinger they had found the secret of success which had so long eluded them. On 9 March they revived another Massinger play, *The Duke of Milan*, with Kean in the role of Sforza. The play was a failure and, after being given seven performances to diminishing receipts, it was withdrawn.

Around this time an incident occurred which showed how Kean's debauchery was beginning to affect the attitude of the public towards him. On 26 March, when he was advertised to play in *The Duke of Milan*, he did not turn up at the theatre. After waiting until seven o'clock, Rae apologised to the audience. He told them that he feared some accident had happened to Kean, as this was the first time he had ever missed a performance. Kean, at that moment, was lying dead drunk in a tavern at Deptford, where he had been with some companions since performing Overreach the previous night. On the day after his non-appearance, so many scandalous rumours were circulating round London that the subcommittee, after a hurried consultation, issued a statement saying that Kean, returning from the country at a very quick pace to keep his engagement at the theatre, was thrown out of his carriage and had his arm dislocated, besides being stunned and very much bruised. To give substance to this story, Kean was driven home, propped up with pillows and his arm in a sling.

This subterfuge fooled nobody and the newspapers had a great time with the story. The subcommittee then announced that Kean had told them he would appear, on the advice of his doctors, 'if it be not in a character requiring too much bodily exertion', and suggesting Shylock. The subcommittee had agreed and *The Merchant of Venice* was announced for 1 April. When Kean made his entrance, with his arm in a sling, he was greeted with a mixture of applause and hisses. Considering that he had missed only one performance since his début, the hissing was unfair, but some members of the audience were using the incident as an opportunity to express their distaste for his infamous behaviour offstage.

After the failure of *The Duke of Milan*, the subcommittee were at a complete loss as to what Kean's next new play should be. Then Byron came up with *Bertram*, a tragedy by the contemporary writer, Charles Robert Maturin. Sir Walter Scott had recommended this Gothic tragedy to Byron, who, in turn, thought highly of it. He persuaded the other members of the subcommittee to buy it for Kean and so provided the actor with one of the biggest successes in his career. The character of Bertram was perfectly suited to Kean's genius and to the taste of his audience. Bertram was the epitome of the Romantic hero, a man of lofty mind, but twisted with hatred when his love for Imogene is thwarted by her forced marriage. In the last act he has been driven by circumstances into becoming a murderer, insanely bent on revenge, but his attitude softens when he sees the result of his vengeance in the madness and death of Imogene. Kean's audience responded with sympathy and pity to his moving portrayal of Bertram. The play was first produced on 9 May and was performed twenty-two times before the season closed on 26 June.

For his benefit on 5 June, Kean chose Ben Jonson's comedy, *Every Man in His Humour*. He had been urged to play the part of Kitely by Sir George Beaumont, who had demonstrated to him how Garrick had performed it. But Sir George was disappointed when he saw Kean in the part. The following day, at Farington's, he expressed the view that Kean 'was deficient in giving the nice touches of character in which Garrick excelled'. Hazlitt, on the other hand, having no recollection of Garrick to modify his judgement, was pleased with Kean, especially in the reconciliation scene, where to show his confidence in his wife, Kitely tells her that she may sing, go to balls and dance, then interrupts this list of concessions with the restriction, 'though I had rather you did not do all this'. Hazlitt thought this 'a master-stroke'. He wrote: 'It was perhaps the first time a parenthesis was ever spoken on the stage as it ought to be. Mr. Kean certainly often repeats this artifice of abrupt transition in the tones in which he expresses different passions, and still it always pleases—we suppose, because it is natural.'

The season closed, on 26 June, with a performance of *Bertram*. The previous evening Kean had been presented with a large silver cup, costing three hundred guineas, in commemoration of his performance as Overreach. The money had been subscribed by the committee and players of Drury Lane, and their names were inscribed on the cup. Two names were missing, those of William Dowton and Joseph Munden. Both had refused to subscribe, Munden from meanness and Dowton from jealousy. During the season, Kean had played seven new parts, two of which—Bertram and Overreach—were to stay in his repertory. Chiefly because of these two parts, the season had been a good one for him, but the total receipts of the theatre for the entire season were only £58,017, over £9,000 less than the previous year, while Covent Garden's total was £78,000. It was widely feared that the parsimony of the subcommittee was rapidly bringing Drury Lane to the same state of bankruptcy as that achieved by the extravagance of Sheridan.

In the summer of 1816, Thomas Colley Grattan visited London. He had resigned his commission in the army and now lived in Paris, where he earned his living by writing. He decided to call on Kean, whom he had not seen since the Waterford days six years previously. He had no sooner sent up his card than the servant returned and asked him to go upstairs to the drawing room, but before he could even reach the stairs, Kean had sprung halfway down them to greet him. Kean was so anxious to see his old friend that he had darted from under the hands of his hairdresser, and one side of his head was beautifully curled, while the other was a tangled mass of hair. Grattan wrote: 'Had he received the visit of a powerful patron or generous benefactor, he could not, or at least need not, have shown more gratitude than he evinced at the recollection of my slight services, in passing some tickets for his *Chimpanzee* benefit, so long before.' Grattan considered his welcome 'a fair test' of Kean's character. He wrote: 'It was thoroughly disinterested, and was not a mere burst of good feeling, nor a display of ostentation—for these would have been sufficiently satisfied with a momentary expression. But his whole behaviour, during a couple of months that I remained in London at that time, was a continuance of friendly attentions.'

Grattan dined frequently at Kean's house and met much good company there. He wrote: 'Persons of high respectability, and many of them of rank, were among his constant guests. His dinners were excellent, but his style of home living did not appear extravagant; and the evening parties were extremely pleasant with a great deal of good music.' Kean himself sang and gave impersonations of well-known vocalists, such as Incledon, Braham and Kelly. Grattan found Mary friendly and hospitable. He wrote: 'She was in her own house, and surrounded by everything that might dazzle the mind's eye and dizzy the brain of almost anyone, a fair specimen of natural character. Her head was evidently turned by her husband's fame, and the combined consequences were bodied forth with exquisite *naiveté*. But there was withal a shrewdness, an offhandedness, and tact quite Irish; and, what was still more so, a warm-hearted and overflowing recognizance of ever so trivial a kindness, or tribute of admiration offered to "Edmund" before he became "a great man".'

During these summer weeks Grattan often went to the theatre with Kean. He was introduced to many players, but he never saw more than one or two of them at Kean's house. He knew that Kean was in the habit of passing the night at some tavern or other, and that he sometimes went to one straight from the theatre, sweating, panting and excited; but he had no idea of the kind of company he kept there. One night that summer he was to find out. He had asked Kean to dine quietly with two friends of his at the Sablonière Hotel in Leicester Square. At six o'clock Kean's carriage drew up at the door and he stepped out of it in full evening dress, silk-lined coat, white breeches and buckled shoes. Grattan wrote: 'He apologised for coming in so flashy a style to a simple bachelor's dinner, saying, that he must leave me as early as nine to attend a party where he was particularly expected. When that hour arrived, we none of us thought of breaking up. The dinner had gone off well; and some excellent wine marvellously aided in keeping up the sociability of the evening. The valuable horses were kept waiting somewhat unmercifully, and messenger after messenger came in search of my unpunctual guest, only to be treated with the same neglect as their predecessors. At length the clock struck midnight, Kean said it was impossible for him "to break his engagement"; and he proposed that my friends and myself should accempany him.'

They all squeezed into Kean's carriage, and after a short and furious drive, drew up at the head of a narrow passage. They stumbled down this passage and through the open door of a tavern. They went up the stairs, watched by a score of waiters and women. Kean flung open the folding doors of a first floor apartment, where some sixty persons were assembled at a long supper table. The Wolves were in session. A shout of welcome greeted Kean and he was escorted to the head of the table. Grattan wrote: 'I had no notion of what sort of company I was in; and no clear conception of anything but lights, looking-glasses, bottles and decanters.' The following day he was angry with Kean for expecting him and his friends to participate in what had been nothing less than an orgy. Kean, for his part, was ashamed that Grattan had seen him in such company, and by tacit consent neither one of them ever mentioned the incident again.

CHAPTER FIVE

THE DESTROYER OF DRURY LANE

On 7 July 1816, Richard Brinsley Sheridan died and the sub-committee planned a memorial series of his plays, to begin early in September with *The School for Scandal*. Douglas Kinnaird wrote to Kean, on behalf of the subcommittee, asking him to play the secondary role of Joseph Surface. This angered Kean and he replied: 'Mr. Kean returns to the Committee the character of Joseph Surface, which he has, with surprise and mortification, received this day. Mr. K. wishes submissively to bring to the recollection of the gentlemen, that the material service which he has rendered to the establishment over which they preside, has been by peculiar success in the *first* walk of the Drama; and he will never insult the judgment of a British public, by appearing before them in any other station, but the important one to which they have raised him.' Kean objected not so much to being asked to play in a comedy, as being asked to play a secondary role; this he had sworn never to do. To his neurotically suspicious mind, it seemed that the suggestion was part of a plot by the subcommittee to denigrate him in the eyes of the public. As the letter had come from Kinnaird, Kean believed him to be the prime mover in this plot. He wrote to Kinnaird: 'I have, with the just indignation of insulted talent, returned, to the Committee, Joseph Surface. I cannot conceive the Committee's intentions towards me, unless it is to destroy my reputation as an *actor*, and interest as a man. But, without disguise or subterfuge, I tell them—I'll be damned if they do either.' The suggestion was dropped.

The violence of Kean's reaction shows how jealously he guarded the pre-eminent position he now occupied. There was no other tragedian who came anywhere near to replacing him. At Covent Garden, Thomas Harris had never stopped searching for an actor who could overthrow Kean. He had already brought many contenders into the field, among them Conway from

Dublin with his Othello, Terry from Edinburgh with his Shylock, Edwards and Cobham with their Richard the Thirds; but as fast as they came, Kean flung them back into obscurity. It was widely believed that he did not rely solely on his talents to defeat them; that he used the members of the Wolves Club as an organised claque to howl them down. While this may not have been strictly true, it was certainly believed at Covent Garden.

In his fourth season at Drury Lane, Kean attempted a new Shakespearean role when he appeared as Timon in *Timon of Athens* on 28 October 1816. His interpretation did not express the whole character. 'We beheld in him the bitter sceptic,' Procter wrote, 'but not the easy, lordly and magnificent Timon.' Hunt thought that Kean's finest scene was the encounter with Alcibiades. He wrote: 'We never remember the force of contrast to have been more truly pathetic. Timon, digging in the woods with his spade, hears the approach of military music, he starts, waits its approach silently, and at last in comes the gallant Alcibiades with a train of splendid soldiery. Never was scene so effectively managed. First you heard a sprightly quick march playing in the distance,—Kean started, listened, and leaned in a fixed and angry manner on his spade, with frowning eyes and lips full of the truest feeling, compressed but not too much so; he seemed as if resolved not to be deceived, even by the charm of a thing inanimate;—the audience were silent; the march threw forth its gallant notes nearer and nearer, the Athenian standards appear, then the soldiers come treading on the scene with that air of confident progress which is produced by the accompaniment of music; and at last, while the squalid misanthrope still maintains his posture and keeps his back to the strangers, in steps the young and splendid Alcibiades, in the flush of victorious expectation. It is the encounter of hope with despair.' Despite such great moments, the play was not a success. After seven performances it was withdrawn and Kean never played the part again.

His next new offering was on 23 November, when he played the part of Sir Edward Mortimer in *The Iron Chest,* a popular melo-drama by George Colman the Younger. Macready thought Sir Edward Mortimer was one of Kean's 'most finished portraitures'.

He wrote: 'Throughout the play the actor held absolute sway over his hearers: alike when nearly maddened by the remembrance of his wrong and the crime it had provoked, in his touching reflections on the present and future recompense of a well-regulated life, in pronouncing the appalling curse on Wilford's head; or, when looking into his face, and in the desolation of his spirit, with a smile more moving than tears, he faintly uttered—"None know my tortures!" His terrible avowal of the guilt that had embittered existence to him brought, as it were, the actual perpetration of the deed before us; the frenzy of his vengeance seemed rekindled in all its desperation, as he uttered the words—"I stabbed him to the heart." He paused as if in horror at the sight still present to him, and, following with his dilated eye the dreadful vision, he slowly continued—"And my oppressor rolled lifeless at my foot!"'

Hazlitt wrote: 'The last scene of all, his coming to life again after his swooning at the fatal discovery of his guilt, and then falling back after a ghastly struggle, like a man waked from the tomb, into despair and death in the arms of his mistress, was one of those consummations of the art, which those who have seen and have not felt them in this actor, may be assured that they have never seen or felt anything in the course of their lives, and never will to the end of them.'

Kean's face was capable of expressing every shade of emotion. 'One of his means of effect,' Lewes wrote, 'sometimes one of his tricks—was to make long pauses between certain phrases. For instance, on quitting the scene, Sir Edward Mortimer has to say warningly, "Wilford, remember!" Kean used to pause after "Wilford", and during the pause his face underwent a rapid succession of expressions fluidly melting into each other and all tending to one climax of threat; and then the deep tones of "remember!" came like muttered thunder. Those spectators who were unable to catch these expressions considered the pause a mere trick; and sometimes the pauses were only tricks, but often they were subtle truths.' Admirers of Kean congregated in the pit, close to the stage, in order that they might not miss any of these expressions. Indeed, Hazlitt declared that 'those who have only seen Kean at a distance, have not seen him at all'.

The Iron Chest was given seventeen times, but this was not the success it seems, for the houses were not very good.

On 20 January 1817 he appeared as the Royal Slave in a revival, of *Oroonoko*, a tragedy by the seventeenth-century dramatist Thomas Southerne. Macready thought the finest moment in the play was Oroonoko's prayer for his wife, Imoinda. He wrote: 'After replying to Blandford, "No, there is nothing to be done for me!" he remained for a few moments in apparent abstraction, then with a concentration of feeling that gave emphasis to every word, clasping his hands together, in tones most tender, distinct, and melodious, he poured out, as if from the very depths of his heart, his earnest supplication:

> Thou God adored! thou ever glorious sun!
> If she be yet on earth, send me a beam
> Of thy all-seeing power to light me to her . . .'

For Hazlitt, the most striking part in the whole performance was in the uttering of a single word. When it is suggested to Oroonoko that 'Imoinda will become the mother, and himself, a prince and a hero, the father of a race of slaves, he starts, and the manner in which he utters the exclamation; "Ha!" at the world of thought which is thus shown to him, like a precipice at his feet, resembles the first sound that breaks from a thunder-cloud, or the hollow roar of a wild beast, roused from its lair by hunger and the scent of blood.' *Oroonoko* was another failure and was given only nine performances. He continued to act his old characters and these, for the most part, attracted the largest audiences, although the receipts were by no means as high as they had been.

At the beginning of February 1817 Thomas Harris heard of a young provincial actor named Junius Brutus Booth, performing at Brighton, whose style of acting was said to resemble Kean's. Booth, who was born in 1796, was nine years younger than Kean. His father, a lawyer of classical tastes, had named him after his favourite Latin satirist. Booth, Snr. had hoped that his son would become a lawyer, but, at the age of seventeen, the boy went on the stage. He was a romantic-looking youth, with aristocratic features framed in lustrous black hair and, like Kean, he was below average height. Harris went to Brighton and saw Booth play Richard III. He was astonished to find that the performance was an exact copy of Kean's. Booth's dress, tones, gestures, movements, entrances and exits, everything even down to the smallest details of stage business, was identical. It struck Harris that this was just the sort of novelty to attract audiences. He invited Booth to play at Covent Garden and promised him a contract if he were successful. To Booth, not yet twenty-one years old, this seemed a golden opportunity.

He made his London début, at Covent Garden, on 12 February, as Richard III. At first the audience were amazed at his audacity in copying Kean's performance, but by the time the curtain had fallen, their reaction was more favourable than unfavourable; some even thought him better than Kean. These attitudes were reflected in the newspapers, some dismissing him as an impostor and others thinking well of him. One thing at least was certain, Booth had captured the interest of the public. At his second appearance he was given an enthusiastic reception. His head was completely turned by his success, and he demanded a three-year contract at a weekly salary of fifteen pounds; but Harris, fearing that the public would soon tire of the novelty, would offer him no more than five pounds a week with annual increases. Booth rejected this offer, and the next time he was due to perform he did not turn up at the theatre.

Over at Drury Lane, Kean had not been pleased when he heard of this young actor who resembled him so closely. He hated all rivals, but one who dared to copy him deserved to be punished in a special way. The quarrel between Booth and Harris gave him his opportunity. He talked the subcommittee into offering Booth a three-year contract at a substantially higher salary than Harris had offered him. On the face of it, the contract seemed attractive, but, in effect, it tied Booth to playing secondary roles to Kean. The subcommittee must have known that they were trapping a young actor into a contract detrimental to his career, but they gave way to Kean. Booth said later that everything had happened so quickly that he accepted without sufficient thought. He came over to Drury Lane, where Kean welcomed him like a brother. Harris was blazing when he learned that Drury Lane had put Booth under contract. He accused the subcommittee of breaking the agreement drawn up between the two patent theatres in Sheridan's time, that in case either theatre had been in treaty with an actor within a year the other theatre would not engage him until it had ascertained that all negotiations were ended. But, urged on by Kean, the subcommittee refused to give up Booth.

The announcement that Booth would play Iago to Kean's Othello on Thursday, 20 February, excited great interest. On the night, Drury Lane was packed for the first time that season. The occasion had more the spirit of a prize fight than a theatrical event. Both men were given a great reception on their first appearance. Booth seemed nervous, but he soon overcame this, and during the second act, he earned several rounds of applause. His Iago was a spirited imitation of Kean's manner of playing the part. He had also adopted Kean's habit of walking diagonally from the middle of the stage into a corner and then going halfway across the footlights. When both men moved this way at the same time, the effect produced was ludicrous. As the tragedy unfolded, Kean's power increased, and the younger man was no match for him in the great scenes in the third act. 'When he ceased to speak,' the *Morning Post* stated, 'he was lost among the subordinate characters, and it required an effort of memory to recognise him as the chief attraction of the evening.'

'But Kean!' Procter wrote; 'no sooner did the interest of the story begin, and the passion of the part justify his fervour, then he seemed to *expand* from the small quick resolute figure which had previously been moving about the stage, and to assume the vigour and dimensions of a giant. He glared down upon the now diminutive Iago; he seized and tossed him aside, with frightful and irresistible vehemence. Till then we had seen Othello and Iago, as it were, together: now the Moor seemed to occupy the stage alone. Up and down, to and fro, he went, pacing about like the chafed lion, who has received his fatal hurt, but whose strength is still undiminished. The fury and whirlwind of the passions seemed to have endowed him with supernatural strength. His eye was glittering and blood-shot, his veins were swollen, and his whole figure restless and violent. It seemed dangerous to cross his path, and death to assault him. There is no doubt but that Kean was excited on the occasion, in a most astonishing degree; as much as though he had been maddened by wine. The impression which he made upon the audience has, perhaps, never been equalled in theatrical annals.' At times Booth appeared to be half-stunned. After one scene, he fled to the green room and had to be coaxed back to the stage. Between acts Kean led him forward to share with him the applause, like some benevolent father dragging forward an over-modest son to receive the honours due to him.

The subcommittee, anxious to profit from the excitement, announced the same play with the same parts for Saturday, 22 February, two nights later. Again Drury Lane was packed, but when the performance was due to begin, Rae, as stage manager, came before the curtain to announce that a letter had just that moment been received from Booth stating that owing to the agitation he had been subjected to that week, he had become too unnerved to play and had gone out of town to recuperate. Rae asked the disappointed audience for permission to act in Booth's place, and after some opposition, this was granted. Before the performance ended, the subcommittee received another letter from Booth.

'Gentlemen', he wrote. 'In an unguarded moment I quitted Covent Garden Theatre (where the most eligible situation for the exertion of my professional talents was open to me) to go over to Drury Lane, where I have since found, and felt to my cost, that every character which I was either desirous or capable of playing was already in possession, and that there was no chance of my appearing in the same. What occasion, therefore, could you have for me, unless to crush any talent I may possess in its infancy? I have now seen through my error, and have therefore renewed the negotiation which was so unfortunately interrupted with the proprietors of Covent Garden Theatre, and have just signed a regular article with them for three years; consequently, I have no longer the power of appearing again at Drury Lane Theatre, and you will have the goodness to take my name entirely out of your bills. I have heard, Gentlemen, that your treasury has benefited considerably from my appearance on Thursday last; I ask no pecuniary recompense for it. I only request that you will not seek to persecute or molest a young man, just entering into life, and who cannot afford either to be shelved (according to the theatrical phrase) at Drury Lane, or to be put into such characters as must infallibly mar all his future prospects.'

Booth had realised that the only future for him at Drury Lane was playing secondary roles to Kean, which meant that for the next three years he would have to repeat over and over again the terrible experience of Thursday. It was a prospect to unnerve any man.

Placards were posted over London stating that Booth had entered into a new agreement with Covent Garden and would appear on Tuesday, 25 February, as Richard III. In reply the Drury Lane subcommittee issued a circular stating that the previous Monday Booth had signed a three-year contract with them and that they meant to hold him to it. Booth was now in a dilemma similar to the one which had caused Kean such agony, when he was unable to play either at the Olympic or Drury Lane, but it is to be doubted that he felt any sympathy for Booth. It was now open warfare between the two theatres. On Monday, 24 February, the Drury Lane subcommittee filed a bill in Chancery against Booth and Covent Garden for an injunction to restrain him from acting at any theatre except Drury Lane. In reply to this action, the proprietors of Covent Garden issued a statement entreating that Booth should not be made the victim of disputes between the two theatres, 'his youth and inexperience alone having placed him in a dilemma, from which it is hoped the candour and liberality of an English public will rescue him'. The following day, on reflection, the Drury Lane subcommittee withdrew the bill, and that night Booth appeared at Covent Garden, as Richard III, as advertised.

The theatre was crowded. When Booth appeared on the stage, he was greeted by a storm of boos and hisses. He had supporters among the audience, but his enemies were determined that he should not be heard. Every voice on stage was drowned in the clamour, which rose to a frenzy of abuse whenever he made an entrance. In the middle of the second act, a player entered with a placard reading, 'Mr. Booth wishes to apologise,' but the uproar continued. Booth came forward and by gestures implored the audience to hear him, but this only made matters worse and he was forced to retreat under a bombardment of oranges. Another player appeared with a placard reading, 'Can Englishmen condemn unheard?' But nothing could quiet them. Among the howls and groans could be heard the shouts of Booth's supporters, 'No shelving', 'No Wolves', 'Booth for ever'. The din continued after the play had ended and the farce begun. Even when the entire performance was finished and the lights extinguished, the row still went on, and it was almost midnight before the audience dispersed.

The extent to which Kean was responsible for this demonstration against Booth is not fully known, but it was widely believed at the time that he was deeply involved. On Tuesday, 25 February, he was indicted indirectly in the *Morning Post*, which stated, 'The Proprietors of Covent Garden have received a notification from a person, who states that he was at a place called the *Coal Hole* on Sunday last, where a club called The Wolves are accustomed to assemble, and that he heard the whole party pledge themselves to drive Mr. Booth from the Stage. If such a conspiracy exists it is severely punishable by law.'

Kean's answer to this charge was published in the *Morning Post*, of Thursday, 27 February. He wrote: 'I think it is my duty in justice to a society of which I once had the honour of being a member, to refute a most malicious piece of calumny. The *Wolf Club* seems to have been the foil, with which the friends of the *rival theatre* have, for the last two years, parried the public censure against their unsuccessful candidates. I wish, therefore, through the medium of the public prints, to inform their *fears*, that such a society is no longer in existence, has not been for the last nine months, and when it was, the principles of the institution were founded in integrity and *universal philanthropy*. The misrepresentations, with regard to this society, laid before the public, rendered it, unjustly, an object of reprobation, and in acknowledgement of my duty to the public, I resigned it. With regard to Mr. Booth, that I have the highest opinion of his talents I gave proof when I recommended his engagement to the Drury-lane Committee. If anyone should assert that I would, individually or accessorily, do anything detrimental to the interest of Mr. Booth, I should be happy, in person, to tell the propagator of such a report that it is a falsehood.' Kean's statement was corroborated by the landlord of the Coal Hole, who issued a statement on the same day stating that the Wolves had ceased to exist many months before.

Two nights later, Booth again played Richard III at Covent Garden. From early afternoon, the streets leading to the theatre had been blocked by excited crowds. When the doors opened, there was a desperate struggle for places. Inside the theatre Booth's supporters raised banners reading, 'He has been punished enough—let us forgive him', 'Beware the artillery of Drury Lane', 'The pit forgives him'. Fights broke out between the rival factions, and by the time the curtain rose, the auditorium was all confusion and riot. Again the players were unheard, but this time Booth's obvious distress began to arouse the sympathy of the audience. The disturbances at Covent Garden had become so serious that the Lord Chamberlain intimated to both theatres that if the present disorder continued he would consider it his duty to prevent Booth from appearing on either stage. By 6 March, however, when Booth again played Richard III at Covent Garden, the opposition had worn itself out and he was allowed to act in peace.

His playing of Sir Giles Overreach two nights later attracted a large audience, curious to see him in Kean's famous role. The similarity of his Overreach to Kean's was uncanny. At one point only did he vary his performance and this was a startling effect in the last act, when Overreach goes mad. One of the supporting actors had concealed a small sponge dipped in rose pink fluid, which he passed to Booth, who slipped it secretly into his mouth and squeezed it with his teeth. Blood seemed to ooze from his lips, and many in the audience believed that in his paroxysm of rage he really had burst a blood vessel. For a while, the controversy over the justification of this effect helped to keep his name before the public, but his imitations of Kean in all his great roles soon palled and he ceased to draw the crowds. His name appeared less and less on the Covent Garden playbills and by the end of the season he was almost forgotten.

That same season saw the London début of William Charles Macready, who was to prove a more formidable rival to Kean than Booth. Macready's father, the manager of a provincial circuit, had wanted his son to be a gentleman and had sent him to Rugby, but the father's social ambition was not matched by his business ability and, when the boy was barely sixteen years old, he had to leave school and help his father out of his financial difficulties. He trained as an actor and worked hard to pay off his father's debts. When his father was imprisoned, he ran the circuit. But Macready found the theatre distasteful and was always wanting to escape from it. He detested the vulgarity and uncouthness of his fellow players. He always avoided their company offstage and, in the theatre, he rarely entered the green room. Like Kean, he was morbidly sensitive on the subject of his social status as an actor, and this was aggravated by the years he had spent at public school. He had thought of leaving the stage, taking a degree at Oxford and entering the Church. Yet the power he felt within himself to become a great actor kept him in the theatre. This was his state of mind, when, at the age of twenty-three, he was invited to perform at Covent Garden. He made his début on 16 September 1816, as Orestes in *The Distrest Mother*, Ambrose Philips' adaptation of Racine's *Andromaque*. The play had been chosen with Kean and the Wolves in mind. Macready later recalled: 'A club much talked of at the time, that bore the name of *The Wolves*, was said to be banded together to put down anyone appearing in Kean's characters. I believed the report not to have been founded in strict fact; but it was currently received, and had its influence on the Covent Garden deliberations. Orestes was the part finally resolved on, as least likely to provoke party criticism.'

Macready had few physical advantages as an actor. He had fair hair and blue eyes, but his face was flat and heavy, and he was not more than an inch taller than Kean in height. A knowledgeable audience were present at his début, Kean among them, conspicuous in a private box. The play went well and Macready knew his success was assured when he heard the loud applause that followed his vehement burst of passion in the line, 'O, ye Gods! give me Hermione, or let me die!' He noticed that Kean was generous with his applause throughout the performance. Hazlitt, in the *Examiner*, had 'not the slightest hesitation in saying, that Mr. Macready is by far the best tragic actor that has come out in our remembrance, with the exception of Mr. Kean.' This favourable reception resolved Macready's doubts about his future career. He decided to devote himself single-mindedly to his ambition to become the first actor in England.

On 25 October 1816, five and a half weeks after Macready's début, Kemble began his series of farewell performances, at Covent Garden, with Addison's *Cato*. Macready was anxious to see every performance, in order that he might judge for himself how far Kemble's talents had been exaggerated by his admirers and belittled by his detractors. The theatre was only moderately filled for *Cato*. This surprised Macready, who had expected a great display of public enthusiasm. 'But there was Kemble!' he wrote. 'As he sat majestically in his curule chair, imagination could not supply a grander or more noble presence. In face and form he realised the most perfect ideal that ever enriched the sculptor's or the painter's fancy, and his deportment was in accord with all of outward dignity and grace that history attributes to the *patres conscripti*.' The five acts of declamatory verse on the themes of patriotism and liberty tended to have a drowsy effect on the audience. 'But,' Macready wrote, 'like an eruptive volcano from some level expanse, there was one burst that electrified the house. When Portius entered with the exclamation,—

> "Misfortune on misfortune! grief on grief!
> My brother Marcius . . ."

Kemble, with a start of unwonted animation, rushed across the stage to him, huddling questions one upon another with extraordinary volubility of utterance—

> "Ha! what has he done?—
> Has he forsook his post? Has he given way?
> Did he look tamely on and let them pass?"

Then listening with intense eagerness to the relation of Portius,—
how

> "Long at the head of his faithful friends
> He stood the shock of a whole host of foes,
> Till, obstinately brave, and bent on death,
> Oppressed with multitudes, he greatly fell—"

as he caught the last word he gasped out convulsively, as if suddenly relieved from am agony of doubt, "I am satisfied!" and the
theatre rang with applause most heartily and deservedly bestowed.
This was his great effect—indeed his single effect; and great and
refreshing as it was it was not enough so to compensate for a
whole evening of merely sensible cold declamation. I watched
him intently throughout—not a look or tone was lost by me; his
attitudes were stately and picturesque, but evidently prepared;
even the care he took in the disposition of his mantle was distinctly observable. If meant to present a picture of Stoicism, the
success might be considered unequivocal, but unbroken, except by
the grand effect above described; though it might satisfy the
classic antiquary, the want of variety and relief rendered it unin-
teresting, and often, indeed tedious.'

Throughout the farewell season, from a seat in the dress-circle,
Macready saw Kemble in all his great roles—Hotspur, Macbeth,
Hamlet, Wolsey, Brutus, Octavian, King John and Coriolanus.
Of these he preferred King John, Wolsey, Brutus and the incomparable Coriolanus. For Kemble's last performance as Macbeth,
Mrs. Siddons came out of retirement to play opposite him.
Covent Garden was crowded for this great theatrical event. But
the years had done their work on the great tragedienne and there
was no sign of her awesome genius. Her performance amounted
to little more than a reading of the text. Kemble himself was not
much better. Macready wrote: 'Throughout the whole first four
acts, the play moved heavily on: Kemble correct, tame, and

I   KEAN AS SHYLOCK
From a painting by W. H. Watt

2 KEAN AS RICHARD III
From a painting by Samuel Drummond
Reproduced by permission of its owners, the Governors of the
Old Vic Theatre, London, and of the University of Bristol
Theatre Collection, to which it is on loan

3(a) JOHN PHILIP KEMBLE
From a painting by M. A. Shee

3(b) JUNIUS BRUTUS BOOTH
AS RICHARD III
*Photo Radio Times Hulton Picture
Library*

3(c) ROBERT WILLIAM ELLISTON
From a painting by G. H. Harlowe

3(d) JAMES WINSTON
From a painting by Samuel De Wilde

6(a)
MRS ALDERMAN COX
KEAN'S 'LITTLE
BREECHES'
From a pencil and
watercolour sketch by
Samuel De Wilde, 1814
Photo: A. C. Cooper Ltd

6(b)   KEEN-ISH SPORT IN COX'S COURT!! *or* SYMPTOMS OF
CRIM. CON. IN DRURY LANE MAY 1824

From an engraving, attributed to George Cruikshank,
published by J. Fairbairn
Harvard Theatre Collection

7 KEAN AS ALANIENOUIDET, HONORARY HURON CHIEF
From an engraving by G. F. Storm after a painting by
Frederick Meyer, Jr
Harvard Theatre Collection

8

KEAN'S THEATRE
AND HOUSE AT
RICHMOND,
SURREY
From a print
published by
T. Woodfall
*Harvard Theatre
Collection*

ineffective; but in the fifth, when the news was brought, "The queen, my lord, is dead," he seemed struck to the heart; gradually collecting himself, he sighed out, "She should have died here- after!" then, as if with the inspiration of despair, he hurried out distinctly and pathetically, the lines:

> "Tomorrow, and tomorrow, and tomorrow
> Creeps in this petty pace from day to day . . ."

rising to a climax of desperation that brought down the enthusi- astic cheers of the closely-packed theatre. All at once he seemed carried away by the genius of the scene. At the tidings of "the wood of Birnam moving", he staggered, as if the shock had struck the very seat of life, and in the bewilderment of fear and rage could just ejaculate the words "Liar and slave!" then lashing himself into a state of frantic rage, ended the scene in perfect triumph.'

Covent Garden was crowded again on 23 June 1817, when Kemble ended his career with a performance of Coriolanus, the role in which no one, not even the most fervent admirer of Kean, could deny his pre-eminence. When the curtain fell, the roars of cheers and the thunderous applause celebrated not only the close of Kemble's career but the end of an era in the history of the English stage.

When Grattan next visited Kean, in the summer of 1817, he found him much changed from the previous year. He noticed how bitterly Kean spoke of those members of the aristocracy whom he used to claim so proudly as his friends. Grattan wrote: 'He made it a boast that he refused their invitations, and despised their patronage; and that he knew they meant him no honour by these distinctions, which were only so many negative tributes offered to their own importance.' When asked to 'recite' at a party given in honour of the Duke of Wellington, he had refused, complaining that he had been asked not as a gentleman but as a wild beast to be stared at. Kean had recognised at last that the aristocracy would never accept him as an equal, and he was morbidly conscious of the condescension with which they treated him. His resentment took the form of a savage hatred for all aristocrats. Grattan wrote: 'Kean thought that as he could not fawn upon title, he must necessarily shun everyone who was a "lord" merely because he was one.'

Grattan also perceived in Kean some characteristics which had not been apparent during his previous visit to London. The chief among these was 'an evident affectation of singularity, an over-strained boldness of demeanour, a rage for being conspicuous, not merely as an actor, but as a man'. Kean's life had become one of wildness and display. He craved to be admired and talked about, to excite admiration and wonder. He kept a pet lion, and it was a common sight to see them seated together in the stern of a wherry, being rowed up and down the Thames. The wherry had become his favourite mode of transport. He owned a small fleet of these passenger boats and had inaugurated an annual race for wherry-men. In a moment of drunken enthusiasm, he had bought a beautiful yacht. He employed a private secretary, an unheard-of thing for an actor. The secretary, whose name was Phillips, had been a supporting player at Drury Lane. In addition to his normal duties, he was expected to wait up half the night at some tavern and remain sufficiently sober to get his employer safely home. Kean had bought a black stallion, which he named Shylock, and in the early hours of the morning, when he was roaring drunk, he would ride the horse up and down the steps of Drury Lane. Some nights he would ride into the country, jumping the turnpikes at full gallop, until the horse was foaming at the mouth, when they would return home and sleep together in the stable. He attended every important prize fight and was friendly with all the champions. He sometimes sparred in his dining room with Mendoza and Richmond the Black. He no longer attempted to hide his affairs with women, for he was anxious to be regarded as a man of gallantry; but these episodes were so gross that they aroused not admiration but only disgust.

Much of Kean's sodden life-style shows the influence of Byron. Grattan maintained that Byron had modelled himself on Napoleon and that what Byron was to Napoleon, Kean was to Byron. 'And, after all,' he asked, 'which was most a stage-player of the three?

Was not the political world the great theatre of Napoleon's deeds
—the social world of Byron's doings? Did not both act a part from
first to last? and was not Kean more an actor in the broad gaze of
London life than on the narrow boards of Drury Lane? The
generic signs of genius were common to them all; and they were
undoubtedly of the same species of mind. Had their relative
positions been reversed, their individual careers had probably
been the same, or nearly so. Reckless, restless, adventurous,
intemperate; brain-fevered by success, desperate in reverse; seeking to outdo their own destiny for good; and rushing upon
dangers and difficulties, which they delighted first to make, and
then to plunge within . . . They were each, on their several
stages, acting the self-same part—straining for the world's
applause, not labouring for their own delight; and though there
was more greatness in one instance, and more glory in the other,
the inspiration was, perhaps, precisely similar in all. The grand
distinction in favour of Napoleon was, all through, not that he was
an emperor, but that he was an original. Bryon was an extravagant copy; Kean an absurd one.'

Byron, like Napoleon, was now in exile. The moral indignation of the British public that was shortly to fall upon Kean had
already fallen upon the handsome crippled poet and driven him
from the country. During February and March of the previous
year, London had buzzed with ugly rumours of his cruelty,
neglect and infidelities. His wife had left him after a year of marriage. He was accused of incest and sodomy; compared to Nero,
Caligula and Epicurus; ostracised in public and in private; abused
in the newspapers and insulted in the streets. Undecided whether
he was unfit for England or England unfit for him, he had sailed
from Dover on 25 April 1816, never to return.

While Kean was living this dissolute life, he continued to fulfil
numerous engagements in the provinces. These, together with his
commitments at Drury Lane, were a great strain on his health. In
the autumn of 1817, on the night before Grattan left London for
the south of France, he went with his brother to Drury Lane to
see Kean act Othello. After the play they went to Kean's dressing
room. Grattan wrote: 'We found him, as was usual after the

performance of any of his principal parts, stretched on a sofa, retching violently, and throwing up blood. His face was half-washed—one side deadly pale, the other deep copper colour. He was a very appalling object, certainly, even to those who were accustomed so to see him; and my brother was quite shocked and alarmed, from the apparent danger of the tragedian.'

Kean was only thirty years old, but he was rapidly decaying. From this time on, he was to be frequently absent from the stage. Some of these absences were no more than strategic moves in the game of power politics he was playing at Drury Lane and others were the result of drunkenness, but there were times when he was simply too ill to make an appearance. From Grattan's description of Kean's condition after a performance, it would seem that the actor suffered from tuberculosis. He definitely had venereal disease, probably syphilis as well as gonorrhea. His poor state of health would account for many of his temperamental difficulties, and these were further aggravated by his excessive use of alcohol. His dissipated way of life was, perhaps, a manifestation of an hereditary urge towards self-destruction. His father had committed suicide and his maternal great-grandfather, Henry Carey, had also taken his own life.

His reputation was chiefly based on the parts he had perfected during his years in the provinces, Richard III, Othello, Hamlet and Shylock. During his first season at Drury Lane, he had shown the public what he could do with these characters, but, apart from Macbeth and Overreach, he had done little since then. Perhaps the hardship, poverty and driving ambition of his early life had been a necessary discipline for his art, restraining his tendency towards dissipation. Perhaps after he achieved success and threw off this restraint, the viciousness of his life, together with his organic diseases, drained him of the energy to master new parts.

Yet he was always able to give a good performance in any of his old parts, and the reason for this lay in the nature of his acting. People spoke of Kean as an impulsive actor, not realising that, during his years in the provinces, he had patiently rehearsed every detail; every tone of voice, every look and gesture until he was satisfied, and having once perfected these, he never changed them.

Lewes observed: 'The consequence was that, when he was sufficiently sober to stand and speak, he could act his part with the precision of a singer who has thoroughly learned his air. One who often acted with him informed me that when Kean was rehearsing on a new stage he accurately counted the number of steps he had to take before reaching a certain spot, or before uttering a certain word; these steps were justly regarded by him as part of the mechanism which could no more be neglected than the accompaniment to an air could be neglected by a singer. Hence it was that he was always the same; not always in the same health, not always in the same vigour, but always master of the part, and expressing it through the same symbols. The voice on some nights would be more irresistably touching in "But, oh! the pity of it, Iago!"—or more musically forlorn in "Othello's occupation's gone"—or more terrible in "Blood; Iago; blood, blood!" but always the accent and rhythm were unchanged; as Tamberlin may deliver the C from the chest with more sonority one night than another, but always delivers it from the chest and never from the head.' So Kean continued to repeat his old parts, and the public came to see them, regardless of the threadbare costumes and the tattered scenery, knowing that the miracle would still happen and the fire from heaven blaze again on the stage of Drury Lane.

Kean was aware that his powers were declining, but he was determined to remain the leading tragedian at Drury Lane. He had neither the strength nor the inclination to maintain his position by a continuous striving for perfection in new parts and so he schemed against anyone whom he thought might be a threat to him. The chaotic conditions prevailing at Drury Lane gave him ample scope for intrigue. The 1816–17 season had been a disastrous one for the theatre. Kean's other offerings—*Manuel*, a new tragedy by Maturin; *The Surrender of Calais*, by George Colman, Jr.; *Barbarossa*, by John Browne—had all been failures. The duel with Booth had brought in £500, but the nightly average was only £197, and the total receipts for the season were £41,060 almost £17,000 less than the previous season. Before the season ended, the shareholders had already lost all confidence in the subcommittee. At a general meeting held in March, it had been alleged that the theatre was £40,000 in debt and that the value of £100 shares had dropped to £20. The majority of the share-holders were of the opinion that the time had come to place the affairs of Drury Lane in the hands of a professional man of the theatre, and a motion was adopted to let the theatre on lease, provided adequate rent and security could be obtained.

It was three years since the subcommittee had come into power, and of the five original members, Byron had left the country, Kinnaird had resigned, and Lord Essex had lost much of his interest in the affairs of the theatre. The only two effective members now were George Lamb and Peter Moore. They were virtually running Drury Lane, with Lamb in charge of the artistic direction and Moore handling the administration. In these three years there had been no less than six stage managers. Before the 1817–18 season Rae had been dismissed and Raymond, who had been dismissed the previous summer, was re-appointed. Raymond died in October, 1817, and his assistant, Henry Johnstone, succeeded him. Kean disliked Johnstone and he issued an ultimatum to the subcommittee, telling them that he would not serve under him. The subcommittee dared not discipline Kean for his insubordination, because he was still their main source of income. Admittedly, he played many nights when the receipts did not cover the running expenses, but even these amounts were better than those of the nights when he did not play. The subcommittee, therefore, came up with a compromise solution, by which it was agreed that Kean would have the right to choose his own plays and that on the nights he performed he himself would become stage manager. This was to prove an expensive decision, for the four new plays Kean chose that season were all lavish productions and all were failures.

The first was *Richard, Duke of York*, adapted by Merivale from several of Shakespeare's plays. This was given on 22 December 1817, and lasted only seven performances. Next came *The Bride of Abydos*, an adaptation of Byron's poem by William Dimond. It was hoped that the combination of Kean and Byron would ensure a long run, but the play ran for only fourteen performances. For his next production Kean turned again to the

Elizabethan theatre in the hope of finding another golden part like Overreach. On 24 April he played Barabbas in a revival of Marlowe's *The Jew of Malta*. This lasted only eleven performances. On 1 June he made another mistake when he played in Shakespeare's *King John*, one of Kemble's great roles. Kean's performance did not match Kemble's and the play was only given three performances. The receipts on the third night were £87, the lowest to which he had yet fallen.

It seemed that the subcommittee could do nothing right. At the beginning of the season they had lighted the theatre with gas. This was a major reform, but it was resented by the public, who accused the subcommittee of trying to poison them. *The Times* stated: 'All admit that after having sat a whole evening in the theatre, they feel a burning and prickling sensation in their eyes, a soreness about the throat and generally a violent headache which sometimes lasts for two or three days.' The subcommittee had also transformed the saloon into an exotic Chinese pavilion, but many people thought it looked more like some kind of brothel, and the subcommittee were accused of encouraging prostitutes to congregate at Drury Lane, as if there were not already enough there as it was. The subcommittee was in worse trouble at the end of the season, when it was found that the total receipts had dropped to £43,068, more than £4,000 below the cost of running the theatre.

In desperation, Peter Moore inaugurated a drastic economy drive. Production costs were cut to the bone. The scenery and costumes were used over and over again. Good players were dismissed and inferior ones recruited. On 29 May 1818, a meeting was held between the Drury Lane company and the subcommittee to discuss the crisis. A report was submitted showing debts totalling £80,280 13s. 5d. The subcommittee recommended that all players earning more than £4 a week should have their salaries reduced, and that the system of management be changed and the theatre put in the hands of a professional man of the theatre. The company protested vehemently against the reduction of salaries and, in the end, neither of the recommendations was adopted. The situation deteriorated so much that some weeks the treasury had not enough money to pay the salaries of the company. This led to several good players leaving Drury Lane, and they were not always replaced.

There is reason to believe that Kean encouraged the sub-committee in their methods of economy. Certainly, the situation suited him. He welcomed the inferior acting talent which now surrounded him, for in his opinion, this made him shine all the more. Few leading actors of the day believed in ensemble playing, but most realised that they needed some adequate support, or if they did not, their stage manager did. But Kean, because of his special arrangements with the subcommittee, was a law unto himself, and he was now acting virtually alone on the stage, expecting the public to come for him and for no other reason. He was notorious for his jealousy of other players in the company. Oxberry has reported that after Miss Somerville's promising début in *Bertram* Kean would not act with her again. He said she was too big for him, but everyone knew he meant she was too good.

From then on she was given only secondary roles, and so was forced to leave the company. It was believed that he dropped *Manuel* because Rae, as De Zelos, outshone him. Another actress to incur his displeasure was Miss Macauley, who joined the Drury Lane company in 1818. After playing Constance opposite his King John, he accused her of acting so badly that she had spoiled some of his effects, and, as a result of this, she was dismissed. For the most part, he was hated by the other members of the company, the only exceptions being toadies like Pope, who, when acting with him, were always careful never to do anything that would distract the attention of the audience away from him.

In the summer of 1818, Kean, accompanied by Mary, visited Paris, where he was received with honour by François-Joseph Talma and other members of the Comédie-Française. Talma was acknowledged as the greatest French tragedian. He had been responsible for many reforms in French acting and had done much to suppress the exaggerations of the declamatory style. Kean saw him play Orestes in Racine's *Andromaque*. He especially admired him in the mad scene, although he was convinced that he could play the scene better himself and was anxious to show the London public what he could do with it. He left Paris for Switzerland and, on his return to London, he claimed, quite untruthfully, that he had climbed to the summit of Mont Blanc. On 22 October he played Orestes in *The Distrest Mother*, Ambrose Philips' adaptation of Racine's tragedy. This was the play Macready had chosen for his début two years earlier. Kean was not so good as Macready in the part, and the play was withdrawn after six performances.

His growing list of failures was halted on 3 December with the production of *Brutus*, a new verse drama by the American writer, John Howard Payne. *Brutus* was not a great play, but it was highly effective on the stage, and it gave Kean some splendid opportunities for the physical indication of mental states, a technique of his that was much admired by Hazlitt. This was best demonstrated in the judgement scene, where Brutus's duty as a citizen overcomes his feelings as a father and he sentences his son to death. The reflection of Brutus's mental anguish was seen in the contrast between Kean's stern look and the convulsive movement of his hands. *The Times* stated: 'We can recollect no instance of an actor who could stand silently on the stage for minutes together, and by calling up in succession all the shades and degrees of passion into his countenance, move his audience to silence and tears of truest sympathy.' *Brutus* ran for thirty-nine consecutive performances and, by the end of the season, it had been given fifty-two times. The average receipts were only around £300, but, in the present condition of Drury Lane, the play was a triumph.

In 1819, the complaints against Kean's behaviour inside Drury Lane were given a wider currency when they were made the subject of pamphlets and newspaper reports. His debauchery was already common knowledge, but now the public learned of his vicious behaviour towards his fellow-players and also those unfortunate authors who submitted plays that did not measure up to his requirements. This knowledge added to the considerable body of hostile opinion which had already built up against him. One of the first broadsides was fired by Miss Macauley, whom he had caused to be dismissed the previous year. She published a pamphlet denouncing him. 'Mr. Kean,' she wrote, 'stands in general estimation, as the enemy of his profession, and the public; as one, who to raise himself to a climax of theatrical grandeur, has bartered the best feelings of human nature; as one who has endeavoured to sacrifice the feelings, fortunes, and even hopes of Actors, and Authors, unless they made themselves subservient to him; as one who repayed the generosity of the public, by keeping from them all prospects of amusement but what centred on himself.'

One of the authors who had suffered at his hands was Miss Jane Porter, a writer of historical romances. She had written a play especially for him entitled *Switzerland*. The subcommittee wanted him to do the play during the 1817–18 season, but this had not suited him and he proposed *The Jew of Malta* instead. As the subcommittee had agreed to allow him to be the manager of his own plays, there was nothing they could do. But all the plays Kean chose that season were failures, and the following season the subcommittee reminded him of this fact and suggested again that he should do *Switzerland*. This time he agreed. He studied his part assiduously. He flattered Miss Porter by asking her to attend rehearsals so that he could consult with her over the interpretation of the character he was playing. At the final rehearsal he acted so well that he drew applause from the other players. When the play opened on 15 February 1819, Miss Porter took her seat with every confidence of success. 'Think, then, my astonishment,' she wrote, 'when on the night of Public Representation, the Curtain drew up, and discovered all this promised energy, transformed into an almost motionless Automaton! He appeared to have lost his memory, and his power of action: the other Performers became disconcerted in their parts: and the confusion on the stage, being now answered by an equal confusion amongst the audience, the whole became a chaos of uproar: "Shame!—Shame, Kean!" burst from every part of the House; contending with the vociferous yells of a set of wretches, who could only have come from the lowest orgies of the Western Hustings of that day.'

The newspapers were indignant and laid the blame squarely on Kean, who, as the *Theatrical Inquisitor* stated, 'did not in one single instance condescend to display his powers'. Moreover, he was suspected of organising the claque which had howled the play down. *Switzerland* was far from being a masterpiece, but whatever its faults, it had not been given a fair trial. The *Morning Herald* stated: 'Miss Porter's tragedy was certainly ill-adapted for the stage; but it will be some consolation to her to know, that the noblest piece of Sophocles or Shakespeare, if represented like her play, would meet the same destiny. It would seem, as if the whole theatre had conspired against it, even to the scene-shifters. Two scenes fell flat upon the stage during the performance, and presented a strangely confused spectacle of back lights, naked machinery, and more than the bustle of a ship's deck in a storm. But the greatest outrage was the behaviour of MR. KEAN. He went through his part, of course the principal one by many degrees, with as much slovenliness, as if he was merely rehearsing it.'

Poor Miss Porter realised that she had been the innocent pawn in a power game between Kean and the subcommittee. He had used her to show the subcommittee that he would tolerate no interference from them and that no play could succeed without his approval. The *Champion* voiced the disquiet of the public when it stated: 'Mr. Kean, it is true, for the want of a better, stands at the very head of his profession; and if he enjoyed his eminence with discretion, we should be happy to swell the chorus of his reputation. But if he will suffer no other merit, among actors, to appear beside him on the boards; no production of authors to be accepted or to succeed, that does not make his character *the exclusive object of attraction*; and no wish or promise of managers to be fulfilled, that does not chime in with his ambition to shine, not only superior, *but alone*, it is high time for criticism to look at the other side of the picture: and Mr. K. may assure himself, that there are still faults enough to be pointed out in his elocution and acting, to place, without discolouring or exaggeration, even his very best characters in a much less favourable point of view, than they have generally been regarded by an indulgent public.'

Within a few weeks of the *Switzerland* débâcle, the public learned, in the fullest detail, of another episode concerning Kean, which proved conclusively that the present monarch of the English stage was nothing less than a tyrant. Early in November, 1817, a writer named Charles Bucke had submitted his tragedy, *The*

Italians, to Drury Lane. The subcommittee accepted the play enthusiastically and promised him that it would be performed with the best actors at their command. The play was given to Kean to read and, as he was equally enthusiastic, it was announced for immediate production. Then Bucke was told that this arrangement must be changed and *The Italians* give way to *The Bride of Abydos*, but he was assured that his play would be produced immediately after this. *The Bride of Abydos* was performed, but then Kean suggested that this should be followed by a comedy. Bucke agreed on the understanding that his tragedy would be next in line. *The Castle of Glendower* was chosen by Kean and while this comedy was in rehearsal he told Bucke that he wished to revive Marlowe's *Jew of Malta* for his next production. Again Bucke agreed to waive his prior claim, the subcommittee and Kean giving him their solemn promise that his tragedy would appear immediately after Marlowe's. This happened towards the end of February 1818. Bucke suggested to Kean that he would use the interval to revise some of the script, but Kean assured him that he was perfectly happy with the play as it was and that any minor corrections could be attended to during rehearsals.

Towards the end of April, while *The Jew of Malta* was being presented, orders were given by the subcommittee for the immediate production of *The Italians*. The music was arranged, the scenery painted and everything going to Bucke's satisfaction, when, one evening, in the green room, Kean, who was to play the part of Albanio, hinted to him that the character of Manfredi was 'too much in his line', that the Blind Man was 'too good', that the Page would excite too much 'interest', and that no one should write a tragedy for Drury Lane 'without making the entire interest centre in the character HE should perform'. Bucke was astounded. He related the incident to a member of the Drury Lane committee, who replied 'that he, and most of the performers, were well aware of the unfortunate jealousy of Mr. Kean; and that if Miss Kelly were to perform the part of Scipio, as I wished, such was the interest she would excite, that he was certain Mr. Kean would immediately throw up his part'. Bucke was now thoroughly disquieted. He mentioned this conversation to a literary friend, who told him 'that he had himself sent a Tragedy to the Committee, of which Mr. Lamb was a leading member, and a letter to Mr. Kean; who had returned for answer, that unless the entire interest centred in the character, designed for him, it would neither suit his reputation, nor the interests of the Theatre, that it should be accepted'.

The morning after his conversation with Kean, Bucke received a letter from Peter Moore suggesting that the play be laid by for the time being. Bucke objected so strenuously that the sub-committee decided to put the play into rehearsal immediately. Bucke attended the rehearsals, and as he grew aware of the hostility that existed between the management and the players, he became convinced that to allow his play to be produced under such inauspicious circumstances would be 'the height of superlative folly'. He wrote: 'A Nightmare seemed to sit upon the House; all was treason within; and all was clamour without . . . the House stood upon the brink of ruin:—the benches were deserted; and the treasury was losing nearly two hundred pounds every night: It was prudent, therefore, to withdraw.'

But Bucke had not given up hope of his play being performed, and the following season he again approached the subcommittee. They told him that they were willing to present the play providing Kean agreed to play the leading part. On 14 January 1819, Bucke wrote to Kean telling him of the subcommittee's attitude and requesting an interview. Kean replied '. . . I have nothing to do with the management of the theatre: if the Committee think your tragedy worthy of representation, I am the servant of the establishment, and have neither right nor wish to offer any impediments; and for my own sake, shall make the most of the materials that are allotted me: further explanation on this subject is unnecessary, when the prompter sends me the character, I shall enter on its study.' The coldness of this reply made Bucke pause, uncertain whether to proceed or withdraw. Then an event happened that made up his mind for him. Miss Porter's tragedy, *Switzerland*, was produced at Drury Lane. Bucke was present on the first night and as soon as the play was over, he went to the committee room and told Moore that he wished to withdraw his play.

He was now determined that everyone should know the truth about the state of affairs at Drury Lane, and so he published *The Italians* with a preface telling the story of the past year. In the course of this preface, he stated that 'every person, capable of taking a wide view of subjects in general, and who is even only superficially acquainted with the management of Drury Lane Theatre, knows, and knows well, that though MR. KEAN is saving that establishment with his right hand, he is ruining it with his left'. Kean issued a statement denying completely the accusations made against him by Bucke, saying *The Italians* 'was the worst of all bad Tragedies, the only feelings it excited among the performers were uncontrollable laughter'. The public interest in the quarrel was so great that by May seven editions of *The Italians* had been printed and several pamphlets published in Kean's defence. The public felt an injustice had been done and demanded an apology from Kean. He made this apology before a performance of *Brutus*. It was so perfunctory that the audience roared their disapproval, but as it became obvious that this was all they were going to get from him, their shouts gradually subsided to a few discontented murmurs which continued until the end of the performance. Some newspapers were perturbed at Kean's contemptuous treatment of authors, believing that his behaviour was nothing less than an insult to English literature and that for so great a crime, no apology, however ample, could ever be adequate. The *Morning Herald* stated: 'To men of literary talent, and of that high spirit, to which eminent talent is a natural and a becoming appendage, we have one advice to give—"never write for Drury-Lane Theatre, so long as the present system continues; you but waste your noble energies; and subject yourselves not only to disappoint, but to insult".'

To appease public opinion, the subcommittee put *The Italians* into rehearsal, with Rae in Kean's role, and the play was presented on 3 April 1819. The majority of the audience disliked the play, although Bucke claimed, as had Miss Porter, that the performance was booed down by an organised claque. The play was given a second time before a poor audience and then dropped. It was never performed again. In Kean's defence, it might be argued that neither of the plays he did his best to ruin was of any great merit, but this was not the point. His arrogance was discouraging the best contemporary authors from writing for the stage. This is clear from Sir Walter Scott's reply to Robert Southey, who, as a result of a newspaper rumour that Scott was writing a play, had written to him hoping that this was true. Scott, who had been following the quarrel between Bucke and Kean, replied: 'To write for low, ill-informed, and conceited actors, whom you must please, for your success is necessarily at their mercy, I cannot away with. How would you . . . relish being the object of such a letter as Kean wrote t'other day to a poor author, who, though a pedantic blockhead, had at least the right to be treated as a gentleman by a copper-laced, twopenny tearmouth, rendered mad by conceit and success?'

CHAPTER SIX

UNDER NEW MANAGEMENT

In June 1819, the Drury Lane committee decided to resign their powers into the hands of a lesseee manager. The 1818–19 season had been the most disastrous to date, with receipts totalling £34,337. They realised that this state of affairs could not be allowed to continue, and they invited tenders from anyone willing to rent the theatre for a number of years. Kean was among the first to apply. His letter to the secretary of the committee reads like the ultimatum of a soldier-king demanding the surrender of a besieged city. 'These are my proposals,' he wrote. 'I offer eight thousand pounds per annum for the Theatre Royal in Drury Lane, and its appurtenances, scenery, dresses, chandeliers, books, &c. &c. In a word I shut my doors against all committees, expecting an immediate surrender of their keys and all privileges in possession. I select my own officers, my own performers,—"My reason's in my will,"—and can only be accountable to the proprietors for payment of the rent, and to the public for their amusements. This is my offer—if they like it, so; if not, farewell. Read this aloud to the proprietors, and as much in earnest as I write it.'

The first letter was quickly followed by a second, in which Kean increased his bid to £10,000. He had learnt that his old enemy, Robert William Elliston, was in the running for the theatre. He had recently received an attractive offer to tour America and he threatened to accept this, if he did not secure Drury Lane. He wrote: 'The public has witnessed the mismanagement that has brought this magnificent theatre to ruin; its restoration can only be achieved by a popular professional man. I now stand forward to devote my property, reputation, and experience to this great cause—to cleanse the Augean stable, and "raise a new Palmyra". I cross the Atlantic should the proprietors reject my proposals, which are these—rent and taxes ten thousand pounds a year. The committee may pay my watchmen and firemen (persons in whom they place so deep a trust) if they please; but no servant except my own shall have ingress on my property. I shall propose such securities as the committee cannot think objectionable. Now, sir, everything else I reject *in toto*. Read this to the committee with emphasis and discretion. I have seen and known their errors; the world has seen and known them too. *Et vitio alterius, sapiens emendat sum.* Let me hear from you immediately, that in one case I may be making my arrangements for the restoration of Drury's monarchy, or be preparing for crossing the Atlantic.'

The committee were not impressed by Kean's lofty aim to 'raise a new Palmyra'. They knew that he was as responsible as anyone for the present predicament of Drury Lane. Elliston, on the other hand, was the obvious choice. Not only was he experienced in theatre management, but he had also made a more attractive bid. He had offered to take the theatre for fourteen years and, during that time, to spend £7,000 on the interior. He would pay a rent of £8,000 for the first year, £9,000 for the second and £10,000 for the remainder of the term. He also offered security to the value of £25,000. The committee accepted this offer and, on 8 September, Elliston added to his chain of theatres the brightest jewel of them all. From now on, he was styled the Great Lessee, or the Napoleon of the Stage.

Around this time, Elliston met Charles Lamb in the street. 'Grasping my hand with a look of significance,' Lamb wrote, 'he only uttered "Have you heard the news?" Then, with another look following up the blow, he subjoined, "I am the future Manager of Drury Lane." Breathless as he saw me, he stayed not for congratulation or reply, but mutely stalked away, leaving me to chew upon his new-blown dignities at leisure.' But, characteristically, having acquired the first theatre in England, Elliston could not find the time to devote himself fully to its interests. He appointed James Winston as 'acting manager', and then left for the provinces to fulfil his acting engagements and to visit his theatres in Leamington, Cheltenham and Shrewsbury.

From the provinces, he bombarded Winston with instructions for the coming season at Drury Lane. The interior of the theatre was to be completely redecorated. New scenery and costumes were to be ordered. Some members of the company were to be sacked and new players engaged. His policy was to build up the comedic and operatic sides of the company. For the past three seasons, because of the influence of Kean, Drury Lane had become almost entirely dependent on tragedy, but Elliston was not going to allow the fortunes of his theatre to be subject to the whims of one actor. For the time being, however, he needed Kean, for the actor was the only money-spinner he had, but it proved difficult to get the actor to agree to serve under him. Having failed to secure Drury Lane, Kean had announced his intention of visiting America. Elliston begged him to reconsider. He assured him that he would continue to be the leading tragedian and that even he, Elliston himself, would think it 'no degradation' to play Cassio to his Othello.

Kean sent back an insolent reply. He wrote: 'The lovers of the drama will hail with rapture a minister to their amusements so transcendent in his art and so mature in experience as Robert William Elliston. With regard to myself, I expressed my determination at the close of last season to leave England. My arrangements are made—*Cras ingens iterabimus aequor*—I quit the kingdom! This has not been kept a secret. On my return I may treat with you; but it will not be consonant with my feelings to act in any theatre where I have not the full appropriations of my own talents & this I am aware can only be obtained by *nightly* engagements. But I shall allow the field open to my compeers, and heartily wish success to all aspirants—this for the sake of the drama, which should be immortal. I have prepared Mrs. Kean to answer any inquiries that may be necessary in my absence. *Richards* and *Hamlets* grow on every hedge, & I doubt not but I shall shortly hear of some Dramatic Meteor, whose refulgence shall shrink into insignificance the twinkling Capacities of yours, Edmund Kean.'

He added a withering postscript: 'If I shou'd go by water to the next world, I shou'd certainly relate to our great Master you thought it no degradation to act his Cassio!!'

Kean wanted no dealings with Elliston. This was the man who had almost jeopardised his career at its very outset by holding him to the Olympic contract when Drury Lane wanted him. He suspected that under Elliston's management his own pre-eminence was threatened; that, despite his soft words, Elliston would replace him at the first opportunity. Since hearing from Elliston, he was more anxious than ever to go to America. A year away would give him the chance to see how things were shaping at Drury Lane.

By the terms of his contract, Kean had to forfeit £1,000 if he failed to appear at Drury Lane. He tendered this sum to Elliston, but the manager refused to accept it. On 24 September, Elliston told Kean that he had posted his name in the list of performers for the coming season. He suggested that if Kean really wanted to go to America, he could have a year's leave of absence at the close of the season. On the surface, Elliston's approach was friendly, but each word carried a hidden threat. The following day, Kean learned from his solicitors that Elliston could come down on him for damages of £10,000 for breach of contract. Kean realised that again, as in the case of the Olympic contract, Elliston was playing a cat-and-mouse game with him. He had no alternative but to abandon his plans for America and agree to play at Drury Lane.

For the first two months of the season, Elliston concentrated on the comedic and operatic powers of his company. He had two excellent comedians in Joseph Munden and William Dowton. On the operatic side, he had persuaded John Braham, the popular singer, to return to Drury Lane, after an absence of four years. These tactics worked and for the first time in five years, Drury Lane had larger audiences than Covent Garden. The fortunes of Drury Lane were helped by the fact that the rival theatre was going through a difficult time. Eliza O'Neill was absent on leave and, although no one yet knew it, she had already made her last appearance, for before the end of the year, she married and left the stage. Two of the most popular performers, John Liston, the comedian, and Kitty Stephens, the singer, were ill. Charles Mayne Young, the tragedian, had quarrelled with Harris and left the company. There were now deplorable gaps in what had been the most attractive company in London. .

All this was a blow to Covent Garden, but the circumstances provided a breakthrough for Macready. Since his début three years previously he had been mainly employed playing second to Young, but, with Young's departure, he was promoted to leading tragedian. For the first six weeks of the season he played Henry V, Othello, Hotspur and other parts. The public now had the chance to see how great an actor Macready had become. Like Kean, he had mastered the gradations of passion and the transitions from the formal to the colloquial. He did not copy from Kean, but had evolved his own style. His performances were well received, but he could not play every night and, when he was absent, the theatre was almost empty. Salaries fell into arrears and Harris afterwards declared that he never knew in the morning whether he should not shoot himself before night. He believed that some novelty was needed that would arouse the curiosity of the public and he suggested to Macready that he challenge Kean in the role of Richard III. Macready was reluctant to do this, because the names of Kean and Richard III had become synonymous, and he feared that any comparisons the public might make would be to his disadvantage. This could retard the splendid progress he was making and perhaps even annihilate him. So he prevaricated, pleading with Harris for more time to study the part; but Harris refused, telling him that the situation was too critical for any delay. As Macready still hesitated, Harris made up his mind for him by having playbills posted all over London announcing him in the part.

On 25 October 1819, *Richard III* was performed at Covent Garden. Macready was nervous, but after the first scene, a fellow-actor whispered, 'It's going well,' and this encouraged him. His success was assured at the point when Buckingham enters. Macready recalled: 'I rushed at him, inquiring of him, in short broken sentences, the children's fate; with rapid decision on the mode of disposing of them, hastily gave him orders, and hurrying away, exclaimed, with triumphant exultation, "Why then, my loudest fears are hushed"; the pit rose to a man, and continued waving hats and handkerchiefs in a perfect tempest of applause for some minutes. The battle was won.'

A fortnight later, on 8 November, Kean made his first appearance of the season at Drury Lane as Richard III. The rival Richards became a great attraction and both theatres were well attended on the nights Kean and Macready played the part. At first, their rivalry was unembittered. Of Macready's success as Richard, Kean declared: 'Such a man could do nothing short of excellence.' Macready, not to be outdone in courtesy, owned that he could never appear as Othello without 'blushing through his black' at his inferiority to Kean. But this affability was to be short-lived. On 29 November, Macready scored a hit as Coriolanus. Kean had never played this part, knowing that he could not match Kemble's interpretation, but he could not allow Macready to succeed in a role that he dared not attempt himself. The play was put into rehearsal at Drury Lane and performed on 25 January 1820. Kean failed as Coriolanus; he could not portray the stoicism and dignity of the character. The critics compared him unfavourably not only with Kemble but also with Macready. Kean now realised that Macready was the most powerful rival ever to challenge him and he was frightened of him.

He was aware of his own dwindling popularity. Apart from Richard III, he played to poor houses and did best on the nights he was supported by Elliston. It was obvious that, on his own, he was no longer the great attraction he had been. The comedic and operatic side of the company were not doing too well either. The return of John Liston and Kitty Stephens to Covent Garden had restored the balance of power between the two theatres. By the beginning of March, the average receipts at Drury Lane had become so poor that it was doubtful if the theatre would make a profit that season. Elliston seemed unconcerned about the shakiness of his financial position, but his deputy, James Winston, felt the cold fear of bankruptcy. It seemed to Winston that Elliston was revealing to a greater degree the same pattern of extravagance, absenteeism and mismanagement that he had displayed during his years at the Olympic. He was convinced that Elliston had lost all his judgement after purchasing Drury Lane. It was becoming difficult to get him to make any decisions. He was frequently out of town and Winston found himself virtually responsible for running the theatre.

James Winston was hardly the ideal man to leave in charge of
Drury Lane. For the past four years, he had been Elliston's deputy
at the Olympic Theatre, where he was detested by the entire company for his mean and pettifogging approach towards his duties.
Elliston and he were an ill-matched pair. Around this time, they
were both in their late forties and age was about the only thing
they had in common. Winston was a colourless man, short and
thin, with a pointed nose, while Elliston was florid, round-faced
and paunchy. Winston was thrifty, cautious and scrupulously
honest, while Elliston was extravagant, impulsive and totally
corrupt.

Elliston was not the easiest of masters; he was belligerent and
bullying with all his underlings and erratic and devious in his
dealings with them. But, for better or worse, Winston was to
stand by him, probably because he needed a profligate, such as
Elliston, against whom he could measure his own righteousness.
Elliston, for his part, needed a dependable deputy, as his multi-
farious interests often took him from town. Throughout his seven
years' tenure of Drury Lane, he was rarely to be found there. He
was either away in the provinces, or too drunk to attend to
business, or confined to his house by one of his 'attacks'. These
attacks were to occur with increasing frequency and the symptoms
described by Winston suggest epilepsy.

During his first weeks at Drury Lane, Winston had already
made himself unpopular by his obsession with the need for
economising, so much so that the company called him 'the Stage
Screw'. Joe Cowell, the comedian, wrote of him: 'It was his
province to measure out the canvas and colours for the painters,
count the nails for the carpenters, pick up the tin-tacks and bits of
candle, calculate on the least possible quantity of soap required for
each dressing room, and invent and report delinquencies that
could in any way be construed into the liability of a forfeit.'
Winston disliked actors. He had been on the stage himself before
he went into the administrative side, and he resented actors with
all the acrimony of a man who has failed where others have
succeeded. Above all, he resented Kean, not only for his triumphs
but also for the chaos to which he had reduced Drury Lane.

When Winston came to Drury Lane, he found that Kean considered himself to be above all the rules and regulations of the theatre. When Kean intended to spend the night drinking, he expected rehearsals on the following day to be postponed from the morning until the afternoon, so that he could catch up on his sleep. He was always altering the nights on which he was scheduled to play and varying the frequency of his performances. It had become almost impossible to print a playbill with any accuracy. He had soon made it clear that he had no intention of altering his habits to suit the new management. He paid no attention to Winston's protests, but openly ridiculed his authority. He was often absent through illness, sometimes real, sometimes assumed. While Winston did not believe half the medical certificates that were delivered to him, there was nothing either he or Elliston could do about it. Although Elliston could have claimed heavy damages from Kean in the event of breach of contract, he was powerless to do anything if the actor could prove that he was not fit enough to appear at Drury Lane. The medical certificate had become one of Kean's greatest weapons against the new management and he was to use it ruthlessly, whenever it suited his purpose.

Winston kept a diary and, like some malevolent recording angel, he wrote down every incident and every piece of malicious gossip that could discredit Kean. As Professor Alfred L. Nelson, the editor of the diaries, has said: 'It was almost as if Winston had been hired to spy upon the great actor.' In the diaries, Kean is shown as 'a conceited braggart, a brawler, a hypochondriacal malingerer, and a compulsive lecher'.

Prostitutes thronged his dressing-room. He shocked Winston, perhaps deliberately, by telling him that he frequently had three women during a performance and that two waited while the other was served. On the nights he played, the length of the intervals between acts could never be calculated with any accuracy, for he copulated in his dressing-room regardless of the waiting audience. One night, on being asked if the intervals between the acts of *Richard III* would be long, he replied that they would not, as his veneral disease was too active. Winston recorded with disgust that later that same night a woman went to him.

Not only prostitutes went to Kean in his dressing-room but also actresses and even leading ladies, among them Mme Storace and Mrs. MacGibbon. When Elliston did turn up at Drury Lane, he made no attempt to discipline Kean. Indeed, he shared his tastes in drink and women and they would drink together, either in the manager's office, or the actor's dressing-room, where they were usually joined by some women. Kean was not fussy about where he copulated, but Elliston preferred to have his women in the seclusion of a private box. The effect of all this on the discipline of the theatre was disastrous, and Winston was convinced that Drury Lane would be ruined unless Elliston could rid himself of Kean. Elliston, in his devious mind, was as much aware of the problem as Winston, but he was not yet in a position to replace Kean and so, for the time being, he did nothing to antagonise him.

Then, in April, when receipts were at their lowest, Kean reversed his poor showing and scored a success in *King Lear*. The play had not been performed for ten years out of respect for George III's madness, but the king's death on 30 January had released it for the stage. The news that Kean was to play the part caused great interest. It was widely reported that he was studying the character with great care, even visiting lunatic asylums to observe the effects of madness. Everyone knew of his boast that he would make the audience as mad as himself. He disturbed Mary by wandering about the house with his eyes alternately vacant and filled with fierce light.

When Harris learned that Kean was to appear in *King Lear*, he immediately put the play into rehearsal at Covent Garden. He wanted Macready for the part, but Macready refused, knowing that Harris's objective was to hurry out a production, no matter how ill prepared, in order to beat Drury Lane. Kean's friends said that the real reason for his refusal was that he feared comparison with Kean. In Kean's place, Harris engaged Junius Brutus Booth. On 13 April, Booth played Lear at Covent Garden. He failed in the part and the play was withdrawn after three performances.

On 24 April, Kean played Lear. As at Covent Garden, the version used was that of Nahum Tate, the Restoration 'improver'.

Betterton, Garrick and Kemble had all acted in this travesty of Shakespeare's play, in which Cordelia survives to marry Edgar and Lear recovers his wits. For over a century, this version had been preferred to the original on the grounds that the culmination of Shakespeare's tragedy was more than any audience could be expected to bear. Although Kean had played the part in the provinces, this was the first time he had played it in London. The audience and most of the critics were pleased with his performance, but Hazlitt was disappointed, chiefly because Kean had preferred Tate's version to Shakespeare's original tragedy. When the play was banned, Kean had often bragged that the public had never seen what he could do until they saw him over the dead body of Cordelia, yet when he was given the chance, he balked at it. Although Hazlitt believed the part of Lear to be beyond the range of any actor, he had hoped that Kean, who, in the past, had 'dared so much' might succeed where all others were sure to fail.

In the *London Magazine*, he wrote: 'We had thought that Mr. Kean would take possession of this time-worn, venerable figure, "that has outlasted a thousand storms, a thousand winters", and, like the gods of old, when their oracles were about to speak, shake it with present inspiration:—that he would have set up a living copy of it on the stage. But he failed, either from insurmountable difficulties, or from his own sense of the magnitude of the undertaking. There are pieces of ancient granite that turn the edge of any modern chisel; so, perhaps, the genius of no living actor can be expected to cope with Lear. Mr. Kean chipped off a bit of the character here and there; but he did not pierce the solid substance, nor move the entire mass.' In Hazlitt's opinion, the only 'electric shock' came in the imprecation scene, when Kean 'threw himself on his knees; lifted up his arms, like withered stumps; threw his head quite back, and in that position, as if severed from all that held him to society, breathed a half-struck prayer, like the figure of a man obtruncated'.

King Lear was a hit, but that season Kean had the chance of an even greater success, and, ironically, he allowed it to go to Macready. Kean had suggested to Sheridan Knowles, the dramatist, that a good play might be made out of the story of Virginius.

Knowles wrote the play within three months, but when he submitted it to Drury Lane, he was told that a Virginius play by
George Soane, their resident playwright, had already been
accepted. Knowles then sent his play to Macready, who persuaded
Harris to buy it for him. On 17 May, at Covent Garden, Macready
scored a personal triumph in *Virginius*. It was not a great play,
but compared to other tragedies of the time, it was a masterpiece.
Following the usual policy, Drury Lane broke off the run of *King
Lear* to rush Soane's *Virginius* into production, with Kean in the
title role. Soane's play was much less effective than Knowles's and
was given only three performances. Kean had not only lost one of
the best parts of the century, but he had given Macready the
greatest triumph of his career.

On 8 July 1820, the season closed. The total receipts were
around £44,000, £10,000 more than the previous year. At first
sight, it would seem that Drury Lane, after floundering under the
direction of the committee, was at last heading for success with
Elliston, but this was not so. Expenditure had been high and the
receipts yielded only a small margin of profit.

At the end of the season, Kean held Elliston to his promise of a
year's leave of absence to tour America. He was more anxious than
ever to go there and this was not only for the financial rewards,
which he expected to be considerable. There was another, more
personal, reason: a visit to America would give him the opportunity to withdraw, for a time at least, from a romantic situation
which was becoming increasingly complicated. That spring, he
had embarked on the great love affair of his life with a married
woman named Charlotte Cox. He had first met her four years previously, in 1816, at Taunton, in Somerset, where he was acting
Othello. The circumstances of their meeting were unusual. Charlotte and her husband were watching the performance from a stage
box, when, overcome by the power of Kean's acting, she rose to
her feet, cried out and then fainted away, to the great interest of
the audience, whose attention had been distracted from the play
by her distress. Kean immediately stopped the performance and
she was lowered gently from the box and carried over the stage,

Kean directing the manœuvre. He also ordered his dressing-room to be placed at her disposal. The next day her husband called on him to thank him for his solicitude and followed this up with an invitation to visit them upon his return to London.

A close friendship grew up between the Coxes and the Keans. They dined regularly at each other's houses. Both Kean and Mary were flattered by the connection, for, in their eyes, Robert Albion Cox was a person of some consequence. He was a man of property, an alderman of the city of London and a member of the Drury Lane general committee. He was middle-aged, but his wife was considerably younger. Kean was later to tell his solicitor: 'I imagine Mrs. Cox's age to be about 45 when she first flapped her ferret-eyed affection upon me.' But when he wrote this, he was disenchanted with her. At the time they first met, she was no more than thirty-two years old.

From all accounts, she was a vulgar woman, predatory and over-sexed, for whom, as her maidservant was to observe in court, two men were not sufficient. She made no impression on Grattan, who met her at Kean's house in the early summer of 1817. Eight years later, he was to be astonished that so insignificant a woman could be the cause of Kean's downfall. He wrote: 'She was so little remarkable in any way that I can scarcely remember her appearance. She had nothing attractive about her certainly either as to person or manners.'

By the spring of 1820, Kean and Charlotte had become lovers. She was thirty-six years old and he was thirty-two. 'From the first moment I saw you,' he wrote to her, 'I loved every hour; that passion has increased; and, in the possession of your heart, I acknowledge with gratitude, that I have obtained the very summit of my wishes. Do not doubt me, Charlotte; I write you from my heart, a heart overflowing with love, for a heart that while it beats shall own no other mistress. Dear, dear, dear girl, more than fame, more than wealth, more than life, more than heav'n—I love you.'

He had never been so happy. He had a lady for his mistress, and he found her a delectable change after his usual diet of prostitutes and actresses. Charlotte was no more than the discontented wife of a bourgeois businessman, but to Kean she was a great lady, and sleeping with her gave a wonderful boost to his self-esteem. Although he claimed to have rejected high society, his love-hate attitude towards it still remained; he scorned it because he wanted to be a part of it. Mounted on Charlotte's hot, exciting body, he was not only entering most intimately into that society but also proving his dominance over it. To his delight, he found her to be a lady at table and a harlot in bed. Their excesses were considered too gross to be repeated when his letters were read aloud in court. He had no need to be reticent with her about his recurrent venereal disease; she understood that there were times when he could not go near her.

Charlotte had never been a great theatregoer, but, after they became lovers, she went to Drury Lane every night he played. Sometimes she was escorted by her husband, but more often she was accompanied by Anne Wickstead, Mr. Cox's unmarried niece, who lived with them. They were accommodated in one of Kean's private boxes. In his diary, Winston complained about Kean being allowed two boxes, 'one for his wife and one for his whore'. Anne Wickstead was in Charlotte's confidence, and on the nights they went together to Drury Lane she would remain in the box while Charlotte made her way under the stage to visit Kean in his dressing-room. Newman, his dresser, would guard the door, while they made love on the sofa. Then Kean would put on his costume, while she hurried back to the box. From there she would watch him make love to Ophelia or Desdemona, knowing that the words he spoke on stage were addressed to her. This was a lovely secret shared between them and while it appealed to Charlotte's romantic mind, she could not help thinking how much more piquant it would be if everyone else in the audience knew about it. Indeed, she wanted the whole world to know that she was the mistress of England's greatest tragic actor.

This was the last thing Kean wanted. He lived in daily terror of someone finding them out and carrying the news to Mary and Mr. Cox. From the start he had insisted that their affair must remain a secret, and he took every precaution against discovery. Aunt Price was in his confidence, and to her house he addressed all his letters to Charlotte under the name of Mrs. Allen. He was aware that

Charlotte bridged most dangerously the gap between his irregular life and the family circle at Clarges Street. Until now, he had managed to keep these two worlds apart, but Mary frequently entertained the Coxes and on these occasions, he observed, with alarm, a growing tendency on Charlotte's part to show her feelings for him.

Charlotte saw no reason to hide her feelings. The demands for secrecy were all on Kean's side. She did not ask for marriage; all she wanted him to do was to acknowledge her openly as his mistress. But this did not suit Kean at all. He knew that Mary of all people, with her genteel background, would never agree to such an arrangement. He needed Charlotte badly, but he would not take any steps that might damage the interests of his family. Next to his career, their wellbeing was the chief motive in his life. By the summer the situation had become very difficult and he looked forward to his American tour for the respite it would give him. Charlotte wanted to go with him, but he argued that by doing so she would lose her 'rank in society', as he termed it. This did not trouble Charlotte, but she could not persuade him to take her with him.

Kean had told Elliston that he planned to leave in the autumn and the manager could not have been more co-operative, even suggesting that the theatre should re-open for a short farewell season. Kean agreed and Elliston quickly got a company together and engaged Junius Brutus Booth as Kean's replacement for the following season. Booth was also free to support Kean during his farewells. Kean was pleased that Booth had been picked as his replacement. He feared no comparison with the actor he had crushed so convincingly three years previously, and he was certain that after a season of Booth the Drury Lane audiences would be delighted to welcome him back. The following year Booth himself was to go to America, where he gained a greater reputation than he had ever enjoyed in Britain. He settled there. One of his sons, Edwin Thomas Booth, became the first great American actor, and another, John Wilkes Booth, made a name for himself far beyond theatrical circles when he assassinated President Abraham Lincoln during a performance at Ford's Theatre, Washington.

On 15 August, when the farewell season started, Kean was in great form. He was anxious to give of his best, so that the audiences would have something to remember him by. The first performance went well, but, on the second night, everything turned sour. The play was Otway's *Venice Preserved*, a popular Restoration tragedy, with Kean as Jaffeir and Booth as Pierre. The action of the play was held up for a few minutes while everyone waited for Kean to make his entrance. 'I always take a shag before the play begins,' he explained to Winston, as he strode on to the stage. The combination of Kean and Booth had attracted a full house, but this time the audience witnessed no one-sided contest. Booth had improved tremendously and at the fall of the curtain, they called for him as well as for Kean. This did not please Kean and he told Elliston that *Venice Preserved* was not to be repeated. Then, on 21 August, the play was *King Lear*, Kean's greatest triumph that year. Booth played Edgar and Mrs. West played Cordelia. After the play, Kean had a stormy interview with Elliston. He told him that *King Lear* was not to be repeated, as it showed Booth and Mrs. West to advantage. He went on to object to all of Elliston's arrangements, and insisted on playing only four nights a week for the remainder of the season.

The publicity surrounding Kean's departure for America caused many of his creditors to insist on a settlement of their accounts, in the event of him perishing on the high seas, or being carried off by Red Indians. It was not only his creditors who were anxious that he should put his affairs in order before he left the country. On 11 September, at Bow Street Court, a young woman brought paternity proceedings against him. Kean claimed that during the relevant time, the previous October, he had been away from London, but the court ordered him to pay seven shillings and sixpence a week for the upbringing of the child. On 14 September, he was up at Clerkenwell Court for a similar reason, but when the girl was called upon to give evidence, she admitted that she could not be certain who the father was.

On Saturday, 16 September, the farewell season came to a close. At the end of the play some members of the audience called for Kean, but Winston believed that this demonstration had been pre-

arranged, as Kean gave a prepared speech. After the performance, Kean attended the celebrations organised in his honour by
the Drury Lane company. The previous week, he had given
Elliston a bust of himself, with instructions that it be placed with
appropriate ceremony in the green room, on the last night of the
season. At first Elliston had demurred, as the only busts admitted
to the green room were those of famous players of the past. He
had questioned the propriety of putting the bust of a living actor
among those of the revered dead, but Kean had been so insistent
that in the end he had given way. On the last night, the bust was
carried in procession to the green room. Elliston made a speech
and so did Kean. The bust was then placed in position. There it
would remain to keep Kean's memory fresh in the minds of the
company while he was away, and to remind those who might be
foolish enough to hope otherwise that he would be coming
back.

The arrangements for Kean's American tour had been made by
Stephen Price, of New York. Price was the first great American
theatre manager. He was the equal of Charles Frohman in the
scope of his enterprises and of Phineas Taylor Barnum in his flair
for publicity. At the height of his career, he was to control theatres
on both sides of the Atlantic. In 1820, he was the manager of the
Park Theatre, New York. Ten years previously, he had brought
over George Frederick Cooke and this venture proved so successful that he began the regular importing of English stars. American
cities were not large by English standards, but Price worked out
an arrangement with the managers of the theatres in Boston,
Philadelphia, Baltimore, and Charleston by which he supplied
them with his stars. This enabled him to offer the stars not only a
season in New York but also a tour of the main cities on the eastern
seaboard and so make an American visit financially worthwhile.
More and more English players crossed the Atlantic and Price
became known as 'Star Provider to the United States'.

No star so brilliant as Kean had ever visited America and the
terms he got were the highest ever offered to any actor. For his
first New York season of sixteen nights, he was to receive £50 a

night for fourteen performances and half the profits of the remaining two. There was tremendous interest when it was announced that he was coming. Every theatregoer in America knew of his sensational triumphs at Drury Lane. It was by no means certain, however, that he would have a friendly reception. George Frederick Cooke, who had spent the last two years of his life in America, until his death in 1812, still had his devoted followers, who were unwilling to allow that any other actor could equal his naturalistic style. There were also the supporters of the classical style, who were saying that Kean's acting consisted of nothing more than sudden starts, unexpected pauses, and other cheap stage tricks. His arrogance towards dramatists, actors and audiences was common knowledge, as was the depravity of his private life. There was not only prejudice against him but also hostility.

On 29 November 1820, Kean opened in New York as Richard III. He played at the Anthony Street Theatre, as the Park Theatre was being reconstructed after a disastrous fire. Every seat was taken and disappointed crowds stood outside. At first the audience were confused by the strangeness of his style, but when the curtain fell the applause was overwhelming. On the whole, the New York press was for him, and he found two staunch champions in Major Noah, editor of the *National Advocate*, and William Coleman, editor of the *Evening Post*.

Throughout December, Kean played all his great parts— Richard III, Othello, Shylock, Hamlet, Lear, Macbeth, Overreach and Bertram. It was the most brilliant season New York had ever known. As had happened at Drury Lane, some of the audience did not know exactly what to make of him, but his style gained converts every night. The audiences followed the plays in a profound silence, unwilling to break the spell with applause. By the end of the month, most theatregoers were agreed that he was the greatest actor they had ever seen.

It was the same story at Philadelphia, where, in January 1821, he played fourteen nights at the Walnut Street Theatre. His terms were even better than New York. He was on a profit-sharing basis and the receipts were so good that, at the end of his engagement, he was able to remit $4,444.44—£1,000 sterling—to Coutts &

Co., his London bankers. He did even better at Boston, where he played sixteen nights during February and March. On the first night, there was a great rush for tickets, many of which were resold at an enormous profit. To avoid this abuse, it was decided that tickets for the boxes would be auctioned and the profits distributed among various charitable institutions. By the end of the season, Kean had made $5,454.26 and the amount raised for charity was $2,999.75.

At the end of his final performance, on 7 March, the audience shouted for him to extend his stay. He said that he regretted his engagements did not allow him to do this, but if in the future he could arrange it, he would be delighted to revisit the 'Literary Emporium of the New World'. This cumbersome compliment to the pre-eminence of Boston as the centre of culture delighted the Bostonians, but irked the citizens of the other towns in which he had played. From Boston, he returned to New York, where he gave seventeen performances. On 9 April, he revisited Philadelphia for a short season of six nights. On 23 April, he began fourteen nights at Baltimore. The tour was proving to be more successful than he had expected.

Indeed, these past months in America had been like his first glorious season at Drury Lane all over again. There was the same adulation and the same heated arguments over his style of acting. Here he could forget his declining popularity and relive the happiest days of his life. Miraculously, America had given him a second chance, and this time there was no aristocracy to seduce him. American society held no terrors for him. Prominent people invited him into their homes, but their friendliness and informality were more to his taste than the cold ceremonials of Lord Essex's drawing room. He liked them and they liked him. Dr. John Francis, of New York, a patron of the theatre wrote: 'He won my feelings and admiration from the moment of my first interview with him. Association and observation convinced me that he added to a mind of various culture the resources of considerable intellect; that he was frank and open-hearted, often too much so, to tally with worldly wisdom.' He had resolved to make none of the mistakes he had made in England. He avoided late nights and parties. He showed none of the arrogance or Byronic seeking after notoriety that was expected of him. He lived an exemplary life, earning the good opinion of everyone who met him.

His associates at Drury Lane would not have recognised the Kean of the American theatre. Edmund Simpson, stage manager of the New York company, wrote: 'We find him extremely agreeable in the Theatre & are agreeably disappointed in finding him in manner and conduct exactly the reverse of what we expected.' Elliston and Winston would have been surprised to learn this. William Wood, manager of the Walnut Street Theatre, Philadelphia, found him 'a mild, unassuming and cheerful man, wholly free from every affectation of superiority or dictation. His suggestions as to business on the stage were always given with a gentleness of manner which secured their immediate adoption. The deficiencies of humbler performers were treated with indulgence, and created even in the most careless of them a desire to excel. His presence in the green room was always a source of enjoyment.' This had hardly been the experience of the Drury Lane company. The trouble with Kean in America was that he was acting a part offstage as well as on. Sooner or later, the real Kean was bound to rise up and destroy him as it had destroyed him so often in the past.

For the time being, however, everything was going favourably. Since his arrival he had remitted £1,000 each month to his English bankers. On 19 March he wrote to Douglas Kinnaird: 'I am making money and fame by bushels.' Having discovered the dollar-strewn shores of America, he was reluctant to leave them. He believed that if he stayed long enough he could make enough money to retire. He asked Elliston for a year's extension of leave, telling him that he reckoned this would bring his total to fifteen or sixteen thousand pounds—'& then farewell Critics, Authors— Greasy Corps of Whistlers'.

Although he was in no hurry to get back to Drury Lane, he could not hear enough about the place, for he was anxious to know how the theatre was getting on without him. He asked Mary and Charlotte to send him all the news. He was pleased to learn that Booth had not proved to be a sufficient attraction; that Elliston had added John Cooper and William Wallack to the tragic side, and that they, in turn, had failed. In spite of these failures, Elliston was having a good season, because, from the beginning of the year, he had concentrated on opera and melodrama. He had sensed that the public taste was turning away from legitimate drama and he was finding that musical productions did best at Drury Lane. By the end of the season, productions of opera and melodrama were to outnumber those of legitimate drama by two to one.

Kean was unaware of this shift in public taste. He concluded that the success of opera and melodrama at Drury Lane was a temporary phenomenon caused by his absence, and that the balance would right itself on his return. In the meantime, he reasoned that Elliston's success in these fields would give him no excuse for refusing to extend his leave of absence. His reasoning proved correct. Elliston willingly granted him an extension and Kean made plans to stay in America until the following spring. Now he could continue his regenerated life, behaving as people expected a great actor to behave, with dignity but also humility; a kinglike king, who knew that the crown of gold upon his head was also a crown of thorns: but he was to ruin it all in Boston.

Early in May, Kean announced his intention of revisiting Boston. James Dickson, manager of the Boston Theatre, was against the idea. He told Kean that people were not inclined to go to the theatre so late in the season, and he suggested postponing the visit until autumn. But Kean could not believe that the city which only two months previously had begged him to extend his stay would not turn out for him again. He considered himself to be a draw at any time of the year, and he insisted on coming to Boston against Dickson's advice.

On Wednesday, 23 May, he opened at the Boston Theatre as Lear. It was a poor house, and the following night, when he played Jaffeir, it was even poorer. On the Friday, he was announced as Richard III. He went to the theatre at the usual time and, looking through the curtains, he saw only a few people in the auditorium. He told Dickson that he would not play to so few and he refused to dress for the part. When the curtain was due to go up, there was still only a handful of people in the theatre and Kean now declared that it was impossible for him to play. Dickson asked him to perform that night at least and then wind up his engagement in Boston. Kean would not consider this and he left for his hotel, saying that he intended to leave for New York the next morning.

He had no sooner left the theatre than the boxes filled up and there was quite a fair house. Dickson sent word to Kean, telling him this, but Kean would not return. As the audience were getting restless, John Duff, the stage manager, went out and told them that Kean had refused to play that night and was preparing to leave the town. He asked them if the play should go on without him. There were loud affirmatives from the audience. When the curtain rose, Duff was called for again. This time the audience wanted to know the reason for Kean's refusal to play. Duff told them it was want of patronage.

Boston was enraged. 'KEAN—DECAMPED!' was the headline in the *Commercial Gazette*. A notice appeared in the newspapers:

ONE CENT REWARD

RUN away from the 'Literary Emporium of the New World', a stage-player, calling himself KEAN. He may be easily recognised by his mis-shapen trunk, his coxcomical, cockney manners, and his bladder actions. His face is as white as his own froth, and his eyes are as dark as indigo. All persons are cautioned against harbouring the aforesaid vagrant, as the undersigned pays no more debts of his contracting, after this date. As he has violated his pledged faith to me, I deem it my duty thus to put my neighbours on their guard against him.

PETER PUBLIC

Even Kean's greatest admirers turned against him. They said that only a second-rate actor could have behaved in such a manner. He had deluded them on his first visit. They had been fooled by a tricky style of acting from a very tricky man. At first, New York and the other cities where Kean had played were amused at the discomfiture of the 'Emporium', but the press blew up the incident until it assumed the proportions of a gross insult by a foreigner to the great American nation. Then the whole country rallied to Boston's side.

As citizens of a young nation, Americans were sensitive to all foreign criticism, but especially that of the British. Although they had broken away from British rule, they were still tied to the old country by bonds of race, language and culture. They were morbidly conscious that the British attitude towards them was one of condescension, that the British regarded them as boorish citizens of a fourth-rate nation. This excessive touchiness made them see Kean's action as the latest in a long line of British insults to America.

He was attacked by the press throughout the country. In New York, Noah, of the *National Advocate*, and Coleman, of the *Evening Post*, stood by him. They pleaded that Kean be allowed to give an explanation before condemning him. On 1 June, Kean's explanation was published in the *National Advocate*. He wrote: 'At an immoderate expense, and with all the additional cost which falls to the lot of a stranger, I repaired to Boston to fulfill my engagements. Had I been acquainted with the customs of the country, I should have made different arrangements; but my advisers never intimated to me that the theatres were only visited during certain months of the year; that when curiosity had subsided, dramatic talent was not in estimation. I never could or would believe that the arts in this country were only encouraged periodically, or that there could be any season in which Shakespeare was diminished in value; but as I am now initiated in these mysteries, I shall hereafter profit by my experience.'

After this piece of heavy sarcasm, he went on to remind Americans that he had to support his family by his professional exertions. 'I had performed two of my principal characters, without hope of remuneration in that town, where my efforts had, two months before, contributed largely to augment the public charities. I repeat, I had acted two characters to the very extent of my abilities without profit. On looking through the curtain at seven o'clock, on the night I was to represent *Richard III* (that character which had been the foundation of my fame and fortune), I counted twenty persons in front of the theatre. I then decided, hastily, if you please, that it was better to husband my resources for a more favourable season, and, in this decision, no disrespect was contemplated to the audience, slender as it was. The managers apparently concurred with me, deplored the unfortunate state of the times, and we parted in perfect harmony and confidence.'

The managers had done no such thing, as Kean well knew, but he hurried on to discuss another aspect of the affair. People were saying that he had played to equally bad houses in England, and this he denied. 'The present existence of the first theatre in Europe is founded on the abilities which they affect to despise. The provincial managers of England, Scotland, and Ireland, have thankfully rewarded my efforts by sums equal to what I receive from my friend, Mr. Price, the worthy and efficient manager of the theatre in this city. For the first three years of a career unprecedented in dramatic annals, I was in receipt of double that sum, in every theatre in which I acted, and even allowing a trifling diminution in the space of seven years, what am I to think of a city in which I have been received with equal enthusiasm, and witness a total desertion in the space of three months? But the public say I was too precipitate—that I should have performed that evening, and then closed my engagement. Granted. Our feelings frequently mar our better judgements, and from trifling causes lead to results which we subsequently regret. The error was venal, but who is exempt from error? But all unprejudiced people will, I trust, take into consideration the unprofitable labour of acting *Richard the Third* to a solitary few, who subsequently acknowledged themselves perfectly satisfied with the gentleman who represented the character.'

Kean's explanation aroused the Americans to fury. It was arrogant and conceited; it contained no apology; it inferred that they did not appreciate Shakespeare and that they were happy with second-rate actors. Dickson and Duff immediately issued a joint denial that they had concurred in his decision to withdraw. The Boston *Commercial Gazette* stated: 'His first fault might, after a suitable and humble apology, have been overlooked, but his disingenuousness in attempting to throw the fault on our Managers, and afterwards insulting the whole American public, by charging them with a want of taste for Shakespeare, as well as disinclination to patronise genius, has fixed the climax of contempt on his character in the United States.' Kean's statement had finished him in America. His friends, Noah and Coleman, warned him that he would not be able to play in any town without causing a riot. The opposition was too great; public opinion was running too high. They advised him to go home.

On 7 June he sailed for England. The following day, another statement from him appeared in the *National Advocate*. It was proud and unrepentant. He had no doubt that the conduct he had pursued was that which 'every man of reputation would pursue under the same circumstances, in that country where Shakespeare was born and Garrick had acted'. The second chance was over; the old Kean had conquered the new, and he sailed away the poorer by £1,000 a month. But he could not believe that he had ruined himself irretrievably with the American public and he hoped to return, perhaps in a year's time, when the outcry against him would have died away.

CHAPTER SEVEN

IN DEFENCE OF THE THRONE

KEAN arrived in Liverpool on 20 July 1821, the day after the coronation of George IV, and immediately wrote to Elliston: 'With those feelings which an Englishman alone can understand, I have touched once again my native land. I shall be at the stage-door of Drury at noon, on Monday next. Do you think that a few nights now would be of advantage to you? I am full of health and ambition, both of which are at your service, or they will run riot.' Elliston was about to close the theatre for the season, but, within a few hours, huge bills were posted over London, announcing the return of Kean and his reappearance the following Monday as Richard III.

The friend who had delivered the letter suggested to Elliston that Kean would be gratified if his entrance into London were marked by some token of professional respect. Elliston was pleased to co-operate. On Monday, 23 July, Kean's carriage was met on the outskirts of London and a cavalcade was formed. A vanguard of six horsemen was followed by Elliston, seated alone in his carriage. Next came Kean, in his own carriage, drawn by four magnificent black horses. A troop of horsemen brought up the rear and these were followed by an interested rabble, which increased in numbers and noise as the procession made its way through London. At Drury Lane, Kean alighted and was escorted into the theatre by two liveried attendants.

That night he played Richard to a large audience, who showed that they were pleased with his return. The next night he could not play, because of hoarseness. He played Shylock on Wednesday, Othello on Thursday and then told Elliston that he was too exhausted to continue, leaving the manager with a re-opened theatre and no attraction with which to fill it. For some weeks, Elliston had been considering mounting a lavish Coronation pageant and the loss of Kean now impelled him to put this into immediate production. On 1 August, the *Coronation* was presented at Drury Lane and, from the very first night, it was a smash hit. It was the greatest spectacle ever seen on the English stage. All the gorgeous robes worn at the coronation of George IV had been carefully copied. The stage was thronged with bishops, ambassadors, lords and ladies. Elliston, as George IV, dressed in robes and crown, threaded his way among them, to the cheers of the audience. The crowded theatre, the brilliant assembly on stage, the orchestra, the choirs, his own exalted and drunken state, all this affected him strangely. When he lifted his hand in benediction and exclaimed, 'Bless you, my people,' he really believed himself to be the king.

Over the past year, Elliston's eccentricities had become more marked. He now suffered from delusions. He frequently complained that, when he went home at night, some stranger sat beside him in the coach, whispering to him. One night he had stopped at a doctor's house to have the carriage searched by candle light. He was concerned about interruptions that he believed were caused by water falling from the ceiling. He had taken to kicking the backsides of anyone who disagreed with him. He did this regardless of rank, and members of the committee, authors, actors and actresses had all been assaulted. It had reached such a stage that no one dared turn their back on him. Always prone to drinking and wenching, he had abandoned all restraint after the death of his wife four months previously. He was now living with Maria Cubitt, a young singer in the company. Winston records that, when Elliston first brought her to his house, she was insulted by his landlady, who said that she refused 'to wait upon her or any other of his Drury Lane whores'.

Kean, too, was having romantic difficulties. He had written regularly to Charlotte from America, addressing his letters to Mrs. Allen, care of Aunt Price. In every letter he assured her of his love. He wrote: 'Do believe me when I tell you that every hour of absence I feel more and more the influence you have over my heart; one moment I think of my folly of not encouraging your proposal of coming with me, and the next, applaud my fortitude in respecting the foremost of my wishes; but we shall meet again sweet.' Charlotte had found the separation hard to bear. She was used to having another man apart from her husband, but she dared not start an affair for fear of spoiling her chances with Kean. While he was away, an event had occurred that gave her more reason to value their relationship. Her husband's business affairs, which had been unhealthy for some time, had taken a turn for the worse and he was now bankrupt. She had begun to take an interest in the financial side of Kean's tour. 'You ask me what money I am making,' he wrote. 'My love, it is almost incredible. I am living in the best style, travelling magnificently, and transmitting to England £1000 each month.'

She had looked forward to his return, for life with Kean promised to be more rewarding than with a penniless alderman. She was certain that he loved her; it was impossible to doubt the feelings of a man who wrote: 'How shall I thank my darling girl for all her solicitude and affection, and how shall I tell her how much I love her, and how great my desire to have her once more in my arms? In my heart she reigns triumphant, and ever will reign there while one pulsation throbs to recollection.' No woman could have hoped for more ardent a lover, yet, when he returned from America and she urged him to acknowledge her openly as his mistress, he told her that it would be dangerous to declare themselves too soon and insisted that their affair continue to remain a secret. Then, that summer, despite all his precautions, the worst happened: Mary discovered one of Charlotte's letters to him. This, in Kean's words, 'created a most terrible explosion'.

Ever since their marriage, Mary had been aware of his need for other women and, although this disgusted her, she had come to accept it. She had never been a satisfactory partner sexually; she could not shed her gentility with her clothes. Moreover, she was older than he was: she was now forty-one, while he was only thirty-three. The marriage had never been a happy one. It is significant that both Aunt Price and Aunt Tid were to take his side over Charlotte and also help him to deceive Mary. Although, on Aunt Tid's side, there had always been animosity towards Mary, yet, taken in conjunction with Aunt Price, her acceptance of Charlotte shows that she had reason to believe that Mary was not the best of wives.

In marriage, Kean and Mary had reached a compromise. She had everything she wanted; a fine house, a carriage and servants; her sister, Susan, to keep her company; a busy social life and the devotion of her ten-year-old son, Charles. Kean behaved discreetly at Clarges Street and did nothing to embarrass her. In return, she allowed him his other women. But she would not tolerate Charlotte. His prostitutes and actresses were not a threat to her; Charlotte was. Kean had no wish to harm Mary. He was bound to her by so much shared experience: the poverty and hardship of their early years together; their grief over the death of Howard and their protective love for their remaining son. For Kean, the well-being of his family was an over-riding concern. So he agreed with Mary that all friendship with the Coxes must end, and he promised never to see Charlotte again.

But his desire for Charlotte proved too great and soon they were meeting again. He doubled his precautions against discovery, for Mary was now suspicious and watched him closely. In August, he told Charlotte: 'The eyes of Argus may be deluded, but those of a jealous wife impossible. Even now I am on tenterhooks. I expect the door forced open "and what are you writing?" the exclamation, or Susan to see if everything is comfortable, or Charles, with a handful of endearments for his dear papa, all tending to the same thing, what is he about?' He changed both Charlotte's pseudonym and the receiving house for letters. He now sent his letters to Mrs. Simpson, care of Aunt Tid. He made furtive arrangements for their meetings. 'On no account come near the park,' he wrote in November. 'I shall cross over Waterloo Bridge on Tuesday between 1 and 2 o'clock. I will see you on Wednesday at 12 in the saloon of the theatre. I have declared you are in the West Indies. If you are seen, I am ruined.'

There was no tranquillity for him either in his personal life or in his work. Following his return from America, he had been confounded when his arbitrary decision to cut short his season at Drury Lane had caused so little inconvenience. The enormous success of Elliston's *Coronation* production had more than compensated for the loss of Kean. He now realised that, as a result of Elliston's shift towards light entertainments, his own position had been undermined and he was no longer indispensable to the fortunes of Drury Lane. He resolved that, in the coming season, he must assert his authority, and he believed that his contract gave him the means of doing this.

The conditions under which he acted at Drury Lane were the same as those he had negotiated with the old committee and his contract still had three years to run. It included a clause that gave him the right to direct the plays in which he appeared. The degree to which he had exercised this right in the past varied considerably. He had been willing enough to leave the production of his plays to others, if everything suited him, but he had never hesitated to use the clause whenever he felt himself threatened. So, during his farewell season, in 1820, he had forbidden any further perform- ances of *Venice Preserved*, because Booth had scored a success in it and of *Lear*, because, he claimed, that it showed Mrs. West to advantage. Now, in the autumn of 1821, he was to invoke the clause again, in an attempt to strengthen his position at Drury Lane.

He announced that he would appear in a revival of Joanne Baillie's tragedy, *De Montfort*. Elliston was certain that the play would fail. Kean had chosen as his leading lady an inexperienced actress named Miss Edmiston, and Elliston was convinced that to draw a crowd nowadays Kean needed strong supporting players. His appearance with an unknown actress could only have a disastrous effect on the box office. On 14 November, Elliston sent his treasurer, William Dunn, to reason with Kean. This was not the first time Elliston had used his treasurer in a matter calling for diplomacy, and Winston suspected that Dunn was beginning to replace him as Elliston's right-hand man. Dunn suggested to Kean that Mrs. West would be more suitable than Miss Edmiston. At this, Kean turned nasty and said that if Mrs. West were engaged he would not act with her. So Dunn let the matter drop.

On 27 November, *De Montfort* was performed and, as Elliston had foreseen, was a total failure. To bolster up the poor receipts, he suggested that the next time the play was given the *Coronation* should be included in the programme. Kean objected to this. He said that his drawing power was every bit as good as that of the *Coronation*. Elliston let him have his way, but the receipts proved to be so bad that Kean agreed not only to allow the performance of the *Coronation* but also to replace Miss Edmiston by Mrs. West. This defeat made him very truculent. According to Winston, he went about the theatre 'very drunk and very abusive'.

For the rest of the season, Kean continued to produce his own plays. In an effort to recapture his audiences, he tackled three new parts, but failed in all of them. The first of these was the title role in *Owen, Prince of Powys*, by Samson Penley, which he produced in January 1822. This play had little merit and Elliston had only bought it because Kean had insisted, yet, by the end of rehearsals, Kean did not even want to play the part, saying that it was not big enough and that he would not act unless he was paramount. In the circumstances, it is not surprising that his performance was a complete fiasco. In March, he appeared in a second role new to him—Sir Pertinax Macsycophant, in *The Man of the World*, the part made famous by Macklin (its author) and later by Cooke. Again, he was unsuccessful. In May, he played for the first time Cardinal Wolsey in Shakespeare's *Henry VIII*. This had been one of Kemble's best parts, but it turned out to be one of Kean's worst. At the fourth performance, the receipts were barely £60.

His best audience was on 21 May, when the theatre was crowded for the farewell benefit for Aunt Tid, who was retiring after forty years at Drury Lane. At the end of the performance, Kean brought her back onto the stage. They stood together, the supporting actress who had never played a lead and the great star in whom she had inspired the love of acting. It was one of those emotional occasions so loved by theatregoers and the audience were generous with their applause. Elliston stood in the wings, with the tears rolling down his cheeks, and he embraced them both as they came offstage.

By the end of the season, however, Elliston had no kindly feelings at all towards Kean. On the nights he played, the theatre was three-quarters empty. There were complaints that his performances had become lax and his acting too mannered. Kean himself was depressed, for there seemed no doubt that the public had tired of him. He thought of going to America, but he was uncertain of the reception he would get there. He even considered retiring from the stage altogether and, with this in mind, he purchased a property in Scotland, a house with twenty acres of land at Rothesay, on the Isle of Bute, at the head of the Firth of Clyde. In addition to his worries about his career, he was also oppressed by the constant fear that Mary would find out about Charlotte, or that Cox would find out about him.

It is not certain how much Cox knew about his wife's affair with Kean. He must have had his suspicions when Mary broke off relations with his family, yet he continued to make Kean welcome in his home. Kean often went there for supper after the theatre. He was also in the habit, when drunk, of knocking them up in the early hours of the morning, demanding brandy and a bed for the night. On one occasion, at three in the morning, he arrived by coach and, after rousing the Coxes from their beds, insisted that they accompany him to Croydon, where he was to play that night. Cox, Charlotte and Anne Wickstead got into the coach and Kean drove them down. Later that morning, Cox returned to London, leaving Charlotte and Anne in Kean's charge. He left them together until the following day.

There was a time that summer when his behaviour was even more incomprehensible. In July, Kean and Charlotte met in Birmingham, where he was playing for a short season. She had told Cox that she was going to visit her mother at Brighton, but, for some reason, he had her followed by Robert Cox, his son by his first marriage. Robert found Kean and Charlotte together and reported this to his father. Kean was alarmed at what Cox might do, but as the days went by it became apparent that he was going to do nothing at all. He did not even mention the incident to Charlotte. The most probable reason for his silence was that Kean was helping him financially and it suited his purpose to say nothing. He was to claim in court that he had been completely hoodwinked by Kean, but not even the sympathetic judge could swallow this entirely. On the other hand, there was no doubt that Kean had made every effort to deceive Cox, and this was to weigh heavily against him.

When Kean learned from Charlotte that Cox was ignoring the Birmingham incident, his relief was heartfelt. 'My little Darling,' he wrote. 'Thank Heaven, all is well: and let us be more wary in the future.' She did not share his relief; she found his furtiveness tiresome and degrading. She wanted to be admired by all the world as his mistress. So far she had failed to achieve this, but there was a promising development that made her hope for better things. Cox was talking of settling abroad and she had told Kean that if this were to happen she would not go with him. Kean had promised that if Cox left the country he would set her up as his mistress. He believed that with Cox out of the way he could do this without a public scandal. Charlotte did not realise that he still had no intention of acknowledging her openly. He planned to set her up discreetly in a separate establishment and continue living with Mary. He saw the removal of Cox as the solution to their problem. On 21 July, he wrote: 'I know the necessity of his departure, and I would then hold my little darling to my heart and sleep in spite of thunder. I am so surrounded by visitors that I can scarcely seize the moment to dictate to my love the sincere emotions of my heart; but that I love her better than all the world, and will continue to do so till the end of life, is a feeling that I can never be dispossessed of. Do not mind my short letter. I really am so bothered I cannot sit down one moment.'

His agitation was increased by Charlotte's growing carelessness and when she addressed a letter to him under his own name he was completely unnerved. 'My dearest, though imprudent, little Girl,' he wrote, 'for such I see you are determined to remain, in spite of admonition and experience, why did you direct to me in my own name, when the others answer just as well? Letters may miscarry. I have not heard from her lately. She may be on the way to me—they may follow me—we have had one dreadful instance of that! My dear love, for Heaven's sake be guarded.' There were times when he cracked under the strain. 'What the devil is the matter with you, you little bitch,' he wrote, 'if you do not be quiet, I will kick your arse. If I do not see you before I leave London, I will take care that you will be with me shortly after.'

This was hardly the language of a resolute lover, but Charlotte was sustained by the knowledge that on one thing at least he was decided: let Cox leave the country and he would claim her for his own. Most annoyingly, Cox kept postponing his departure, but she was gratified by the violence with which Kean raged against the delay. 'O God! Charlotte, how I love you,' he wrote, in August. 'If such a feeling is a crime, why are we given it? I did not seek it. The power that will condemn has placed you in my way: the same inspiring hand that framed my better qualities pointed to you as the object of my love—my everlasting love. I must not doubt the justice of the Great Being, and have little or no faith in the general Tempter. What ere it be, "You are my fate—my heaven or my hell." ' This passionate declaration was modified by the final sentence: 'Caution be our password.'

By the autumn Cox had abandoned his plans for going abroad and this brought matters to a crisis. Kean pleaded with Charlotte for more time before making a move, but she would have none of it. She asked him how he could reconcile his love for her with his procrastination. On 3 November, from Carlisle, in the north of England, he replied: 'Do not let the thought enter your brain for one moment that I intend you unkindness, or that my love is undiminished: you shall find me ever the same, though I say with Coriolanus, "World, I banish you." She left me yesterday for London; if that had not been the case, I could not have written to you now. I am watched more closely than Buonaparte at St. Helena, independent of which I have never been three days in a place. I am setting off now for Whitehaven, where I play till Friday 8th, and set off after the play for London; if you could manage, without a shade of suspicion, how happy I should be; but beware, my brain is overclouded now with care, and you must lighten not increase it . . . remember, caution is the word, and true love will rather shield its object from dangers than incur them.'

The cares that 'overclouded' Kean's brain were caused by

Elliston's new policy at Drury Lane. The past season had been the worst since Elliston had taken over the management of the theatre. It was not only that Kean had failed; legitimate drama itself was becoming less and less popular. The public were demanding opera, melodrama and spectacle. This was the fare provided by the minor theatres. Forbidden by law to produce legitimate drama, they had concentrated on lighter entertainments, with such success that the major theatres were now being forced to provide an increasing proportion of similar amusements in order to retain their audiences. It was a crisis that called for heroic measures, and no one was more capable of these than Elliston. In August, the interior of Drury Lane was gutted. The shape of the auditorium was changed from a three-quarter circle to a horse-shoe. The size of the pit was reduced and the number of boxes increased, although the capacity of 3,100 remained unchanged. The stage was deepened, making it more suited to spectacle. All this was completed within fifty-eight days and cost £10,000, a third more than the sum he was obliged to spend under the lease.

He also looked around for fresh faces with which to liven up the company, and the situation at Covent Garden gave him the opportunity he was seeking. In the spring of 1822, Harris had handed over the management of Covent Garden to a committee of four shareholders which soon ran into trouble. Three of the leading players—Charles Mayne Young, the tragedian, John Liston, the comedian, and Kitty Stephens, the singer—had demanded a rise in salary. The committee had refused, and so the three of them terminated their contracts. Ignoring the agreement between the two major theatres that no player leaving the one should be engaged by the other before a year had elapsed, Elliston offered the three players more money than they had been asking at Covent Garden. Young, who had wanted his salary raised from £20 a week to £25, was offered £20 a night for thirty nights. This precedent of enormous salaries, established by Elliston, was eventually to ruin both major theatres, but for the time being the balance of power had been tipped overwhelmingly in favour of Drury Lane. Macready, held fast by his contract, would continue to play at Covent Garden, but he was the only star they had. The rest were all at Drury Lane, and the coming season there promised to be very exciting. Elliston was arranging a series of gladiatorial contests in all departments: in opera, Stephens would play against Vestris; in comedy, Liston would play against Munden; and in tragedy, Young would play against Kean.

Elliston had yet to inform Kean that a tragedian of equal status would be acting with him during the coming season. Characteristically, he delegated the task to his treasurer, William Dunn. Kean was at his Scottish home when he received Dunn's letter. As he read it, he became more and more angry. He regarded the engagement of Young as an attack on his own supremacy at Drury Lane. One 13 October, he wrote to Elliston: 'Your Treasurer has written me a letter so charged with *we* and *us* that it is with difficulty I could extract the subject but the drift I find is—that as Mr. Young is engaged for *30* nights & my services are wanted— to act with him—now this I call exceedingly impudent, & I hope without your authority—The Throne is mine, I will maintain it— even at the expense of expatriation—go where I will I shall always bear it with me—& even if I sail to another quarter of the globe, no man, in this profession, can rob me of the character of the first English Actor.'

His first reaction had been to refuse to act with Young, but he recognised that if he were to do this, Elliston could come down on him heavily for compensation. He had been put in an intolerable position, but decided that if he were forced to act with Young, it would be on his own terms. In his letter to Elliston, he continued: 'When I come to London Elliston I open in Richard the *3d* my second character *Othello*!! *Hamlet*—*Lear*—& so through my general cast. If Mr. Young is ambitious to act with me, he must commence with *Iago*—& when the whole of *my* characters is exhausted we may then turn our thoughts to Cymbeline & Venice Preserved—at the same time I do not wish to influence your Dramatic Politicks, if you think Mr. Young will answer your purpose better than me.'

Elliston informed Kean that he had no intention of altering his plans. He had broken up the successful Macready-Young com-

bination at Covent Garden in order to replace it with a Kean-
Young combination at Drury Lane. Kean and Young represented
opposite schools of acting. With the retirement of Kemble, Young
had become the chief exponent of the classical style. The announcement that he was to act with Kean had already aroused interest
among theatregoers. Nor was Elliston willing to allow Kean any
say in the parts Young was to play. Young had come over to
Drury Lane on the understanding that he was to be equal to Kean
and that, apart from their joint efforts, he was to be a star in his
own right. So, in his reply to Kean, Elliston evaded the question
of the order of the plays.

On 17 October, while Kean was still in Scotland, Young opened
at Drury Lane as Hamlet and, a few nights later, he followed this
with Macbeth. Both times, he played to better houses than Kean
had had for years. When Kean learned of this, he was not only
jealous but also frightened. Hamlet and Macbeth were his parts
and he was dismayed that another actor had been allowed to play
them at Drury Lane. Moreover the audiences had applauded
Young, and had turned out in greater numbers than when he
himself had played these roles during the previous season. He was
jealous of Young for other reasons. With his gentlemanly background and urbane manners, Young mixed easily at all levels of
society. Unlike Kean, he had never tried to be the equal of the
aristocracy and, as a result, he had achieved an easy relationship
with them that Kean envied. Kean thought bitterly that the
aristocracy would turn out in force to support Young against him.
He was convinced that they had never wanted him as the leading
tragedian; that they would much prefer Young, an actor who
knew how to behave himself. He suspected that there was a plot to
get rid of him. He dreaded the confrontation that awaited him in
London and he continued to skulk in Scotland, reluctant to leave
the security of his island retreat.

Elliston ordered him to return and, on 23 October, Kean
replied: 'I cannot according to the arrangements I have made, be
in London till Monday, the 11th. You can if you please advertise
me for Richard on that night—You must forgive my being
jealous of my hard earned laurels. I know how brittle is the

ground I stand upon—& how transient is public favor—Mr. Young has many advantages that I have not, a commanding figure, sonorous voice—& above all lordly connexions—I had too much regard for my own happiness not to kick all such trash to the devil. I am therefore coming to meet an opposition, made up of my own enemies (which like locusts—can almost darken the sun) Mr. Young's *friends*—& his very great abilities—with nothing but humble genius to support me, a mere ephemera— always at the command of caprice—& the same breath that nourishes the flame this day—tomorrow puts it out.'

Throughout his life, he had always believed that no one had ever wanted him, but he had fought his way to the top of his profession and he could not allow this position to be taken from him. He must be predominant at Drury Lane. He had made this clear to the committee prior to his début, when he had come up from Dorchester and stood before them in his shabby greatcoat. He re-stated his position to Elliston, with the same quotation he had used then: 'Aut Caesar, aut Nullus, is my text. If I become secondary in any point of view, I shrink into insignificance. I shall not trouble the world longer than the two years I am engaged to you—I have taken a house in Scotland for the purpose of retire- ment with my family at the termination of my engagement & all I ask of you—is to let me retire with my reputation Undiminished, that I may enjoy the retrospection, when I am the world forget- ting, & by the world forgot—as the Covent Garden Hero—comes upon my ground, the Challenger!'

He did not want this fight, but if it were forced on him, then he would use every advantage he had. If, at their first appearance together, Young were to play Iago to his Othello, then, at the very outset, he might annihilate him as he had once annihilated Booth; but if they opened with *Venice Preserved*, with Young as Pierre, one of his best parts, and himself as Jaffeir, then Young might score the first success. Therefore, he believed it essential that he should decide the order of the plays. He put this in his letter to Elliston: 'I have doubtless my choice of weapons. He must play *Iago*! before I act Jaffeir. I am told he is extraordinarily great in Pierre—if so—I am beaten—this must not be—I cannot bear it. I would rather go in chains to Botany Bay—I am not ashamed to say—I am afraid of the contest.'

In his reply, Elliston again evaded the question of the order of the plays, and his equivocation convinced Kean that there was definitely a plot to supplant him with Young. He was travelling south from Scotland, and from Carlisle, on 31 October, he wrote to Elliston: 'I never doubted your ingenuity in composing a letter, but you must excuse me when I say, from the first moment of our acquaintance, I have questioned your sincerity. Your letter very cleverly—but not honestly evades the answer of a simple question, is Mr. Young to act Iago with me first or is Mr. Kean to act Jaffeir with Mr. Young's Pierre—You tell me you are surrounded by equal talent in your department—I acknowledge this—but I do not see Mr. Dowton or Mr. Munden or Mr. Knight or Mr. Harley or Mr. ——— in for *Rover Ranger*—I see Mr. Young's name for Hamlet!!! did Mr. Young's Hamlet ever bring to the treasury the same Money mine has. Is there any Country Manager will give Mr. Young £10 for his acting Hamlet. I made *54* for playing it last night—

'Why is Mr. Young engaged for a certain number of nights, when Mr. Kean is attached to the property.

'Elliston. My *dear* Elliston, I *know you*—I see the deep entangled Web you have extended for me but that Providence which has guided me through all the perils of worldly Chicanery—fights for me now & will defeat the plot though *Coutts Bank* flowed into the coffers of my enemy—& his Suite composed of *Lords & Auctioneers*. I am prepared for *war*.'

On 11 November, Kean made his first appearance of the season at Drury Lane. He was in a very sulky mood, when he turned up at the theatre. He pointedly avoided his dressing-room and changed in the second green room. Everyone in the company could see that he was taking things badly. For the first fortnight, he was never sober. On Monday, 18 November, he arrived at the theatre drunk and pugnacious. He had not been home since Friday and, the previous night, had been arrested for disturbing the peace and locked up in the watch house.

On 27 November, he made his first appearance with Young.

The play was *Othello*; in this, at least, he had had his way. The theatre was crowded, for the publoc were hoping for another great duel, like the one with Booth. Both actors had their followers and throughout the play both were frequently applauded. The honours were even until the great scenes in the third act, when Young's precise gestures and icy declamation were ineffective against the passion of Kean's acting. It was not another slaughter; Kean no longer had the energy for that, but he had proved himself to be the better actor.

His victory restored his confidence; he was no longer afraid of acting with Young, but resented his playing starring roles at Drury Lane, above all, Hamlet and Macbeth. He argued that these parts belonged to him, and that no one else should be allowed to play them at Drury Lane. He brooded over this all the time. On 17 December he got drunk in Joey Grimaldi's dressing-room at Covent Garden and decided to settle the matter with Elliston once and for all. He sent word to Elliston that unless he came within half an hour he would go to America. Elliston came and they sat arguing and drinking until the early hours of the morning. Kean kept insisting that Hamlet and Macbeth were his parts; that by playing them he had saved Drury Lane from ruin; that he could not understand why Young was allowed to play them. He said that if Elliston did not want him he should say so; that his contract had only two years to run and then he would be rid of him; that if he persisted in wanting Young at Drury Lane, then he should release him from his contract and allow him to go to America. The discussion ended with Elliston promising to think the matter over and Kean had to be satisfied with this. But Elliston had no intention of altering his plans. He needed both Young and Kean at Drury Lane and he hoped that, in time, Kean would see things his way.

The new year began badly for Kean and Elliston. On 1 January 1823, Elliston was stricken at the theatre by one of his attacks and put to bed. A crowd had gathered in the street outside, drawn there by a burst water main. Elliston left his bed and addressed them from the window, warning them to disperse, because the street might blow up at any moment. Kean was having difficulties with Charlotte, who was now making no attempt at all to hide her feelings for him in public. He was sure that this would lead to trouble and, at the beginning of the year, trouble came.

Kean had arranged to play a short season in the West Country and a party was made up to accompany him, consisting of Charlotte and her husband, Anne Wickstead, Aunt Tid, and the Reverend Benjamin Drury, the son of his old patron. Kean was to pay all expenses. At Salisbury, in front of the clergyman, Charlotte's attitude to Kean was so obvious that Cox could not ignore it. He made a bombastic scene, in the course of which he challenged Kean to a duel. After a while, things calmed down, but next day Cox took his wife back to London, an action which lost much of its force when he borrowed £10 from Kean for the fare.

The whole incident upset Kean badly. Although Cox must have had his suspicions long before Salisbury, he had never revealed them and, as a result, Kean believed that up until then he had been completely hoodwinked. He decided that his best course of action would be to brazen the matter out.

'My dear Cox,' he wrote, from Exeter, on 6 January, 'I have been seriously considering the mass of nonsense uttered by us the last two nights at Salisbury. I must own likewise they have given me a great uneasiness. If I have paid more attention to your family than any other of my acquaintances, the simple motive was to show the world that I valued my friends as much in adversity as when I shared their hospitality in their prosperity. I am sorry my conduct has been misconstrued, as the inference is unworthy of yourself—me—and a being whose conduct, I am sure, is unimpeachable: to remove all doubts upon the subject, and to counteract the effects of insidious men, I shall beg leave to withdraw a friendship rendered unworthy by suspicion.'—

'Had he paused there,' Cox's counsel was to say, 'was it possible for any thing to be better calculated to remove suspicion than this air of injured honour—this protest of angry and insulted friendship—this indignant withdrawal of an intimacy the motives of which were too pure to bear suspicion? But this was not all. Mr. Kean proceeded—and let the jury take from his own pen his own character as written against himself'—

'I must be the worst of villains if I could take that man by the hand, while meditating towards him an act of injustice. You do not know me, Cox: mine are follies, not vices. It has been my text to do all the good I could in the world, and when I am called to a superior bourne, my memory may be blamed, but not despised. Wishing you and your family every blessing the world can give you, believe me, nothing less than Yours, most sincerely, EDMUND KEAN.'

To Charlotte, on the same day, he wrote: 'Dear little imprudent Girl,—Your incaution has been very near bringing our acquaintance to the most lamentable crisis. Of course he will show you the letter I have written him; appear to countenance it, and let him think we are never to meet again, and in so doing he has lost a friend. Leave all further arrangements to me. My aunt desires her best wishes to you, notwithstanding her anger, she says, of your conduct before him, "Love shields the object of its wishes, not exposes it." All shall be shortly as you wish.'

Two years later, when these letters were read aloud in court, they did him irreparable harm. He stood exposed before the world as the most treacherous of deceivers and the most sanctimonious of hypocrites.

Cox took no action over the Salisbury incident, and Kean was careful to give him no further grounds for suspicion. He avoided his house, and his precautions against discovery became even more elaborate. 'I shall so contrive our meetings,' he told Charlotte, 'that a lynx's eye shall not penetrate our retreats.' He chose the most unlikely places, sending her complicated directions and advising her to alter her route each time. He changed their pseudonyms yet again. His letters were sent to Mrs. Elbe and hers to Mr. Sexton.

Throughout the spring of 1823, Elliston did all he could to persuade Kean to accept Young at Drury Lane. His policy of playing off one actor against another was proving a sucess and the theatre was having its best season for years. He matched Kean with Young in *Othello*, *Venice Preserved* and *Cymbeline*. Othello was the greatest attraction, but there were good houses whenever they played together. Kean fought hard against the frequency with which Elliston matched him with Young. One night he complained to Winston, 'I have to play again with that bloody, thundering bugger.' Apart from their joint efforts, each continued to play separately. Kean revived *King Lear*, restoring Shakespeare's ending in place of Nahum Tate's. He had long boasted that no one had any idea of what he could do until they had seen him over the dead body of Cordelia, but he failed in the scene and, after only three performances, returned to Tate's ending.

Young, for his part, continued to play Hamlet and Macbeth, and Kean found this intolerable. Again and again, throughout the season, he threatened to go to America unless Young was removed from Drury Lane. For Kean, America had become the solution to all his problems, professional and romantic. The outcry against him there had died away and he was convinced that he would be given a great welcome. Unfortunately, his contract with Elliston still had another year to run and he knew that the manager would not allow him to go to America before it expired. He dreaded the approach of this final year, as he suspected that Elliston was planning to match him with Macready, whose contract with Covent Garden terminated at the end of the present season. Macready was a far more formidable opponent than Young, and Kean had no wish to act with him. He decided that, before the next season began, he must take steps to prevent the introduction of Macready or any other tragedian at Drury Lane, except on his terms. As always, when he felt himself threatened, he turned to the clause in his contract that gave him the right to direct the plays in which he appeared.

On Monday, 26 May, before the evening performance, Kean asked Winston to come to his dressing-room, where he handed him a sheet of paper on which the clause was written. He told Winston that, by virtue of the clause, he wanted *Hamlet* to be performed next Friday instead of *Town and Country*, as advertised. He said that from now on he was to be the only Hamlet at Drury Lane and that he would play the part whenever he chose. Winston told him that he had better discuss the matter with Elliston.

After the performance, Kean met with Elliston and Winston in Winston's office. He told Elliston that by allowing Young to play Hamlet and Macbeth he was depriving him of half his fame; that these parts were his property at Drury Lane and Elliston had robbed him of them. He told him that he might as well go into his house and take away his furniture as take these parts from him. He warned Elliston that he was fully aware that his policy was to injure him.

Elliston asked Kean to be calm and reasonable. He said that Macready and Young had both played Hamlet at Covent Garden, so why should Kean and Young not do the same at Drury Lane? Kean shouted that he knew nothing about Covent Garden and other actors, that he only knew Kean and there was no other person than Kean. If Drury Lane did not want him, he could be equally attractive elsewhere. In the meantime, he had the right to direct the plays he acted in and, therefore, he directed that *Hamlet* be performed on Friday. He then left the room. Kean's interpretation of the clause confounded Elliston and Winston. It seemed that the actor believed he had the right to 'direct' which plays should actually be performed on given nights.

Two days later, Kean's solicitor, Mr. Broughton, had a meeting with Elliston and Winston in Elliston's office. He said that Kean was anxious to cancel the troublesome clause, but unfortunately the contract had still another year to run. He suggested that a more suitable contract be drawn up immediately, in both Kean's and Elliston's interest. The purpose of Kean's outburst now became clear to Elliston. Kean wanted a contract that would inhibit the introduction of any other tragedian at Drury Lane. Elliston was too wily to fall for this. He told Broughton that he was anxious to further Kean's interests as far as he could, but he saw no reason to draw up a new contract just yet. Kean was talking of going to America for a year, when the present contract expired, and he would allow him to go. When he returned, they might negotiate a new contract, in which, if Kean so wished, he could specify the characters he wanted to play at Drury Lane. But, for the present, he saw no need for a new contract.

Broughton advised Kean to settle for this He cautioned him

that the interpretation he placed on the clause would not stand up in court, if Elliston chose to fight. He also told him that it would be a flagrant breach of contract if he went to America at the end of the present season, and that God alone knew what this would cost him in damages. Kean now realised that once again he had been outmanoeuvred by Elliston, and this made him very angry. He went about the theatre arrogant and belligerent. That weekend there was a doubt as to whether John Liston would be able to act on the following Monday, and Elliston sent Kean a note asking him to play instead. Kean replied: 'I cannot be made a stopgap to the property I have been so long supporting. I, E. Kean, say, "If I play on Monday night, I'll be damned!" '

The season closed on 30 June. It had been a great success, with receipts totalling over £60,000, but Winston feared that not even this magnificent sum could justify the high salaries Elliston had been paying and the huge debt he had incurred. It seemed to him that Elliston was more erratic than ever, promising everything to everybody and then vanishing into the provinces. Whenever Kean came to the theatre to find out Elliston's plans for the coming season, the manager was never there. Kean still did not know if any other tragedians would be playing at Drury Lane, and the uncertainty was driving him frantic. Although he had failed to get a new contract that would have prevented the introduction of other tragedians, he still hoped to have a say in the parts they would be allowed to play.

On Friday, 25 July, he arrived at the theatre late at night. He was very drunk and he slept on the sofa in his dressing-room. The next morning, he came to Winston's office in an aggressive mood and told him that he had something to say to him. He said that he was trying to decide whether to act at Drury Lane next season, or sell up and settle in America. He said that his conditions for staying were these: that Young, or even Macready might be engaged at Drury Lane for melodrama or minor tragedy, but Hamlet, Macbeth and all the other great tragic roles were to be his. He told Winston to communicate these conditions to Elliston. He would give Elliston until Tuesday to reach a decision.

As usual, Elliston was out of town, but by Monday he had sent an answer to Winston. At one o'clock that afternoon, Kean came to the theatre and, after reading Elliston's letter, he appeared satisfied. Before leaving, he gave Winston a sheet of paper with six parts written on it—Hamlet, Lear, Richard III, Macbeth, Shylock and Overreach—which he wished not to be played at Drury Lane while he was touring the provinces. He thought that he had got his way with Elliston, but when he arrived home and read the letter more carefully, he began to wonder, as he had wondered so often in the past, just exactly what Elliston meant. The letter was so evasive that he had no idea where he stood. At half-past-six that evening, he arrived at Winston's house, in Charles Street, drunk and almost insane in his agony. He said that there was something in Elliston's letter that had made him change his mind; that he now wanted to be advertised as playing his last season in England. He said that he would retire to America; that he would have his house there surrounded by walls; that he would let in only those he wished, and then he would be happy. He said that he had acted in provincial companies for only three pounds a week, and he would rather return to one of these than be second where he expected to be first.

He was right to be suspicious of Elliston. The manager was already negotiating with Macready to play at Drury Lane during the coming season. Young had no wish to renew his contract. Acting with Kean had not been a pleasant experience for him and he was going back to Covent Garden. Macready was not happy with his salary of £20 a week at Covent Garden and, at the end of the season, he had declined to renew his contract. Elliston offered him £20 a night for forty nights and he accepted. To avoid all possible grounds for complaint on Kean's side, Elliston raised his salary from £30 a week to £20 a night. This meant that providing Kean continued his usual routine of acting three times a week, his salary had been doubled.

Kean was touring Ireland when he received a letter from Dunn telling him that Macready would be playing at Drury Lane, and that they were to act together. Even though he was totally opposed to the plan, he had no alternative but to accept the terms offered him. On 11 October, he replied: 'I hope Mr. Elliston will not deceive himself in the belief of my renewal of engagement for Drury Lane. The frequent usurpations of my right—the forgetfulness of my former Services & above all the *violation* of *word*, must have excited disgust in a less irritable mind than mine—& I assure you Sir—no Galley Slave—ever sighed for emancipation, more deeply than I to bid farewell—to Elliston & his management. Novelty—is the weapon, which he teaches me to adopt—& by carrying my merchandise to the rival market—I doubt not but the novelty will excite a more than common sensation. I shall now publicly avow my intention of closing my Theatrical career, at Covent Garden Theatre by going through the whole routine of my characters previous to my departure for America—the effects of this I am vain enough to believe—will require very novel attractions in Mr. Elliston to counteract, but his is the speculation—not mine . . . As Mr. Macready is occupying my Situation my Services will not perhaps be wanted so early as the 3d—I am making a vast deal of money in this country—I have no wish to give it up while it chooses to flow. . . .'

On Monday, 13 October, Macready opened at Drury Lane as Virginius. He went on to play Hamlet, Macbeth, Wolsey, Coriolanus, and all his other great roles. Whenever he played, the theatre was well filled, but this was not entirely due to the merits of his acting. That season, Elliston was competing openly with the minor theatres by providing even more operas, burlesques, farces, pantomimes and melodramas. On the nights Macready played, his tragic performances were sometimes supported by a spectacular melodrama entitled *The Cataract of the Ganges*, by Moncrieff, in which horses paraded, military bands played, and a splendid waterfall, fed from the emergency tank, sparkled and cascaded at the back of the stage.

After his Irish tour Kean retired to his Scottish home, pleading ill health. He knew that so long as he stayed away from London, Elliston had no chance of pairing him with Macready. In the middle of November his secretary, Phillips, wrote urging him to come to London and take up the challenge. Kean replied: 'I must differ with you about my coming to London. Fabius Maximus conquered not by fighting a powerful enemy, but by avoiding him. He weakened his resources, and saved the city of Rome.'

The high-minded and fastidious Macready did not care for the chaos and immoralities of Drury Lane: the drunken Elliston forever coupling with some actress in a private box; the filthy state of the corridors and dressing-rooms; the prostitutes enquiring about the return of Kean. On 6 December, when the first part of his engagement ended, he was glad to leave for a three-month tour of the provinces. Two days after Macready's departure, Kean returned to Drury Lane.

He had avoided Macready, but the problem of Charlotte could not be dodged so easily. Throughout the summer and the autumn her demand for an open relationship had become implacable. Again he procrastinated, this time using his projected American trip as his excuse. He begged her to leave any decision over until his return, but she would not agree. She told him that he must make up his mind once and for all. He was in an agonising dilemma, torn between his need for Charlotte and his duty to his family.

'What can I say,' he wrote. 'I love you better than all the world —all beyond. I see no remedy for our disease but patience, and that must be exerted to the utmost. On my return from America all shall be as you wish, till then it is impossible. You must think for a man struggling to obtain competence for his family, which the circumstances of our connection must utterly destroy. I feel for you most sincerely, on my soul, my heart is breaking, but any rash steps would destroy our hopes forever. I long to see you but will not come to your house. If you enter the front door Theatre Royal Drury Lane, I will meet you through the other. Our meeting last night was cold and distant, not as formerly.'

To force him to act, she had begun to flirt with other men and the tone of her letters now disturbed him. He wrote: 'That simple style of writing that you had, and which I used to clasp to my heart, kiss with my lips, and sleep with on my pillow, is changed to the slang of fashionable coquetry. "I did not give the Colonel one smile tonight." Why any night, if those smiles belong to me?' Her flirtations were more serious than he knew. For some time she had fancied her husband's clerk, a young man named What-more, and she had recently taken to sleeping with him at his lodgings in Norfolk Street. But she had not yet given up hope of becoming Kean's mistress and she wrote him a pathetic letter, saying that if he really wanted her, he would take her.

Her letter drove Kean to action. On 22 January 1824, he replied: 'My darling, darling love, writes to me in affliction, and every thought but for her happiness has subsided; she flies to me for refuge; my heart, my whole heart, is open to receive her.' He made one condition: 'All I ask is, that for a few months you will hide yourself, that when the hue and cry is raised, they shall find nothing to criminate me: "If the goods are not found upon the thief, these can be no conviction." ' He suggested that she should meet him at one o'clock, the following Monday, outside the Diorama, in Regent's Park. He urged her to keep the meeting a secret.

On the Monday, they met in Regent's Park and he put to her the arrangement he had in mind: to set her up in a small furnished house, where they could meet discreetly, while he continued to live with Mary at Clarges Street. Charlotte would have none of this, but he told her that he was not prepared to go any further. She looked contemptuously at the nervous little man by her side and was astonished at her own stupidity in ever hoping for better things from him. Was this the great tragic genius with whom she was to have the most famous love affair of the century? Was this henpecked husband the disciple of Byron, whose scorn for morality had scandalised Europe? She was aware that even as they walked together his eyes flickered from side to side in fear that some acquaintance might recognise them. All her feelings for him turned to hatred and she flayed him with her tongue. She told him that she despised him; that she could find other lovers; that she had, indeed, already found one, younger, better-looking and far more virile.

It was the end. One night, while sleeping with Whatmore, she was disturbed by a noise in the street outside. Two prostitutes were howling foul invective at the bedroom windows. The next day she received a note from Kean, saying that he had slept with both women and had then sent them round to Norfolk Street to abuse her.

In March, Cox discovered that Charlotte was having an affair with Whatmore. However complaisant he had been towards Kean, he would not tolerate his wife sleeping with his clerk. There was a terrible row, which ended with Charlotte leaving him and going to live with Whatmore. While packing her belongings, she allowed herself a vindictive action: she left behind all Kean's letters, tied up with ribbon. She left them in an unlocked cabinet in her bedroom, where Cox was sure to come across them. Indeed, he found them the day after she left. He claimed that his discovery of the letters was his first knowledge of his wife's affair with Kean. He threatened publicly that he would kill the actor and, because of these threats, Kean took the precaution of carrying a pistol.

On 7 April, the annual dinner in aid of the Drury Lane Theatrical Fund was held at the Freemasons' Hall. Kean, as Master of the Fund, was waiting to welcome the Duke of Clarence, when Cox forced his way into the room. There was a noisy and confused scene, during which pistols were brandished, but Cox was eventually overpowered and thrown out. Two days later, he took out a writ against Kean for 'criminal conversation' with his wife.

Although it was a little late in the day for Cox to play the part of the injured husband, he may well have been outraged by what he had read in the letters. While it was one thing to turn a blind eye to an affair of which he knew few details, it was quite another to read such explicit letters written by another man to his wife. It may be that Kean's letters made him truly jealous, but in seeking compensation for the loss of Charlotte's affections, he was motivated as much by cupidity as injured pride. Kean, the adulterer, was a rich man, while he, the innocent party, was a poor one. He told his solicitors that his honour would not be satisfied by anything less than two thousand pounds.

From December until April, Kean had played regularly at Drury Lane, but after Easter, when Macready returned, he disappeared. He could not be found anywhere. A messenger sent by Elliston to his house in Clarges Street was told that he had left for an unknown destination. Elliston enquired everywhere, but no one knew where Kean was. Then he learned that Kean had been seen at the Regent Hotel, Brighton. He wrote to him there, but the letter was returned with a note from the landlord, saying that Kean had sailed for France two days previously.

Elliston sent Dunn to Brighton to find out what had happened. When Dunn arrived at the hotel, the landlord insisted that Kean was now in France, but, as they were talking, Dunn could hear sounds of conviviality coming from the next room. He was convinced that Kean was in there, but he said nothing to the landlord about this. Instead, he told him that he was satisfied with his story and would be returning to London that night. He remained in Brighton, however, and arranged for an acquaintance to call at the hotel the following day with a note for Kean. This man told the landlord that he was in Kean's confidence and asked that the note be delivered to him immediately. The landlord said that it would be in Kean's hand within the minute. When Kean opened it, he read: 'Mr. Elliston, with friendly enquiries after the health of Mr. Kean.'

'ELLISTON,' Kean wrote. 'I hate a trickster: you have employed unworthy means to disturb me in my solitude. This was neither manly nor open. It was necessary I should have repose—my health has suffered materially. You have pursued me by a trick, and I should deign you no reply; but I am here, Sir, under the direction of Sir Anthony Carlisle, and will not stir from this place until I have gone through all the routine of medicine and sea-bathing prescribed for me by that great man. The medical gentlemen of Brighton declare also I need repose— "Kean must have repose." If I am pursued either by tricks or openly, I shall retire to "La Belle France", for some weeks. I leave you in no distress—you have Macready! Macready, Elliston!— why should you be anxious about poor Kean? Yet, a breath—a breath, I say, of Kean shall confound a generation of Youngs and Macreadys.'

This time Elliston could not afford to indulge Kean's temperament, for he was facing bankruptcy. His affairs were utterly confused and, admistratively, Drury Lane had almost ceased to function. One of the contributory causes to this was an appointment he had made at the beginning of the season, when he had hired Alfred Bunn as 'assistant manager'. Together with Dunn and Winston, this appointment had given the theatre three officers of equal status and no clearly defined areas of duty. Winston resented the other two receiving the same salary as himself. He particularly resented Bunn and, even allowing for his prejudice, he had good reason to do so, for Bunn was to prove to be one of the greatest adventurers and charlatans in the history of the English theatre. His appointment to Drury Lane, at the age of twenty-five, was an important step in a career that was eventually to bring him control of both major theatres.

He was helped in his ambitions by his wife, Margaret Agnes Somerville, a beautiful actress who had made her début at Drury Lane seven years previously, when she had played opposite Kean in *Bertram*. On that occasion, she had played too well for Kean's liking and, from then on, she had been given only secondary roles. She had then drifted into the provinces, where she had married Bunn. She returned with him to Drury Lane. Under his tutoring, she had learned how to succeed. He encouraged her to sleep with any man who could advance their interests. He knew the weakness of Elliston in this respect and, through his wife's body, he consolidated his position at Drury Lane.

Winston found him incompetent and accused him of spending most of his time sleeping on Elliston's sofa. He called him 'the contented cuckold', a 'pimp', whose existence 'depends solely upon his wife's prostitution'. Elliston thought highly of him, because Bunn always agreed with him. He also encouraged him to mount expensive productions and so hurried him along the road to bankruptcy. In the spring of 1824, Elliston had almost reached the end of that road. There were times when he could not come near the theatre for fear of being arrested for debt. Bailiffs were continually attempting to serve writs on him. In March, Winston had found him hiding in a back room at the theatre.

Elliston had become a public scandal, and the committee were anxious to get rid of him. His rent was badly in arrears and on 10

May, John Calcraft, chairman of the sub-committee, had given him an ultimatum. He had told him that he was a disgrace to the theatre; that his drunkenness had reduced Drury Lane to as bad a shape as it ever was; and that unless he paid £2,000 by 5 July, he would have to go. This was the reason why Elliston was chasing up Kean at Brighton. He hoped that by matching him with Macready he might make enough money to save the theatre. He ordered Kean to return immediately, but Kean, true to his threat, left for France. When Elliston heard of this, he told Winston that he would sue Kean for breach of contract; he swore that he would get compensation from him. It seemed to Winston that, at long last, Elliston had come to his senses.

From Dieppe, on Friday, 21 May, Kean wrote to his old friend, Jack Hughes, the comedian, expressing his fears, both rational and irrational: 'The closer they pursue, the further I shall recede—by the time you receive this Mrs. Kean & myself are on our way to Paris—where I shall remain, till I see the last night advertised of Drury Lane Theatre, the day after you will see me in London. Settle all bills for me: I will discharge them on the instant I return —I shall then quit England for *ever*—but I carry with me the reputation of the first English actor, which if I had allowed them to have their way, I could not have done, if I had acted—I know hundreds were prepared for hostility, & in the bad parts they were forcing me to play with Macready, he must have skimmed the cream of my professional dish—he may now take the whole—& the Public may talk and be damned. I shall be soon out of hearing —& change of Country—I hope will destroy every feeling. However it was not artifice. I was so ill, that if I had attempted to act I am convinced I should have fallen on the stage—Dunn was sent to Brighton & I immediately got into the Packet & sailed— I shall not act anywhere now till August—my *Dublin engagement* & then—Vale Patria.'

Meanwhile the newspapers were filled with rumours about the forthcoming court case. It was known that Kean's letters were to be the chief evidence against him and something was also known of their sensational nature. Thomas Creevey, the diarist, wrote to his step-daughter, Elizabeth Ord: 'Another *slip* is Mrs. Alderman

C. . . . with our tragedian, Kean. . . . He had been at his letters too, one of which to the lady was intercepted by the alderman, and begun—"You dear imprudent little little Bitch". . . . Can anything be more soft or romantic?'

Kean was enjoying his reputation as a great lover. The last three Cantos of *Don Juan* were published that year, and he saw himself as the embodiment of Byron's hero, charming, handsome and unprincipled. He had had some nasty moments with Mary, when she learned that he had continued to deceive her over Charlotte, but when she realised how concerned he had been throughout to preserve their marriage, she had, in the end, forgiven him. He had assured her that their future as a family was secure, and that very summer he fulfilled the second of the two promises he had made to her after his début at Drury Lane: Charles went to Eton to receive a gentleman's education. He made light of the forthcoming trial, and she had no reason to anticipate the terrible scandal that was to break over them.

Kean's insouciance was not shared by his solicitor, Henry Sigell, who had read the eighty letters written to Charlotte. Sigell was convinced that it would be fatal if these were read aloud in court, especially the two written on the same day, one to Cox and the other to Charlotte, concerning the Salisbury incident. He had proposed to Cox's solicitor, Mr. Emery, to let judgment go by default and refer damages to the sheriff's court, but Emery would not agree. It had become a matter of urgency to plan Kean's defence, but the actor did not even bother to answer his letters. On Saturday, 17 July, Sigell called a meeting at Drury Lane to discuss the case. Elliston and Winston were present and also George Robins, a member of the committee. None of them knew where Kean was.

In fact, he was in Boulogne; returning from a leisurely tour through France and Switzerland, he had broken his journey to stay a few days with Grattan. He was in great spirits and seemingly unconcerned about the forthcoming trial. Grattan wrote: 'He spoke of the affair as one which gave him no uneasiness; said he had no fears for the result; and he seemed quite unconscious of the ruinous risk that awaited him. I was rather impressed with the idea that he did not dislike the approaching contest, which was to display him to the world as a man of gallantry.'

On Tuesday, 20 July, Kean arrived back in London and immediately went round to Drury Lane to see Elliston. He had been looking forward to this interview for a long time. He reminded Elliston that the contract between them expired within six days, when the present season ended. He swore that never again would he be bound to Elliston or any other manager; that never again would he endure the humiliations of the past two years. From this day on, he declared his independence; he would play in any theatre he wished, on a nightly basis only and the fee for each night would be not less than £50. These were the only conditions on which he would act again at Drury Lane. Elliston asked him to play the remaining few nights of the season, but Kean said that, so far as he was concerned, his present contract was already terminated.

After Kean left, Elliston told Winston that this time he would definitely sue for breach of contract. He had managed to defer the payment due to the committee, but other creditors were pressing him on all sides. He scorned the idea of paying Kean £50 a night; no actor had ever received such an astronomical sum. He admitted that the high salaries he had given the Covent Garden players had been a gamble which had not paid off, and he was certainly not going to fall into that trap again. Yet, the following day, despite all this brave talk, he agreed to Kean's conditions.

A contract was drawn up for Kean to play twenty-three nights, at £50 a night, between 16 January and 15 March of the following year. Twenty-six parts were listed—all the principal tragic roles— and these constituted the repertory from which he would choose. He could not be made to play any other roles, unless he himself chose to do so. By this contract, Kean placed himself in an impregnable position. Elliston could introduce Young, Macready, or anyone else, but, on the nights Kean played at Drury Lane, he would be supreme. Winston called the contract a 'preposterous and unwise engagement'. Elliston had been given the chance to rid himself of Kean, but he could not bring himself to take it. 'After this,' Winston commented, 'can anyone think him sane'?

The capitulation of Elliston put Kean in a good humour. From now on, he would be the one who called the tune at Drury Lane. After his twenty-three performances there next year, he planned an extended tour of America. In the meantime, there was one very important engagement to be fulfilled, the case of Cox v. Kean scheduled to be heard on 15 January 1825. The press had already dubbed the litigants the Actor and the Alderman. Kean could hardly wait for the great contest to begin. From Belfast, in the autumn, he wrote to Elliston: 'How do you do? Where are all my women? Tell Newman to get some good brandy against the fifteenth of January—to drink damnation to whores and Aldermen.'

CHAPTER EIGHT

COX AND CANT

As events turned out, it was on Monday, 17 January 1825 that the case was heard before the Lord Chief Justice, in the Court of King's Bench, at the Guildhall. Thomas Denman, the Common Serjeant, appeared for the plaintiff and James Scarlett was counsel for the defendant. The public gallery was crowded.

In his opening address to the jury, Denman said that it was his painful duty to bring before their attention the circumstances of that inquiry for which the plaintiff sought redress at their hands, and when he had done so, and established those facts in evidence, he was sure they would be of the opinion that of all the cases of this nature of which they had ever heard, varying as they did infinitely in their degree and characters, this was one most destitute of excuse and most aggravated by the violation of long and steady friendship.

He went on to narrate how this friendship had grown up between the Kean family and the Cox family. He said that during the whole of that period the plaintiff continued to entertain the same confidence in the honour of his friend, and to treat his wife with the same indulgent and tender consideration which had attended their intercourse in earlier years. If the jury were acquainted with the plaintiff, they would know that a man of more frank and unsuspecting disposition, a man of kinder or more generous heart, a man of more open or cordial manners did not live; or a man who, from his very virtues, was more liable to make the victim of treachery like that which had destroyed his comfort for ever.

He told how Cox had discovered the letters last March. He said that he would select a few, which would show at once the criminality of the parties and the care with which this was concealed from the knowledge of the husband. He then read extracts from the beginning of the correspondence in April 1820 down to 22 January of the previous year, when Kean had expressed his readiness to receive Charlotte. He quoted: 'All I ask is, that for a few months you will hide yourself, that when the hue and cry is raised, they shall find nothing to criminate me: "If the goods are not found upon the thief, there can be no conviction".' (Great laughter in which the Lord Chief Justice joined.) But the stolen goods were found on him. (Renewed laughter.) Up to this period, the plaintiff, living in affectionate harmony with his wife, was utterly blinded to her frailty. He had no sense of 'those stolen hours of lust' by which he had been dishonoured. (The quotation from *Othello* was considered a nice touch by those present.)

He had to tell the jury that not only had the plaintiff been hood-winked by the letters already read, but that a yet meaner and baser scheme had been formed and executed to perpetuate that delusion. He referred to two letters written in January 1823—one to Mrs. Cox and the other to her husband—by reading which he should unmask a scene of treachery and of cruelty unexampled, perhaps, in cases of this nature, and lay bare as gross a conspiracy as ever was entered into by a wife and friend to deceive and dishonour a husband.

He then read the two letters written by Kean after the incident at Salisbury, when Cox had challenged him to a duel. He first read the letter to Mrs. Cox, in which Kean told her he had written to her husband that day and that she must appear to countenance the letter and let Cox think that they were never to meet again and that in so doing he had lost a friend. He next read the letter to Cox, in which a seemingly outraged Kean protested his innocence and begged leave to withdraw a friendship rendered unworthy by suspicion. He quoted: 'I must be the worst of villains if I could take that man by the hand, while meditating towards him an act of injustice. You do not know me, Cox: mine are follies, not vices. It has been my text to do all the good I could in the world, and when I am called to a superior bourne, my memory may be blamed, but not despised.'

And this (he told the jury) was the letter Mrs. Cox was to

countenance. He asked them if it were possible, after receiving such a letter, for the plaintiff to suspect that a human being to whom he had been a friend and benefactor was living in habitual adultery with his wife? But he saw that no comment of his was necessary, that the jury had perceived the artifices to which the defendant had resorted, and that they felt justly indignant at such great, such almost unexampled treachery. He was sure that they would feel it was right to manifest their opinion that no imputation rested on the plaintiff, already afflicted with so great and so unmerited a misfortune, and that they would deem it a betrayal of their duty to him and to the public, to withhold from him the amplest compensation which he had demanded.

He then called witnesses to prove that Cox and his wife had been happily married. After the last of these had taken the stand, a selection of Kean's letters was read aloud. The reading was punctuated by shouts of laughter from the public gallery. A particular source of merriment was Kean's frequent references in the letter to 'Little Breeches', a sobriquet he had given Charlotte following a tender episode in his dressing-room, when she had stripped off her clothes and pulled on the short trunks he wore as Richard III. When the letters had been read, there was a short recess, during which the noise in the gallery increased. The place was over-crowded and fights broke out as the struggle for seats continued. At the judge's return, the noise lessened.

James Scarlett, counsel for the defendant, now addressed the jury. He said that Kean's letter to Cox after the Salisbury incident had been that of an honourable man. He would venture to say of any man—he cared not who he might be, if he did not know him previously to be a poltroon and a villain—that if he had been carrying on an intrigue with the wife, and the husband were to reproach him with it, he would boldly and unhesitatingly deny it. If a man was in possession of a woman's honour, he would meet and deserve the contempt of mankind, if, on the husband's charging him with the facts, he should go down humbly before him, and say, 'True it is, I have been in bed with your wife and have debauched her and dishonoured you.' Even if a husband challenged him to a duel, he ought, if possible, to avoid a challenge upon that score and not to fight until he had found every method of persuasion utterly impracticable.

Would he confess his criminality? Certainly not, Scarlett continued. He would make protestations of his own innocence and of the innocence of the lady, which, though they might tell against him when read in a court of justice, no man with the smallest sense of honour would scruple to make when they were calculated to prevent a duel with her husband about her reputation, or the immediate ruin of the woman, who had given up everything to him in the tenderness of love. He called upon them to consider again and again the cruel use his friend had made of the letter which his client had written, blaming him because he had protested to her husband that Mrs. Cox's conduct was unimpeachable. Would it have mended Mr. Kean's case if he had acknowledged to the plaintiff that he had violated his bed and slept with his wife? He must, however, either have done that, or have made such protestations as he did regarding the purity of Mrs. Cox's conduct; and yet this letter was produced to inflict a deep and lasting injury upon the defendant, as if any man could have advised him, under such circumstances, not to pursue such a line of conduct.

Scarlett's defence now followed the line most used in cases of this kind. In the awarding of damages, much depended on the character of the woman and the degree to which her husband had watched over her. If the evidence showed that the wife was immoral and that the husband had done little to guard her against temptation, then it would follow that the husband had suffered little from the loss of her affection and, the damages, if any, would be assessed accordingly. So Scarlett referred to the Croydon incident, when Cox had left his wife in Kean's care for a day and a night. He said that it was odd enough that a man should trust to any other person the care of a wife who was ten or twelve years younger than himself, and who had still all the strength of a summer shoot about her—that shoot which it was admitted was the strongest of all and the most difficult either to control or eradicate. It was still more odd that after determining to entrust her to another, he should select as the person for that trust an insinuating and distinguished actor. If he (Mr. Scarlett) had been consulted on such occasion, he should have advised Mr. Cox not to have selected a clever actor for the guardian of his wife's honour. There was no set of men who were more calculated by their skill in displaying the workings of the passions and in assuming tenderness even when they did not feel it, to produce a powerful effect upon a female bosom. God forbid that he should say that such was the aim of all distinguished actors—he knew that it was not; but still, to a husband jealous of his own honour and his wife's reputation, they must always remain objects of suspicion.

He also suggested that Mrs. Cox had made the first approaches to Kean, that a man in Kean's position would never have had the audacity to make any overtures to her unless he had been previously assured that they would be well received. Therefore, the placing of Mrs. Cox under the care of Mr. Kean was evidence, if not of collusion on the part of the plaintiff, at least of folly. He would prove that Cox had taken his wife to Kean's dressing-room frequently, not only when Kean was dressed but also when he was dressing and half undressed, that this intimacy had continued after Mrs. Kean broke off relations with them. He would prove that there had been at least two other men in Mrs. Cox's life since her marriage and that Cox knew of them.

He drew the attention of the jury to Cox's behaviour after he had learnt from his son that his wife was with Kean in Birmingham. Did the plaintiff put his wife away? Oh no! She was received again into his house. After the explosion at Salisbury, did the plaintiff become more cautious as to the conduct of his wife? No such thing! What would the jury think if he were to prove that the plaintiff and his wife had been seen together, very lovingly, arm in arm, since the commencement of this action; that they were doing this at the time the planitiff was bringing *two* actions for criminal conversation with his wife—one against Kean and the other against his ex-employee, Whatmore. If this were true, then it would destroy all claim of the plaintiff to a verdict.

He would prove that the plaintiff was either in collusion with his wife and had selected the defendant as his victim, because he was able to pay heavy damages, or that he was so negligent that he cared not what she did, or that he and she were colluding together to obtain a divorce, in order that she might live with Whatmore. He said that the plaintiff was seeking damages of £2,000, but he trusted that the question would not be about giving £200 or 200 shillings, but about giving two pence. If the verdict should be for the plaintiff, no damages could be too small, but he trusted that through the evidence he would call, he would oblige them to give a verdict for the defendant, for it was clear law that the husband was not entitled to a verdict when he was the handmaid to his own disgrace.

The first witness called by the defence was Newman, Kean's dresser at Drury Lane, who said that Cox and his wife had often been in the dressing-room while Kean was dressing; that he had seen them there several times when Kean had nothing on but a thin pair of silk drawers, which fitted to him as tight as his skin; that Kean sometimes stripped himself entirely naked to dress and that Mrs. Cox often came to the dressing-room alone. The next witness, John Stuart, a box attendant at Drury Lane, recalled a night, in 1823, when Cox had come to the theatre alone. He asked him if any other persons would be joining him in the box and he said Mrs. Cox, who was then with Mr. Kean in his dressing-room.

Anne Wickstead took the stand and was asked about the Birmingham incident. She said that, on her return home, Cox had never asked her where she had been. She recalled the row between Cox and Kean at Salisbury and the time Cox had left Mrs. Cox and herself in Kean's charge at Croydon. She was questioned about the visits of Sir Robert Wemyss, twelve years previously, when the family lived in Dorsetshire. She agreed that this friendship had been broken off by Mr. Cox because of the attentions Sir Robert paid to Mrs. Cox. She did not know whether Mr. Cox, on returning unexpectedly to the house, had discovered Sir Robert in a closet in his wife's bedroom. She had known Colonel Pearson, who had often visited the house, but was now abroad.

Daniel Henley, a doorman at Drury Lane, said that he had seen Mr. and Mrs. Cox at the beginning of the previous June, in St. Martin's Lane, two months after Cox had started legal proceedings against Kean. Under cross-examination he admitted that he could not tell whether she was brown or fair, because she had a veil on.

In his summing up, the Lord Chief Justice said that the first question to be considered was whether the letters produced in court had really been written by the defendant to Mrs. Cox; if they had been so written, then came the second question—as to which there could perhaps be very little doubt—had the adultery, or had it not, been committed prior to the month of April 1824? For the defendant, several justifications were set up. First, it was said that the plaintiff had connived at his own dishonour, and if that were the case, he could not be entitled to the verdict. Secondly, it had been contended that Mrs. Cox had committed adultery with other persons prior to her intimacy with Kean; that fact, if there were the means of proving it, was one which would go materially to mitigate the damages. Thirdly, it was urged that the plaintiff had not exercised a reasonable caution in the control of his wife, but had exposed her needlessly rather to temptation, and this plea, which would also be material as regarded the question of damages, was perhaps the only one also which would be very important for the consideration of the jury. For the assertion that the plaintiff had connived at his wife's conduct, all the evidence was strongly opposed to it. The letters after the affair at Salisbury made such a supposition almost impossible.

He said that upon the want of caution implied to the plaintiff, a great deal more, certainly, might fairly be maintained. He instanced Kean's access to Cox's house at all hours of the day and night, and the visits of Cox and his wife to Kean's dressing-room. He found it extraordinary that the plaintiff had continued the intimacy with Kean after the Birmingham and Salisbury incidents. The third ground on which it was contended that the plaintiff had little claim to damages, was that from the notoriety of his wife's ill character he had sustained little disadvantage in losing her. The evidence upon that point was very slight. As for the alleged intimacy with Whatmore, he was inclined to lay very little stress upon this, as it had not occurred until after the adultery with the defendant. As to the evidence of Daniel Henley, the doorman, that he had seen the plaintiff and his wife together in June last, it would be for the jury to consider whether the witness might not have been mistaken. Finally, if the jury believed the plaintiff to have been cognisant of his wife's intimacy, he would not be entitled to a verdict. If they thought that no such connivance was made out, then a verdict must pass against the defendant; and the amount of damages, under the facts of the case, it was their province to decide.

After consulting for only ten minutes, the jury returned a verdict for the plaintiff, with damages of £800. While this was £1,200 short of the £2,000 demanded, it was by no means the derisory amount called for by the defence. The jury had shown that although they did not consider Cox to be entirely blameless, they believed Kean to be very guilty. The verdict had gone against him and it was greeted with cheers by the spectators.

Society had waited a long time to punish Kean for his arrogance and immorality. All the resentment that had built up against him was now unleashed in a fury of moral outrage. The powerful *Times* fired the first shot in the campaign that was mounted against him. On the day following the verdict, almost the entire newspaper was given over to a report of the trial, while a leading article stated: 'The public may take his own character as he gives it himself, in the letter dated January 6, 1823, and addressed to Cox, the husband. In that letter, written with the express view to deceive the husband, he says that he should be "the worst of villains" if he "could take that man by the hand", while meditating "towards him an act of injustice"—were he capable of the crime which in truth he was committing all the while. The woman herself was one well worthy of being protected by such a man and by such arts. Some of Kean's letters to her are of so filthy a description that we cannot insert them. Yet have the managers of Drury Lane Theatre the effrontery to present, or to attempt presenting, such a creature as this to the gaze of a British audience, on Monday next. It is of little consequence to the nation whether the character of King Richard or Othello be well or ill acted; but it is of importance that public feeling be not shocked, and public decency be not outraged.'

Most newspapers followed the lead of *The Times*, but the *Morning Chronicle* and the *Examiner* did not. They believed that as Kean had been punished already in a court of justice, the public ought not to punish him further. *The Times* would have none of this. On Friday, 21 January, a leading article stated: 'Mr. Kean is not merely an adulterer, but he is an adulterer anxious to show himself before the public with all the disgrace of a verdict of guilty about his neck, because that very disgrace is calculated to excite the sympathies of the profligate, and to fill the theatre with all that numerous class of morbidly curious idlers who flock to a play or an execution to see how a man looks when he is hanged, or deserves to be hanged. If we had seen no intimation of Mr. Kean's immediate appearance on the stage, we should have made no remark on his private conduct; but when we see the very day se'n night on which he is convicted of adultery, chosen as his first appearance after a long absence—when every person who can read knows that his offence is aggravated by the most shocking circumstances of indecency, brutality, obscenity, perfidy, and hypocrisy—we do say that the public, who have become legally and inevitably acquainted with the conduct of such a man, ought not to be insulted by his immediate obtrusion before them as a candidate for their applause. Let him hide himself for a reasonable time: his immediate appearance is as great an outrage to decency, as if he were to walk naked through the streets at midday.'

The outcry against Kean made the government fear that his appearance at Drury Lane, in three days' time, might lead to a public riot and so Sir Robert Peel, the Secretary of State, sent Sir Richard Birnie to suggest to Elliston that an appearance so soon after the trial was both ill-judged and indelicate. Elliston promised Sir Richard that he would talk the matter over with Kean. Since the trial, Kean had been staying at the Greyhound Inn, at Croydon, and, on Saturday, Elliston found him there, sitting on a couch with a cigar in his mouth and a glass of brandy in his hand, while a prostitute sang to him and an itinerant tumbler vaulted over chairs and tables for his amusement. Elliston proposed a postponement, but Kean would not listen. He had no idea of the strength of public opinion being whipped up against him by *The Times* and other newspapers. He believed that his private affairs were his own concern and that on stage the public would still acknowledge him for what he was, the greatest tragic genius of the age. He told Elliston that, on Monday, he would meet his enemies on that ground, which, by the assent of all England, was his own. 'In the meantime,' he said, 'observe how quietly I am living here.'

He had intended staying at Croydon until the Monday, but later that night he changed his mind and returned to London. Despite his brave words to Elliston, he was apprehensive about his appearance at Drury Lane and he needed the companionship of the taverns to help him through the next two days. He was drunk until Monday morning, when he arrived at the theatre and proceeded to get drunk again, 'having had,' Winston noted, 'Mrs. Bunn in his room at ½ past 11 with Golly and others of the same class.'

That night, the pit and galleries of Drury Lane were filled not with an audience, but with a howling mass of combatants for and against Kean. It was being said that Elliston had bribed people to support his actor, and *The Times* was quick to spread this rumour. 'We had heard,' the newspaper stated, 'and truly the scene did not belie the report, that a great effort would be made to fill the pit and galleries with those who, for a pint of porter, would applaud the worst, or abuse the best, man in society.' This was less than fair, for Kean's supporters were to be found not only among this riff-raff but also among the occupants of the dress circle and boxes. These, however, did not shout their support, but viewed the scene in astonished silence.

The noise was deafening, but this was nothing to the pandemonium when the curtain rose and Kean made his first entrance. The play was *Richard III* and when he came forward to speak his famous opening soliloquy, not a word of it could be heard. The clamour continued throughout his entire performance. He seemed calm enough, but backstage it was obvious that he was struggling to keep a hold on himself. He had many friends among the audience and, at the end of the play, there were more cheers than boos.

This successful outcome for Kean angered *The Times*, which

stated: 'Let not Mr. Kean imagine that he has achieved a victory over public opinion—let him not suppose that the waving of sundry dirty pocket-handkerchiefs, or the throwing up of various greasy hats, has secured to him the battle. If he fancy this, he is wholly mistaken. . . . Let him try the matter and he will have a more terrible fall than he had on Monday week . . . Mr. Kean, we understand, will perform again on Friday next. It must be highly gratifying to him to go through his character as he did last night (and assuredly, such, should he appear, will be the case), without conveying to the audience one syllable of his author. Can any man of genius submit to this? Obstinacy may endure such a situation—genius never will.'

Such vindictive statements were nothing less than an incitement to riot and, unfortunately for Kean, there were other forces working against him. During that week and for many weeks afterwards, a crop of smutty ballads, pamphlets and broadsides concerning Kean and Charlotte found a ready sale in the streets of London. These included reports of the trial, with 'all the love letters'. One pamphlet entitled *Secrets Worth Knowing* claimed to contain 'the suppressed letters'. There were collections of songs such as *Cocks and Cuckledom* and broadsides such as *The Cock of Drury Lane.*

Many respectable people found all this distasteful and *The Times* did all it could to alienate them completely from Kean. On Friday, 28 January, the day of his second appearance, the newspaper stated: 'That obscene little personage (Mr. Kean) is, we see, announced to make another appearance this evening. The ladies from the lobby and the "Wolves" from the Coal-Hole, have undertaken to hear him triumphantly through his ordeal, and he—fit head for such a band—once more ventures to brave the indignation of the respectable and decent part of society. . . . His real friends and supporters, who have hitherto upheld him, because they thought his frailties over-balanced by his talents, must now desert him, when they see him dead even to the lowest degree of shame which distinguishes human from animal nature. We suspect he will scarcely find adequate consolation among his "Wolves" and—we need not add the alliterative adjunct.'

Many decent theatregoers stayed away from Drury Lane that night, in fear of the roughhouse that *The Times* was so confidently predicting. As a result, the theatre was by no means so full as it had been on the previous Monday. The pit was crowded, but only a few people were scattered throughout the rest of the theatre, and these took little part in the dispute. The great scene of contention was the pit. This was filled with the scum of London: prostitutes and their pimps, brothel-keepers, prizefighters, cutthroats and thieves, all drawn to Drury Lane by the prospect of a fight. Some of them were subjects of Kean's tavern kingdom, who had come to show their loyalty to him. It was widely believed that he himself had drummed up their support, but, whether or not this was true, their presence at Drury Lane disgusted respectable theatregoers and lost him a lot of sympathy.

The play was *Othello*, and the appearance of Kean on the stage was the signal for an uproar, which was to last until the end of the play. Not even the imploring looks of Mrs. West, who played Desdemona, could quieten the mob. Whenever Kean, as Othello, touched her, they roared with delight, but when he held her passionately, they screamed, as if in triumph. In the words of *The Times*, 'It was like the yell of Caliban when the prospect of violating Miranda occurred to his lascivious mind.' During the bedroom scene, they shouted obscenities, with many allusions to the recent trial. 'Little Breeches', his sobriquet for Charlotte, had particularly caught the public fancy. No one tried to stop the din. His low friends had come not to get him a hearing, but to shout and fight for him. They made as much noise as his opponents. One of the most vociferous in his defence was a fat prostitute, who clapped and cried 'Bravo!' most emphatically throughout the play. All this happened in the pit, of all places, where Hazlitt, Byron, Leigh Hunt, Crabb Robinson, Tom Moore and other men of taste used to crowd, almost afraid to breathe, for fear they might miss the slightest nuance of his voice and expression.

When the curtain fell, the mob shouted for the manager and Elliston, magnificently drunk, made his way to the front of the stage. After he had bowed obsequiously to them for several minutes, they quietened down.

'Ladies and Gentlemen,' he said, 'You honour me by your silence. I entreat you to attend to me for a few moments; and if any word fall from me which may appear improper, I trust you will attribute it to the agitation under which I labour. (Applause) I stand before you as the servant of the public; I come forward as a peacemaker, and I hope what I shall say will not lower Mr. Kean or myself in your estimation. The engagement which Mr. Kean is now endeavouring to fulfil was made in July last. At that time it was not expected that the question which now agitates the public mind would have undergone any discussion. The engagement was for a period of twenty nights, at fifty pounds a night, to commence on the sixteenth of January and end on the sixteenth of March. The present moment is one of too much interest to me to suffer me to quibble or to go nigh a falsehood. I give you my word as a man —as the manager of this theatre—and, as I trust, you have always found me, as an honourable gentleman, (Loud laughter) that I have stated nothing but the truth.

'I could not break this engagement. (Why not?) Why not? Because Mr. Kean was advertised to appear before you. Could I, Ladies and Gentlemen, withdraw Mr. Kean's name under these circumstances? (Applause and disapproval) If I had done so, I should have made a party against Mr. Kean, and that I will never do . . . I can assure you Ladies and Gentlemen, that the best feelings have always subsisted between Mr. Kean and myself. I have assisted him and he has assisted me. . . . One word more, and I have done. I can assure you, Ladies and Gentlemen, that I have not endeavoured directly or indirectly, by any influence or power I possess, to procure your judgment in favour of Mr. Kean. I have literally suspended the free list—the public press excepted; and I defy any man to say that I have introduced persons into the house for the purpose of influencing your decision. (Applause) Ladies and Gentlemen, Mr. Kean is in the house and if you will have the condescension to hear him, I hope everything may yet be amicably arranged.'

Elliston then left the stage to fetch Kean and found him occupied with a prostitute. The actor told Elliston that he had no intention of apologising to the audience. It took the manager a quarter of an hour to persuade him at least to speak to them. Meanwhile, the mob was bellowing impatiently. When Elliston came onstage, leading Kean by the hand, the uproar increased and the actor had difficulty in making himself heard.

'Ladies and Gentlemen', he said, 'If you expect a vindication of my own private conduct, I am certainly unable to satisfy you. (Applause and disapproval) I stand before you as the representative of Shakespeare's heroes. (Uproar) The errors I have committed have been scanned before a public tribunal; and (here the noise was so deafening that the rest of the sentence was lost). On the occasion, Ladies and Gentlemen, to which I have alluded, I have withheld circumstances from delicacy. (Laughter) If, Ladies and Gentlemen, I have withheld circumstances from motives of delicacy (More laughter) it was from regard to the feelings of others—not of myself. (Applause mingled with boos) It appears at this moment that I am a professional victim. (Laughter) If this is the work of a hostile press, I shall endeavour with firmness to withstand it; but if it proceeds from your verdict and decision, I will at once bow to it, and shall retire with deep regret, and with a grateful sense of all the favours which your patronage has hitherto conferred on me.' He was then led off by Elliston to a mixture of cheers and boos.

Many people were now of the opinion that Kean had been punished enough, and here the matter might have rested, but *The Times* was not yet done with him. The day following *Othello*, the newspaper stated that Kean, in his speech, had endeavoured 'to excite a feeling in his favour by declaring that he had withheld circumstances out of *delicacy* (hear it, ye Gods!) to the feelings of others. We do not believe it.' In another column, a leading article commented on the absence of respectable women at the performance: 'It is gratifying to remark that scarcely one woman, except of the lowest description, was present at the riot of last night. We do not believe that there was a single creature in female attire in the dress boxes.' It went on to sympathise, in the name of 'female purity', with the actresses who played opposite Kean: 'We ask Elliston . . . what women, who are they, and from whence do they come—what women, we again say, are THEY, whom

Elliston WILL bring forward on the stage, to be fawned on and caressed by this obscene mimic?—one, perhaps, as his daughter, another as his sister, another as his wife, and even, in *Douglas*, one as his mother? Is it not shocking that women should be forced to undergo this process with such a creature, for the sake of bread, before an assembled people?'

Other journals, tired of *The Times*' role as the arbiter of morals, were quick to point out that the editor, Thomas Barnes, was himself living openly with another man's wife, but *The Times*, for reasons best known to Barnes, continued to make war on Kean. On Monday, 31 January, three days after *Othello*, Kean appeared as Sir Giles Overreach in *A New Way to Pay Old Debts*. According to *The Times*, a gang of cut-throats and thieves had been organised the previous Saturday to support him. Whether or not this was true, the pit and boxes were crowded with an unsavoury mob from the slums of London. The rest of the theatre was half-empty, for again many regular theatregoers had stayed away to avoid trouble. The curtain rose to a tumult, which reached deafening proportions whenever Kean appeared on the stage. There were cries of 'Off, off', 'Kean for ever', 'Turn him out'. They screamed obscenities and encouragement at him. The prostitutes, who were numerous, cried louder than most. Abraham Belasco, the Jewish prizefighter, was active in support of Kean, hitting out at anyone who opposed the actor.

When Kean came onstage with Miss Smithson, who played the part of his daughter, Margaret, the commotion was terrible. He pointed to her, as if to ask if this were fit treatment for a woman. This drew applause from the respectable sections of the audience. Parts of the second and third acts were audible and some points of the text were seized on by his enemies. When Overreach said to Margaret, 'You will have marriage first and lawful pleasure afterwards. What more can you desire?' they shouted ribald suggestions. When Marrall observed to Overreach, 'I have a conscience not seared up like yours,' they applauded vigorously. When, the negotiations for Margaret's marriage with Lord Lovell concluded, Overreach exclaimed, 'Now all's cock-sure!' they collapsed with laughter. The third act concluded with the words,

'What men report I weigh not.' Kean delivered this line in a defiant voice, which carried clearly above the noise.

On this occasion, his supporters outnumbered his opponents and when the curtain fell, there was a general call for him to come back onstage. At length, he appeared and addressed them, saying: 'I have made as much concession to an English audience as an English actor ought. I hope for the honour of my country—as after twenty nights I shall leave you for ever. (Cries of "No!")—I hope for the honour of my country that news of this persecution may never reach foreign annals.' He then bowed and left the stage.

The following morning, *The Times* gave an alarming account of the riot at Drury Lane and, in a leading article, advised people in poor health to stay away from the theatre whenever Kean played. 'So long as the contest continues,' the newspaper stated, 'we would, from motives of humanity, advise the feeble to stay away from the theatre, as the boxes last night, from top to bottom, were filled with a set of ruffians of the most ferocious aspect and character.' As a result, there were fewer people than ever at Drury Lane, three nights later, when Kean appeared as Macbeth. Most of the audience were in the pit, but not even this was crowded. Nor was the opposition so violent as it had been. Public opinion was turning in his favour and some of the regular theatregoers had banded together to show their support. Placards were raised in the second circle of boxes and in the two shilling gallery. These read: 'One of the dearest rights of Englishmen is not to be tried twice for the same offence'; 'What Kean wrote, the newspapers published. Which is worse?'; 'Let not animosity reign in the bosom of Englishmen'.

Much of the play was inaudible because of the din, but some of it could be heard and lines were seized on, this time by Kean's supporters. When Macbeth said, 'I have lost all taste of fear,' and again, when during his fight with Macduff, he cried, 'I will not yield,' he was loudly cheered. At the end of the play, the audience shouted for him, but he did not appear. They continued to shout through the ballet and the pantomime, but he had already left the theatre.

If such a battle could have a victor, Kean had won. On Monday, 7 February, *The Times* published its last comment on what the editor termed 'this offensive subject'. This took the form of an explanation to those, who either from 'stupidity or malignancy' persisted in 'misrepresenting the motives of our conduct respecting Kean'. The newspaper stated that it would never impugn the private character of any individual, either on or off the stage, but their opposition to Kean had proceeded on the ground that it was 'a monstrous insult to decency' for him to appear so soon after the trial. With this explanation, *The Times* ended its campaign against Kean. From this time on, it was to review his performances quite dispassionately. So Kean had won. His pride in his position as the leading English actor had not allowed him to run away; he had stayed his ground and fought. From the stage of Drury Lane, he had confronted his enemies with dignity and had eventually confounded them.

He played to peaceable houses for the rest of his twenty nights. The rowdies stayed away and the regular theatregoers came back. This was as much a relief for Elliston as it was for Kean. While the manager might have endured nightly riots with capacity receipts, he found little profit in empty benches. Elliston had stood by Kean, because there was nothing else he could do; they were tied together by a bond neither of them could break, for Elliston, believing that it would be to the disadvantage of Drury Lane if Kean were found guilty, had arranged for the theatre staff to give perjured evidence on his behalf.

The strain was now beginning to tell on him; his delusions and mental lapses had become more frequent. On Tuesday, 22 February, he was petrified, when Daniel Henley, the theatre doorman, who had given evidence at the trial, was arrested for perjury. He feared that it would soon be the turn of Newman, the dresser, and Stuart, the box attendant. He wondered how long it would be before he himself was arrested. The thought terrified him, for he was well aware that being arrested for debt was one thing, but being arrested for attempting to pervert the course of justice was quite another. Kean, too, had the same fear, but he hoped that, if the worst happened, he would not have to share a prison cell with this maniac of a manager.

In Winston's opinion, it was impossible to tell which was the madder of the two—Elliston was tottering towards a complete breakdown, but Kean himself seemed barely sane. On Thursday, 10 March, after the play, he took it into his head to walk the twelve miles to Croydon. He started off, but after four miles put up at a waggoner's public house at Brixton, where he stayed that night and all the next day. On Wednesday of the following week, at three o'clock in the morning, he ordered a hackney coach, took a lighted candle and was driven off. He was not heard of until noon on the Thursday, when he was found in his dressing-room, fast asleep, wrapped in a large green coat. They let him sleep until six o'clock, when they woke him and dressed him for the play. He acted, but was still not sober. Winston was praying for the twenty nights to end, when Kean would leave Drury Lane for ever, but to his despair Elliston and Kean signed yet another contract. In this, Kean agreed to play fifteen nights in June and July, the roles, as in his previous contract, to be chosen by himself.

On 26 March, Kean closed his twenty nights with *Othello*. At the end of the play, the audience called for him. He came onstage drained of all energy, not only by his performance but also by the three whores with whom he had spent the intervals between acts. He was befuddled with drink and could hardly speak. He said that he had overcome 'one of the most powerful and malignant attacks to which a professional man has ever been subjected'. He spoke, with gratitude, of the manner in which Elliston had stood by him: 'The manager has acted towards me in the hour of adversity with the affectionate kindness of a father, a brother, and a friend.' Elliston came onstage and they embraced to the cheers of the audience.

This triumph did not mark the end of Kean's agony; the greater part of his suffering was about to begin. In April, he set off on a provincial tour and, wherever he went, met with a hostile reception. As in London, respectable people stayed away and the theatres were given over to a mob. All his great moments onstage were ignored in the uproar: Hamlet's parting from Ophelia; the death of Richard III; the raging of Shylock; the terror of Macbeth; Othello's Farewell. The words of Shakespeare were turned against him in allusions to Charlotte and himself. This nightly laceration of his art was a terrible punishment; even anaesthetised by drink, he felt the pain. Under the continuing hostility, his mind seemed to crack and all the dignity with which he had met his opponents at Drury Lane deserted him. He harangued the audience on his private affairs and turned somersaults, saying, 'I may as well practise, as I suppose I must come back to this.' After this tour, he was never to be the same man again. Grattan wrote: 'Kean sank under his punishment before its rigour was reversed; and I am convinced that he never recovered from the tumult of suffering which then assailed him.'

In June, he was back in London to fulfill his contract for fifteen performances at Drury Lane and now he had to face the greatest consequence of all. There was no hostility towards him, only coldness. His private character had become inextricably entangled with his portrayal of the great tragic heroes. From this time on, audiences would never see him as Richard, Macbeth or Othello without remembering that the character onstage was Kean the adulterer, the little bantam cock of Drury Lane. This tempered their appreciation and modified their applause. He could no longer carry them with him, for they were unwilling to suspend their judgement on him as a man. He had told them that he stood before them as 'the representative of Shakespeare's heroes', but they would not accept him as this. He had become a curiosity. To Kean, the artist, this was death. No longer did he '*dare* so much', for where he had been assured, he was now apprehensive. When confidence is lost, what remains? '*Othello's occupation's gone.*'

Mary had deserted him. While she had condoned his adultery, she had not expected the public disgrace the trial had brought. This had been too much for her. She had stayed in Scotland during the trial and remained there for the spring and summer, leaving him to face his agony alone. She could not stand with him against what she believed to be the justified wrath of an outraged society. She kept Charles with her and let Kean know that they wanted nothing more to do with him. The house in Clarges

Street was closed and the servants dismissed. She was filled with self-pity for the loss of her social life. When the frenzy against him was at its height, she wailed publicly about how badly he had treated her. Her complaint that she had caught venereal disease from him found its way into the newspapers.

The alienation of his wife and son was a hard blow for Kean. However badly he had behaved, their welfare had always been one of his chief motives in life. Throughout his affair with Charlotte, he had done his best to protect their interests. He wondered if Mary had ever really appreciated this; if, indeed, she had any understanding of him at all. He had given her a fine house, a carriage, servants, the company of those she considered to be her betters, and it seemed as if this was all she had ever wanted from him; this and the pleasure of going shopping with her sister, happy in the knowledge that she had sufficient money in her purse to buy anything she fancied. During all his troubles, she had been concerned only for herself; she had not given a thought to the hell he was enduring. After seventeen years of marriage, their life together was reduced to this: her gentility invincible to the end, she was terrified that he had given her a dose of the clap.

He wanted nothing more to do with her. Through his solicitor, Henry Sigell, he made her an allowance of £504 a year, out of which she was to keep Charles at Eton. He also instructed Sigell to inform her that he was in excellent health, quite free from venereal disease. This was a bitter joke and, as he intended, nothing could have hurt her more than the implication that if she had venereal disease, she must have caught it from someone other than himself.

There was nothing to keep him in England, and he pressed ahead with his plans to visit America. He was leaving Drury Lane in its worst financial position since the days of Sheridan. Although he was partly to blame for the theatre's misfortunes, the chief responsibility rested, with difficulty, on the shrugging shoulders of Elliston. Over the past months, the manager had become more extravagant than ever. On 8 April, his fifty-first birthday, he had given his two daughters bracelets costing ninety guineas each, even though there was barely enough money to pay the salaries of the company. By the summer, he had lost all sense of reality. He could not leave his house without being arrested for debt, yet he continued to make grandiose plans for Drury Lane. On Friday, 15 July, Kean, of all people, had him arrested for owing him five nights' salary totalling £250.

The situation was too much even for Elliston; he suffered a stroke. On Friday, 5 August, when Winston called on him, he found him 'in a state of imbecility—melancholy to look at— shocking to contemplate. Thus, in a few weeks, we find a man full of health by now dwindled at the age of fifty-one into a decrepit old man.' He could not sign the papers Winston had brought him, for he had lost the use of his hands.

Next day, in the midst of all these difficulties, Kean came to Drury Lane, at ten o'clock in the morning, accompanied by two prostitutes. He was with them until one o'clock, when Winston and Dunn sent word that the women must leave the theatre. The prostitutes left, but Kean was in a rage, shouting that the town called him a great blackguard and that he gloried in being one.

In September, a few days before Kean left for America, Grattan called on him. 'I never saw a man so changed' he wrote, 'he had all the air of desperation about him. He looked bloated with rage and brandy; his nose was red, his cheeks blotched, his eyes bloodshot; I really pitied him. He had lodgings in Regent Street; but I believe very few of his former friends, of any respectability, now noticed him. The day I saw him, he sat down to the piano, notwithstanding the agitated state of his mind, and sang for me "Lord Ullin's daughter" with a depth and power, and sweetness that quite electrified me. I had not heard him sing for many years; his improvement was almost incredible; his accompaniment was also far superior to his former style of playing. I could not repress a deep sentiment of sorrow at the wreck he presented of genius, fame and wealth. At this period I believe he had not one hundred pounds left of the many thousands he had received. His mind seemed shattered; he was an outcast on the world. He left England a few days afterwards, and I never dreamt of seeing him again.'

Kean went to America with vague plans of settling there, as it did not seem likely that he would ever fully re-establish himself in England. He had little money left and he recalled the £1,000 a month he had sent home during his previous visit. He hoped for a peaceful reception from the American public; he believed that their anger with him over the Boston incident had died away. He was unaware that they had followed the Cox scandal as closely as the British and that the infamous letter to Cox had caused as much revulsion. There was indignation that he was coming to America to escape the moral censure of his own country, as though American morality were more permissive. The New York press advised people to stay away from his performances and promised that they themselves would not comment on them. Coleman of the *Evening Post* was among the editors who had turned against him, but Noah, of the *National Advocate*, still supported him.

Beneath this public outcry, however, the majority of American theatregoers had the sense to separate the private life of the artist from his art. For them, Kean was the supreme tragedian, and they were not going to deny themselves the pleasure of seeing him. Stephen Price, of the Park Theatre, had realised this when he had agreed to Kean's plan for visiting America, but the manager of the other theatres on his star circuit, especially the Boston Theatre, were not so certain; before making a firm booking, they preferred to wait until they had seen how Kean was received in New York.

On 14 November, when Kean opened, as Richard III, at the Park Theatre, the great majority of the audience were for him. The *National Advocate* estimated that out of the two thousand people present not more than one hundred were against him. Unfortunately, his supporters made as much row as his enemies and the result was pandemonium. Scarcely a word of the play could be heard. At one point, an orange, thrown from the gallery, hit him in the chest. He picked it up, displayed it to the audience and then threw it contemptuously into the wings. But after the play, he was completely downcast. He had not yet judged the strength of opinion in his favour and it seemed that he must endure again all the torments he had hoped to leave behind. The following day, a statement from him appeared in the *National Advocate*:

With oppressed feelings, heart-rending to my friends, and triumphant to my enemies, I make an appeal to that country famed for hospitality to the stranger, and mercy to the conquered ... That I have committed an error, appears too evident from the all-decisive voice of the public; but surely it is but justice to the delinquent, (whatever may be his enormities,) to be allowed to make reparation where the offences were committed. My misunderstandings took place in Boston. To Boston I shall assuredly go, to apologize for my indiscretions.

I visit this country now, under different feelings and auspices than on a former occasion. Then I was an ambitious man, and the proud representative of Shakespeare's heroes. The spark of ambition is extinct; and I merely ask a shelter in which to close my professional and mortal career. I give the weapon into the hands of my enemies; if they are brave, they will not turn it against the defenceless.

This statement was received sympathetically. Many of those who had been present at Kean's opening performance were convinced that all his enemies there had come from Boston. This helped to swing New Yorkers behind Kean; they were not going to allow Boston to tell them how to behave. On 16 November, when Kean made his second appearance, the audience were overwhelmingly friendly and there were few interruptions. For the greater part, the play, *Othello*, was heard in complete silence. At the close, Kean made a speech, in which he promised that 'if Lethe's stream were permitted to flow over his former faults, there would be no cause of complaint for the future'. The remaining nine performances went well, especially his final appearance, on 2 December, when he played Lear. From New York, he went to Albany, where he played for six nights. He had not played there before and he found the audiences appreciative. From friendly Albany, he went to Boston.

The managers of the Boston Theatre, encouraged by Kean's favourable reception in New York, had decided to book him. On Monday evening, 19 December, it was announced from the stage of the theatre that Kean would appear for four nights, on Wednesday, Thursday, Friday and the following Monday. There was a mixed reaction from the audience, but it was thought that the majority approved. This test of public opinion, together with Kean's expected apology, led the managers to believe that they had made the right decision. On the Wednesday, Kean's apology appeared in the Boston newspapers:

Sir,—I take the liberty of informing the citizens of Boston, (through the medium of your journal,) of my arrival, in confidence that liberality and forbearance will gain the ascendancy over prejudice and cruelty. That I have suffered for my errors, my loss of fame and fortune is too melancholy an illustration. Acting from the impulse of irritation, I certainly was disrespectful to the Boston public; calm deliberation convinces me I was wrong. The first step towards the Throne of Mercy is confession—the hope we are taught, forgiveness. Man must not expect more than those attributes which we offer to God.

Some Bostonians were inclined to accept Kean's apology, but many treated it with anger and contempt, believing that it did not go far enough. The *Courier* regarded it as an additional insult and stated: ' "Acting from the impulse of irritation" he says, he "certainly was disrespectful to the Boston public." *Disrespectful*, indeed. Does he acknowledge so much? Was he not insolent, impertinent, arrogant, ungrateful?' Most newspapers advised people to show their resentment by keeping away from the theatre, but, during the day, the word was going round Boston that Kean would not be allowed to play and ugly scenes at the box office, on the previous day, when all the tickets had been sold, confirmed the suspicion that, whatever the merits of the apology, some people had already decided on trouble.

That night the theatre was crammed with men; there was not a single woman in the audience. Outside the theatre a great crowd had gathered. The audience were in uproar even before the performance had begun and when Mr. Finn, one of the managers, came onstage to announce that Kean would apologise personally, his voice could not be heard above the noise. Kean then appeared in his everyday clothes. The violence of the outcry against him rocked him on his feet and he was unable to say a word. There were cries of 'Off! Off!' He was assaulted with nuts, cakes, stink bombs and other missiles. There were some cries of 'Silence' and 'Hear Kean', but these were carried away in the fury against him, as he was pelted from the stage. Kilner, one of the actors, came onstage and announced, 'Mr. Kean wishes to make an apology— an humble apology from his heart and soul; but he will not do it at the risk of his life.' There were shouts of 'Off! Off!' and 'His hypocritical heart.' Kean came on again, but was shouted down and he retired to the green room, where he wept like a child.

A placard was then displayed on the stage, which read, 'Mr. Kean declines playing.' This was greeted with derisive laughter. A second placard asked the question, 'Shall the play go on without him?' The response to this was so equivocal that the management thought they might as well retain the receipts and the play began, but not a word could be heard in the continuing din. After the first act, Finn, who had taken the part of Richard III, announced that Kean had left the theatre. He was hoping that this would calm the audience, but it had the opposite effect. Deprived of their quarry, they became a frenzied mob. They tore up the seats, overturned the stoves, pulled down the lamps and broke the windows. The crowd outside, hearing the tumult within, stormed the doors. The few police officers present were helpless. With the exits jammed, there was danger of people being crushed to death and this, together with the fear that fire might break out at any moment, caused a total panic. The occupants of the pit made their escape over the stage, but those in the boxes and galleries were trapped. The windows of the theatre were twenty-five feet from the ground, but one gave out on to the roof of a tenement and many people escaped by this dangerous route.

The 'Boston riot' was to earn a notorious place in the history of the American theatre, but some of those present that night believed that the trouble could have been prevented at the outset by the prompt arrest of no more than a dozen rowdies. Those who had gone to oppose Kean had not anticipated such terrible consequences. They had gone merely to stop him acting, but the spirit of hatred generated had led to a savagery, which they afterwards shamefully realised, had nearly cost the lives of hundreds of people.

Kean had escaped into the house of a Mrs. Powell, which adjoined the theatre. From there, he was driven to Brighton, where he took the stage to Worcester and then went on to New York. He was badly shaken by the ordeal, but it was to have the fortunate consequence of turning public sympathy in his favour. When the news of the events in Boston became widely known, people were sorry for the way he had been treated. They recalled that he had asked only to be allowed to act in America; he had not expected people to accept him socially. In return, he had been abused and persecuted. When he played Lear, in New York, on 4 January 1826, the audience did all they could to show their friendliness. When he spoke the line, 'I am a man more sinned against than sinning,' there was a great burst of applause, as they applied the words not to Lear but to Kean himself. New York wanted to give Boston a lesson in how to treat a genius. Again, the jealousy between the two cities had worked in Kean's favour and, perhaps, in the last analysis, he had reason to be grateful to Boston.

On 18 January 1826, he opened at Philadelphia, where he played successfully until 2 February. He then returned to New York, where he played from 6 February until the 24th. After New York, he went south to Charleston, where he played from 13 March until 24 April. He claimed that America was giving new life to his 'talent, health and fortune'. By the beginning of April, he had saved £2,250. He planned to stay for at least another year and perhaps settle there altogether. From Charleston, he returned to New York, where he played from 11 May until 2 June. He then went to Baltimore to give eight performances, but a disturbance on the first night caused him to run from the theatre. The riot was not so dangerous as he had feared; his supporters were making more noise than his enemies. But Kean's nerves were now completely shattered and he cancelled the remainder of the engagement. From 12 June until the 26th, he played Philadelphia without any trouble and then he rested for a month. He planned to visit Canada and then return to the States in November.

On Monday, 31 July, Kean opened in Montreal for five nights and was given a great welcome. The *Gazette de Quebec* stated: 'It is to the honour of Canada that it has been the *first* of British subjects to redeem the character of Englishmen in everything that regards the first of her tragedians.' Great actors were rare visitors to Canada and the Canadians were not going to forgo the delight of seeing the greatest of them all. He was so well received in Montreal that he extended his engagement there until 28 August.

Moreover, he was accepted socially by the local gentry and on 22 August he was the guest of honour at a public dinner in the Masonic Hall. This touched him deeply, and in the course of his speech he said: 'a waif upon the world's wide common, I expected nothing more than to drag out the remaining portion of my existence in those hard exertions of my public duties; how then I shall thank those beings who have rekindled the social spark, almost extinct, and have lighted up my heart again to friendship and esteem? It is as dew drops to the parched—as sunbeams through the prison gate—the key unlocking the barriers to society —the symbol that I have not *wholly* lost the affections of my countrymen. . . . More than on my own account, I hail this day hallowed—fast as the winds can bear these tidings to the British shores, it will enliven those who in spite of my inconsistencies and errors, watch with anxious eye my progress, and whose grateful hearts will beat like mine at the receipt of that friendship which restores me again to the rank of a gentleman!'

On 4 September, he opened at Quebec and played there until 4 October. Again, on Friday, 6 October, a public dinner was given in his honour. Much as this pleased him, he had been even more gratified the previous day, when, in the presence of local celebrities, four chiefs of the Huron Indians had ceremoniously adopted him into their tribe, bestowing on him the rank of chief and the name Alanienouidet. He was childishly delighted with this honour and, for the rest of his life, never tired of dressing up in the elaborate costume the Indians gave him. He was often to express the desire to leave civilisation and live with the Indians in the wilderness. When his friend, Dr. John Francis, called on him at his New York hotel some weeks later, he found him: 'Full dressed, with skins tagged loosely about his person, a broad collar of bear-skin over his shoulders, his leggings, with many stripes, garnished with porcupine quills; his moccasins decorated with beads; his head decked with the war-eagle's plumes, behind which flowed massive black locks of dishevelled horse-hair; golden-colored rings pendant from his nose and ears; streaks of yellow paint over his face, massive red daubings about the eyes, with various hues in streaks across the forehead, not very artistically drawn. A broad belt surrounded his waist, with tomahawk; his arms, with shining bracelets stretched out with bow and arrow, as if ready for a mark.'

Kean completed his Canadian tour with four performances in Montreal from 19 October until the 30th. Developments in England had caused him to alter the rest of his American plans. The previous year, Elliston had recovered slowly from his paralytic stroke. His debt was estimated at £40,000 and, on 10 November 1825, he had surrendered to the Rules of the King's Bench and gone to the debtors' prison, from where he might be in a better position to make terms with his creditors. The Drury Lane committee had hoped that he would resign, but instead he had made over the management of the theatre to his son. They had not realised that he was legally entitled to do this and they were advised that the only way they now had to break his lease was to have him declared bankrupt. With the help of friends, Elliston compounded his debts and returned to Drury Lane, but this time the committee were ready for him. At a meeting held on 24 May 1826, they demanded payment of arrears amounting to £5,400. They allowed him only three days in which to pay, knowing that it was impossible for him to raise the money in time. Elliston resigned and declared himself bankrupt. The committee then invited offers for the lease of the theatre and the successful applicant was Stephen Price.

In July Price left for London to take over the management of Drury Lane. Once there, he quickly formed the opinion that Kean could be completely rehabilitated with British audiences. He wrote to Kean, advising him to come to London; indeed, he gave him the impression that his return was essential to the success of

Drury Lane. This impression was deepened by a cruel hoax that was played on Kean. While in Canada, he had received a letter, which he believed to come from Price, urging him to return at once and take possession of Drury Lane, which Price was only holding in trust for 'its true inheritor'. Kean was overjoyed, for he had always wanted to manage Drury Lane. In a spirit of unselfishness, he had replied to Price, telling him that they would share the theatre together. He was heartened by his success in the United States and Canada, and now that he had reason to believe that the British public wanted him back, he could not return home quickly enough. He abandoned his American plans and travelled to New York, where he intended playing a short farewell season before sailing for England.

Another reason for cutting short his stay in America was the presence there of Macready. Now that Price was in London, he was to send more and more English stars to the Park Theatre, which he still managed, and Macready had been among the first. His arrival had been awaited with excitement; New York wanted to compare him with Kean. On 2 October, when he had opened as Virginius, the Park Theatre could have been filled twice over. The audience had loved him. The *New York Times* stated that he was an actor who united 'with talents of uncommon eminence, an unspotted private character'. This was a stab at Kean. Macready's Macbeth was praised as a work of great originality and when he revealed his incomparable Coriolanus, he was hailed as a genius. He had played at the Park Theatre until 23 October and then moved on to Boston. The rapturous welcome he had been given by the Bostonians was partly a way of making amends for their disgusting behaviour towards Kean.

On 13 November, Kean began his farewell season in New York. He played to good houses, but the audiences were not enthusiastic. They complained that he had nothing new to offer them. After Macready, they found his performances tired and hackneyed. They were looking forward to 11 December, when Macready would return. When Kean sailed for England five days before, his departure was almost unnoticed.

CHAPTER NINE

GOD DAMN AMBITION!

On Friday, 5 January 1827, Kean came to Drury Lane to claim his inheritance and found that Price had never had any intention of handing over to him the management of the theatre. Instead he was offered a contract for twelve nights at one hundred guineas a night. Price pointed out that this was the highest salary ever paid to an actor, but this did not ease Kean's mortification at finding himself tricked and he left the theatre in a violent temper. Three days later, he faced a London audience once again. It was eighteen months since he had last acted at Drury Lane. He played Shylock, because this made the least demands on his energy. On his first entrance, he was apprehensive, but the audience were friendly and this inspired him to give a great performance. Indeed some critics thought him as good as he had ever been, but the appearance was deceptive: exhausted by his effort he was forced to spend the next day resting in bed.

Throughout January and February, he fulfilled his engagement at Drury Lane. Although he sensed a coldness in some section of the audience, his reception was, on the whole, friendly. This boosted his confidence and his arrogance returned. For Drury Lane, it was soon the bad old days all over again, with Kean arriving drunk and prostitutes thronging his dressing-room. The majority of the company had been glad to see the back of him and no one regretted his return more than James Winston. Winston had hung on after Elliston's departure, but his position under Price was by no means so powerful; the American tended to rely more on Dunn. But Winston was still busy at his favourite task of keeping everybody right. One night when Kean arrived at the theatre drunk, Winston used the occasion to lecture him on the duty of the actor towards his public. Kean listened in astonishment and then said contemptuously, 'Give me bread and cheese and a couple of whores.'

He was living at the Hummums, a seedy hotel near Covent Garden, where he held court in a suite crowded with toadies. He usually received them lying in bed, or on a sofa, for his leg was often too painful to bear the weight of his body. Over the past year, this leg had been giving him considerable pain and, soon after his return to London, he had consulted his doctor, James Carpue. The doctor diagnosed gout, told him that it was curable with care and advised him to live quietly. But Kean ignored this advice; drinking and whoring as much as ever, he had no intention of cutting down on these pleasures. One night, while Kean was dressing for Richard III, John Cooper, a member of the company, noticed that he still had on the same breeches he had worn as Othello four nights previously. Kean told him that his leg had been so painful that he had not been able to take the breeches off, but Cooper also knew that Kean had not been at his hotel since that night and had left the theatre for the tavern not only in Othello's breeches but also with his brown face.

On Saturday, 10 February, when Dr. Carpue called at the Hummums Hotel to dress Kean's leg, he told him that if he rested until Monday, he might be able to act, but if he did not, it would be out of the question. He had no sooner left than Kean went out and did not return until Monday afternoon. On his next visit, Carpue told him that if he continued to live this way, he must be prepared to have his leg amputated, as the only means of saving his life. The sole result of this advice was that Kean went about telling everyone that he had decided to have his leg cut off. Such bravado reflected his chaotic state of mind. One moment he was bragging exultantly of his powers as an actor and the next he was utterly depressed, saying that he would retire to America, where he would drink rum and die forgotten.

In the thirteen years which had elapsed since his début at Drury Lane, he had changed shockingly in appearance. The handsome face and slender figure of the young actor had deteriorated into the emaciated features, pot belly and spindly legs of the alcoholic. Although he was only thirty-nine years old, he looked like an old man. He tottered rather than walked; he was in almost constant pain. Six years later, the autopsy carried out on his body was to reveal that he had suffered from chronic gastritis and gall stones during his final years. He was also troubled by his leg. His doctor had diagnosed gout, but it may well have been a syphilitic lesion, which might explain his disordered mental condition. His venereal disease, if syphilis, could have reached a secondary or tertiary stage, resulting in possible brain damage. Moreover, the mercury compounds with which he treated the disease were certainly poisoning him, and may have damaged his central nervous system.

Since his return to England he had made no attempt to see Mary and Charles, but he was very concerned about his son's future. He wanted to give him a good start in life and so he used his influence to procure for him a cadetship with the East India Company. Mary was advised that this was a good opportunity, but it would mean that Charles would have to live abroad. She could not bear the thought of losing him and she begged him to refuse the offer. On Monday, 26 February, Charles came from Eton to see his father. He was now sixteen years old and every inch the kind of gentleman Kean admired and envied. Charles told his father that he must turn down the offer of a cadetship for the sake of his mother.

Since the Cox scandal, Charles' attitude towards his father had been ambivalent: he detested him for the suffering he had caused his mother and admired him for being so great an actor. For Charles was stagestruck; above all else, he wanted to be a tragedian like his father. When Charles refused the cadetship, Kean was angry. He told him that he must accept the offer, or expect no more help from him. Charles stood firm, so Kean told him that he could finish the present half-term at Eton and then shift for himself. Charles said that this would suit him very well, for it would leave him free to take up the profession of an actor. This disturbed Kean greatly, for he had never doubted that he would be the first and last tragedian by the name of Kean. The interview was too much for him, as he was already sick in mind and body. That night, when he acted Richard III, he had difficulty in finishing the part. At the end, he was so weak that he had to be carried from the stage.

He was about to endure an even greater trial. The news of his successful re-appearance at Drury Lane had reached his old friend, Thomas Colley Grattan, in Boulogne. The previous year, Grattan had submitted to Elliston a tragedy entitled *Ben Nazir*, but the manager had rejected it. Grattan now hoped that the return of Kean might present a more profitable opportunity and so he sent him a copy of the manuscript. The play could not have arrived at a better time. Kean wrote to Grattan, telling him that he had been reading half-a-dozen new plays, but had decided that *Ben Nazir* would be the one in which he would make his 're-generated' appearance, in a new character, before a London audience. He asked Grattan to come to England at once. Grattan was delighted with Kean's reaction. Over the past nine years, he had made a reputation for himself as a journalist and translator, but he also wanted to be known as a dramatist. He knew that his play was no masterpiece, but the fact that the leading part of Ben Nazir, the Saracen chieftain, was to be played by the greatest actor of the day and was reckoned by that actor to be one of the best parts he had read gave him reason to hope for success. He packed his bags and started for London.

On arriving, he went to see Kean. 'When I first called on him at the Hummums, one day early in 1827,' he wrote, 'he was sitting up in his bed, a buffalo-skin wrapped round him, a huge hairy cap decked with many-coloured feathers on his head, a scalping-knife in his belt, and a tomahawk in his hand. He was making up his face for a very savage look. A tumbler glass of white wine negus stood at the bedside; two shabby-looking heroes were close by, with similar potations in their reach; and a portrait painter was placed before an easel at the window taking the likeness of the renowned *Alanienouidet*, the name in which the chieftain (most sincerely) rejoiced.'

Grattan was announced by a black boy in livery. 'I saw Kean's eye kindle, somewhat, perhaps with pleasure at my visit,' he wrote; 'but more so, I thought, from the good opportunity of exhibiting himself in his savage costume. He gave a ferocious roll of his eyes, and a flourish of his tomahawk; then threw off his cap and mantle, and cordially shook me by the hand, producing from under his pillow the part of "Ben Nazir", written out from the prompter's book. The painter quickly retired; the satellite visitors soon followed; having first emptied their tumblers, and paid some extravagant compliment to their patron. Left alone with Kean, he entered fully into his situation. There was a mortified elation in his bearing which is hard to describe.'

Kean told Grattan that he had reached a crisis in his career. Although the aristocracy in the boxes remained cool, he believed that the rest of the Drury Lane audiences were for him and it seemed that he had regained his position as the leading English actor. He was convinced that to confirm himself in this position beyond all doubt, he needed only to display his powers in a new part and that part was now in his hand. Grattan wrote: 'He presented a mixture of subdued fierceness, unsatisfied triumph, and suppressed dissipation.'

Unfortunately, there was no time for further discussion. Grattan wrote: 'My visit that day was interrupted by the arrival of two other persons, gloomily dressed and closely veiled, who were introduced by the black boy with suitable mystery, but whose sex was less doubtful than their character. Kean took care to inform me (in a stage whisper, which they must have heard in the adjoining sitting room) that they were sisters—lovely creatures—the daughters of a clergyman of high respectability; that they had both fallen desperately in love with him, and came up to London together, with the most unlimited offers for his acceptance. I had no wish to pursue the subject further, but left him with the sentimental pair.'

Over the next few days, Grattan paid him several visits and, on each occasion, he was struck by the enthusiasm with which Kean talked of *Ben Nazir*. When Kean signed a contract with Price to act twenty nights in May and June, he stipulated that the play must be performed in the second week of May. At the end of February, his engagement of twelve nights completed, he left on a provincial tour, carrying with him the script, which he intended studying at every opportunity.

At the beginning of May, he was back in London, assuring everyone that he was word perfect in the part. He told Grattan that he hoped to get as much fame from *Ben Nazir* as from Maturin's *Bertram*; that he reckoned upon playing it a hundred nights; that his portrait in the part was to be immediately engraved; that a new wherry being built for him was to be named the *Ben Nazir*; that the costume in which he was to appear was to be the most splendid possible and that to ensure this he was to pay from his own pocket fifty guineas over and above the allowance from the theatre. Grattan wrote: 'Kean's confidence in the part and in *himself* was sufficient to deceive a less sanguine temperament than mine.'

In the meantime, the rehearsals were going well. All the cast knew their parts, but it was impossible to know whether Kean knew his, as he always read his lines from the script. He read them so well, however, that no one doubted the effect he would produce on the audience. He now claimed the privilege of absenting himself from further rehearsals, saying that he was unwilling to lose time from the close study he wished to give to the part. It was thought better to let him have his own way in a matter which was infinitely more important to him than to anyone else. After all, he was the one who wanted to startle London in a new part.

Grattan saw him almost daily and marvelled at the industry with which he laboured at the part. Kean would order his carriage after breakfast and set off for Kensington Gardens, where he studied for a couple of hours; sometimes he sailed his boat on the river and declaimed his lines to the water and the sky. Perhaps the most promising sign of all that Kean was his old self was his insistence that the entire interest of the play should centre on him and on him alone. He suggested several alterations, the most important being that he must speak the last words on stage and that the play must end with his death. In the past, his dictatorial attitude in this respect had caused trouble between authors and himself, but Grattan was happy enough to go along with him.

The first night of *Ben Nazir* had been fixed for Thursday, 17 May. Up to the previous evening, Kean had assured everyone that he was fully prepared. He had refused to attend the final rehearsal, saying that it would only confuse him and perhaps destroy the effect he was reserving for the actual performance. This had caused some uneasiness and Price had to decide whether to go ahead with the production as planned, or put it off for a few more nights. The question was put to Kean that night in his dressing-room. He agreed to a postponement until the following Monday, but, at the same time, insisted on his readiness to perform the part that very night if required.

On the morning of Monday, 21 May, Grattan visited Kean. The actor had taken lodgings in Duke Street and was strutting about the drawing room, decked out in the magnificent costume of Ben Nazir. He was speaking his favourite passages with great expression, but Grattan noticed, with some alarm, that he was still reading from the script. Grattan began to have serious doubts about the night's performance, but he cheered himself with the thought that Kean must at least know the main speeches and any defects on the first night would be eradicated in subsequent performances.

That night the theatre was crowded. The first two scenes of the play went well and Grattan, seated in a private box, waited anxiously for the third scene, in which Kean was to make his first appearance. He wrote: 'The intention of the author, and the keeping of the character, required him to rush rapidly on the stage, giving utterance to a burst of joyous soliloquy. What was my astonishment to see him, as the scene opened, standing in the centre of the stage, his arms crossed, and his whole attitude one of thoughtful solemnity! His dress was splendid; and thunders of applause greeted him from all parts of the house. To display the one and give time for the other, were the objects for which he stood fixed for several minutes, and sacrificed the sense of the situation. He spoke; but what a speech! The one I wrote consisted of eight or nine lines; his was two or three *sentences*, but not six consecutive words of the text. His look, his manner, his tone, were to *me* quite appalling; to any other observer they must have been incomprehensible. He stood fixed, drawled out his incoherent words, and gave the notion of a man who had been half-hanged and then dragged through a horse-pond. My heart, I confess it, sank deep in my breast. I was utterly shocked. And as the business of the play was on, and as *he* stood by, with neverless muscle and glazed eye, throughout the scene which should have been one of violent, perhaps too violent exertion, a cold shower of perspiration poured from my forehead, and I endured a revulsion of feeling which I cannot describe, and which I would not for worlds one eye had witnessed. I had all along felt that this scene would be the touchstone of the play. Kean went through it like a man in the last stage of exhaustion and decay. The act closed—a dead silence followed the fall of the curtain; and I felt, though I could not hear, the voiceless verdict of "damnation". I soon recovered myself and sat out the *butchery* to the end.'

When the curtain fell, James Wallack, the stage-manager, came forward and apologised on behalf of Kean, but the audience, not knowing the play, tended to blame the author as much as the actor. Grattan went backstage, where he saw Kean, supported by two stage-hands, going towards his dressing-room. When he saw Grattan, he lowered his head and said, 'I have ruined a fine play and myself; I cannot look you in the face.' Grattan took his hand, forgetting his own disappointment in the compassion he felt for him.

Everyone else was angry with Kean, especially Wallack, who told Grattan that before the play he had sent three summonses to Kean to come from his dressing-room. At last, he had gone to seek him himself and had found him not even dressed for the part, sobbing and in total despair. Why then, asked Wallack, had he persisted in attempting the character? Why had he ensured the ruin of the play and risked Grattan's reputation as a writer? Why had he not withdrawn and acknowledged that he had been unable to learn the part? He had urged Kean to apologise in person to the audience, but Kean refused, saying that if he attempted it, he would burst into tears. Wallack subsequently suggested to Kean that he write a letter of apology to the newspapers, but again he refused, preferring the public to believe that the fault lay with Grattan.

A few days before leaving for Boulogne, Grattan called on Kean to say goodbye. Kean seemed overwhelmed with remorse. The loss of the power of study, the inability to learn a new part, is just about the worst thing that can happen to an actor and it had happened to Kean. He had been very worried when he first realised that he could not memorise his lines. He had gone to bed early, cut down on his women and drink, but still the words would not stick in his mind. He had forced his exhausted brain to concentrate, but he could only remember odd lines. His pride would not allow him to confess to anyone his fears that his memory was gone, that his career as an actor was finished. He had kept telling himself that the words would surely come, if not today, then certainly the next day. He had deceived himself and everyone else right up to the night of the performance. In his desperation, he had hoped that when he found himself on stage the words would fall into place under the stimulus of the actual performance. He could not believe that he was finished, not at the early age of thirty-nine. As he made his first entrance, he had prayed that the words would come, but they had not come. Grattan understood some of this and pitied him. Kean had let him take the blame for the *Ben Nazir* fiasco and ruined his chances as a dramatist, but he forgave him this, because he realised that Kean's agony was far greater than his own. They said goodbye and they never saw each other again.

For the rest of the season, Kean played his old characters. Although he was unable to learn a new part, he found that he could remember his old ones perfectly. On 28 June, he finished at Drury Lane and then set off on a provincial tour. By the autumn, he was back in London, worn out and discontented. He decided to play one more season and then retire from the stage; he had concluded that this was the best thing to do, as he had nothing more to give the public. He could only go on playing his old round of characters, while Macready and other younger men overtook and passed him by. Rather than allow this to happen, he had decided to retire before any further deterioration of his powers became obvious, so that when the public remembered Edmund Kean, they would remember him at his best.

When Price learned of Kean's decision to retire, he never doubted for a moment that the farewell season would be held any-where except Drury Lane, the theatre that Kean had dominated for thirteen years and was inseparable from his fame. But Kean had still a debt to settle with the man who had refused to share with him the management of Drury Lane and so he arranged to play the final season of his career at Covent Garden.

The manager at Covent Garden was now Charles Kemble, brother of the famous actor. Since taking over the management in 1822, he had staggered from crisis to crisis. The past few seasons had been disastrous, and he was very pleased to have Kean. The playbills announced that Kean was engaged for a limited number of nights, 'having determined to leave the stage at the conclusion of the present season'. When Price learned of Kean's defection to Covent Garden, he was out for revenge. He knew of Charles Kean's wish to be an actor and he also knew that Kean was utterly opposed to this. He was certain that if Charles could be persuaded to come to Drury Lane, this would be not only a sensational attraction but also a slap in the face for Kean. He offered Charles a contract and the stagestruck boy accepted it. This was a great piece of showmanship by Price. He had promised 'a great unknown' to replace Kean at Drury Lane and, when Charles was announced, there was tremendous excitement among the theatregoing public. Kean was annoyed that Price was disturbing the serenity of his last season in this way. He was particularly irked by the manager's publicity, with its implication that Charles would be carrying on where his father had left off.

On 1 October, Charles made his début as Young Norval in Home's *Douglas*. He gave an immature performance more suited to school theatricals and the large audience were disappointed. Charles would have torn up his contract on the spot, but Price persuaded him to continue for the rest of the season. Kean was in Liverpool when Charles made his début, but he had arranged for a report to be sent to him immediately. He was relieved to learn that he had no rival in his son. He loved the boy, but had Charles been a serious contender, then he, too, would need to be regarded as an enemy.

During the season, Kean played at Covent Garden, while his son played at Drury Lane. The different theatre and the different company stimulated him; he played his great parts and he played them well. Then, suddenly, on 22 November, he collapsed

and for several days he was dangerously ill. He was away from
Covent Garden for three weeks and when he returned, the change
in him was frightful; there were ulcers on his face and his nose had
sunk considerably from erysipelas. Kemble doubted that Kean
would finish the season, but he overcame his misgivings and
celebrated the actor's return with an all-star production of
Othello. On 21 December, Kean played Othello to the Iago of
Charles Mayne Young, the Cassio of Charles Kemble and the
Desdemona of Miss Jarman.

He gave a great performance. John Doran, the theatre historian,
wrote: 'To those who saw him from the front, there was not a
trace of weakening of any power in him. But, oh ye few who
stood between the wings, where a chair was placed for him, do
you not remember the saddening spectacle of that wrecked genius
—a man in his very prime, with not merely the attributes of age
about him, but with some of the infirmities of it, which are wont
to try the heart of love itself. Have you forgotten that helpless,
speechless, fainting mass bent up in that chair; or the very unsavoury odour of that very brown, very hot, and very strong
brandy-and-water, which alone kept alive the once noble Moor?
Aye, and *still* noble Moor; for when his time came, he looked about
as from a dream, and sighed, and painfully got to his feet, swayed
like a column in an earthquake, and in not more time than is
required in the telling of it, was before the audience, as strong and
as intellectually beautiful as of old; but only happy in the applause
which gave him a little breathing space, and saved him from
falling dead upon the stage.'

After this performance, it seemed unlikely that he would ever
act again, yet less than three weeks later, on 7 January 1828, he
appeared as Richard III and, three night after this, he played Sir
Edward Mortimer in *The Iron Chest*. In the famous scene with
Wilford, so admired by Macready, the thrilling effect of the line,
'I stabbed him to the heart and my gigantic oppressor rolled lifeless at my feet,' was completely lost, as he was so weak that he had
to sink into a chair in the middle of his speech.

He was forced to cancel his performances for a month. Since
his return from America, he had found that only if he rested

continuously between performances was he able to fulfil his usual commitment of playing three times a week. But he could not stick to this regimen; most of his time away from the theatre was spent in taverns and brothels. Since the Cox scandal, he had lost all respectability in private life; he was ignored by his former friends in polite society, with a few exceptions such as Grattan. He saw no reason now to conceal his depravities. He lived openly with an Irish prostitute named Ophelia Benjamin. She was a handsome woman, probably a gipsy, and she had a ferocious temper. She had moved in with him and insisted on being called 'Mrs. Kean'. Their chief delights, outside of copulation, were drinking and fighting with one another. She was, at times, too much for him and he frequently ordered her from his house, but she defied all his attempts to get rid of her. His cronies were terrified of her. On one occasion, he threw her out and then gave a party to celebrate his freedom, but she burst in upon the company, drunk and belligerent. The guests scattered and the victorious Ophelia was reinstated as Mrs. Kean. In spite of the misery she often caused him, Kean had a deep need of her. He had lost his wife and mistress, but he found some kind of consolation in her stinking, unwashed arms. On a sheet of paper discovered after his death, he stated, 'the Villainy of the Irish strumpet, Ophelia Benjamin, has undone me & though I despise her, I feel life totally useless without her. I leave her my curses.'

For a month, in January, 1828, he escaped from Ophelia to his house in Scotland. The rest revived him and, on his return, he acted with something of his old form. In March, Hazlitt saw him play Shylock and thought the performance as great as it had been on that marvellous night when he had first hailed the advent of Kean. He was disturbed by the obvious reluctance of some sections in the audience, particularly in the boxes, to show their appreciation of the excellent acting they had witnessed. He had been in Italy during the Cox scandal and had recently returned to dramatic criticism. In his review of Kean's Shylock, in the *Examiner*, he used the occasion to attack the hypocrisy of those who made that scandal the pretext for the continued persecution of the actor.

'Let a great man "fall into misfortune",' he wrote, 'and then you discover the real dispositions of the reading, seeing, believing, loving public towards their pretended idol. See how they set upon him the moment he his down, how they watch for the smallest slip, the first pretext to pick a quarrel with him, how slow they are to acknowledge worth, how they never forgive an error, how they trample upon and tear "to tatters, to very rags", the commou frailties, how they overlook and malign the transcendent excellence which they can neither reach nor find a substitute for! . . . Who that had felt Kean's immeasurable superiority in *Othello*, was not glad to see him brought to the ordinary level in a vulgar *crim-con*? . . . Such is the natural feeling; and then comes the philosophical critic, and tells you with a face of lead and brass that "no more indulgence is to be shewn to the indiscretions of a man of genius than to any other!" What! you make him drunk and mad with applause then blame him for not being sober, you lift him to a pinnacle, and then say he is not to be giddy, you own he is to be a creature of impulse, and yet you would regulate him like a machine, you expect him to be all fire and air, to wing the empyrean, and to take you with him, and yet you would have him a muck-worm crawling the earth!'

Leigh Hunt was to add his voice to the defence of Kean. He, too, had noticed that while those who congregated in the pit applauded the quality of Kean's acting, the rest of the audience were reluctant to show their appreciation. The occupants of the boxes behaved as though they had been dragged to the theatre against their will. Hunt wrote, in the *Tatler*: 'Do at least justice to your own discernment, be at the trouble of applauding what you think worth going to see, and let not the town-talk with which a man of genius has been mixed up, and with which his genius has nothing to do, induce you to sit as if you were afraid to applaud him, and had no business where you are.' Hunt and Hazlitt had made their pleas, but to little or no effect. To the majority of theatregoers, Kean was, according to their disposition, a moral leper, a curiosity, or the inspiration of innumerable dirty jokes. After the Cox scandal, Kean was never to carry an entire audience with him. He had the support of the pit, but he was never to bridge the gulf between himself and the rest of the audience. His words evoked no response from them, but drifted away into a void, deep and cold; to a great artist like Kean this was death.

In the spring of 1828, while Kean was acting at Covent Garden, his son was playing to thin audiences at Drury Lane. All the critics were agreed that Charles did not have the genius of his father and that at best he would amount to nothing more than a competent actor, but the boy was determined to make the stage his career and when the season ended, he went to the provinces to learn his trade.

On 1 May, Kean closed his farewell engagement at Covent Garden and left immediately for Paris, where he was to play a short season with the English company at the Salle Favart Theatre. The French Romantics had discovered Shakespeare and this had led to a great interest in the English manner of presenting his plays. Two years previously a permanent English company had been established at the Odéon, made up of players from Drury Lane, Covent Garden and leading provincial theatres. The company was not very distinguished and their greatest star was Harriet Smithson, of Drury Lane. Miss Smithson was well enough liked in England, but had never caused the excitement there that she did in Paris. The French adored her, especially as Juliet and Desdemona, but they were not entirely satisfied by the efforts of the other members of the company. They wanted to see Shakespeare acted by the greatest English tragedians; they wanted Macready and, above all, they wanted Kean. Macready came in April and played to enthusiastic audiences, but the news that Kean was coming caused the greatest excitement. To the French, he was the only Shakespearian actor. They had heard of his illness and they wanted to see him before he died.

On 12 May, when Kean opened in Paris as Richard III, the crowded audience were disappointed. The farewell season at Covent Garden had exhausted him and all they saw was a tired man struggling through his part. When he played Othello to the Desdemona of Harriet Smithson, he seemed like a ghost, but a majestic ghost, leaving the audience to imagine how glorious it had been in life. Three days after Kean's departure for London, Macready returned to Paris, where he was now acclaimed as the greatest Shakespearian actor of the age. On his last night the audience crowned him with a wreath of flowers.

Kean spent the summer resting at his home on the Isle of Bute. Charles, who was playing the Scottish theatres, visited him there. Now that Kean need not fear his son as a rival he was pleased to make up the quarrel between them. In September, he came down to Glasgow to play Brutus to Charles's Titus, in Payne's tragedy. When Brutus fell on Titus's neck and cried, 'Embrace thy wretched Father,' the audience burst into applause. Kean whispered in his son's ear, 'Charley, we're doing the trick.'

The long rest in the summer revitalised him and he was happy in the friendship of his son. With this feeling of well-being, all thoughts of retirement left him. From 13 October, he played regularly at Covent Garden. Whenever his energy returned, so did his ambition and his determination to retain his throne became as strong as ever. Since the *Ben Nazir* fiasco, he had fallen back on his old parts, but now he decided to master a new one. He believed this essential if he were to keep his place as the leading English actor. He knew that the public were tired of his old parts; they had seen them year in and year out. As his performances never varied, they knew every gesture and intonation by heart; they could even count the number of steps he would take on stage between one position and another. Too many people for his liking were saying that Macready had already superseded him, so the role he chose was that of Virginius in Knowles's tragedy. This was a direct challenge to Macready, for the part was one of his greatest triumphs. With difficulty, Kean managed to learn most of the lines and the play was produced on 15 December. The only remarkable thing about Kean's Virginius was that he performed it without loss of memory. In no other way did he equal Macready and, after three performances, the play was dropped.

His new-found energy did not last. On 12 January 1829, while dressing for Richard II, he was seized with a violent ague and the play was cancelled. He was ill for three months and then, in the spring, he set off with Charles on a tour of Irish theatres. At Cork on 9 April, he collapsed, while playing Macbeth, and was laid up for ten days with paralysis of the legs. The doctors thought he would die, but, by the beginning of May, he was acting again. He was out on his feet, like a punch-drunk boxer; he could not even remember the names of the towns where he was engaged to play. He was eating nothing and he kept himself going on brandy mixed with ginger. In Dublin, he collapsed again, but, within a fortnight, he was back on the stage. By the end of the month, he was too ill to continue and he returned to his home in Scotland.

He found little peace there. Ophelia was with him and her behaviour was so outrageous that it became a scandal in the district. She was rapidly alienating his few remaining friends. Charles would not stay under the same roof as her, and that summer she cost Kean the services of his secretary, Phillips. Kean was upset at losing Phillips, who for thirteen years had been a friend as well as an employee. He offered the vacant post to Tom Cunningham, the actor, stating the terms as '£50 a year and as much bub and grub as you can stow in you'. Cunningham declined the post, which was eventually filled by John Lee.

In August, while Kean was in Scotland, Covent Garden was seized by creditors and advertised for sale. Over the past seven years, Charles Kemble had accumulated debts totalling more than £20,000. In this, his latest crisis, the theatrical profession came to his aid. Leading players offered to perform for nothing to help the theatre out of its difficulties. Kean wrote from Scotland, promising three performances. As a result of these offers, Kemble was given a respite by his creditors. Then one of those marvellous events occurred that blaze intermittently across the course of theatre history: out of a conjunction of disastrous circumstances, a star was born.

On 5 October, Kemble opened the season with *Romeo and Juliet*. Juliet was played by his nineteen-year-old daughter, Fanny; it was her first appearance on the stage. She did not want to be an actress, but the situation was serious and her father hoped that her youth and beauty would appeal to the audience. Her début was sensational; no girl had delighted London so much since Eliza O'Neill. Throughout October and November, she played three times a week to crowded houses. She saved Covent Garden from bankruptcy as Kean had once saved Drury Lane.

This was the situation when Kean arrived in London and told Kemble that he would play the three nights he had promised on Monday, Wednesday, and Friday of the week beginning 29 November. Kemble told him that his daughter was advertised for these nights and that he saw no reason to alter this arrangement. He was hoping that Kean, in a spirit of chivalry would give way, but Kean would allow no one to take precedence over him, not even an innocent young girl. He refused to act on the 'off nights', as he termed them and he severed his connection with Covent Garden, patched up his quarrel with Price and went back to Drury Lane.

From December until March of the following year, he played regularly at Drury Lane. He was back where he belonged, and this inspired him to give of his best. While he could still play his old parts with some energy, these efforts to equal past performances were exhausting him rapidly, yet his ambition urged him on to even greater efforts. His success in learning Virginius encouraged him to try another new part and he chose to add to his repertory of Shakespeare's heroes the role of Henry V. The play was scheduled for 22 February, but, at the very last moment, he pleaded illness and the play was withdrawn.

He should have confessed there and then that he had been unable to learn the part, but to have done so would have been an admission that he was no longer the leading English actor. He could not bring himself to believe this; he was convinced that he was as great as he had ever been; he saw no reason to fall back on his old parts while Macready was carrying all before him. He went ahead with his plans to play Henry V, hoping that, in the event of his memory failing him, the magnetism of his very presence on the stage would be enough to overcome the handicap; that he might even invent words that would equal or even surpass those of Shakespeare. So ambition obliterated his judgement and the preparations for the play went forward.

Henry V was produced on 8 March, 1830. Kean appeared on the stage, magnificent in robes of crimson and purple velvet. He was greeted with applause, but it soon became apparent that he did not know the part; not more than four consecutive lines were delivered by him. The other players had to abbreviate and transpose their speeches to retain some coherency. It was *Ben Naẓir* all over again, but this time there was no new play by an unknown author to obscure the issue; this time there was no Grattan to take the blame. Kean stood exposed as an actor who did not know his lines. The audience were outraged and they hissed him at every exit. He looked anxious and bewildered. A long delay between the fourth and fifth act destroyed whatever restraint they had previously exercised and, when the fifth act eventually commenced, their mood was dangerous. Kean came forward to apologise. 'Ladies and gentlemen,' he said, 'I have for many years shared your favour with my brother actors, but this is the first time I have ever incurred your censure. (Cries of "No") I have worked hard, ladies and gentlemen, for your amusement, but time and other circumstances must plead my apology. I stand here in the most degraded situation and call upon you, as my countrymen, to show your usual liberality.' He tried to continue his performance, but he obviously did not know his lines and the play ended in uproar.

The following day, he wrote a letter to the newspapers, pleading 'want of energy' and 'failure of memory', the consequences of 'a long and severe illness'. He urged in his defence that it was only to gratify the public that he had undertaken the arduous study of a new character and if, in this attempt, he had counted too much on his mental and physical strength, this was evidence of zeal in the service of his patrons. He was terrified that he had broken the slender thread of goodwill, which had been established between himself and his public. His spirits had never completely recovered from the outcry that had followed the Cox scandal and the thought of another persecution sickened him. In a personal letter to his friend, W. H. Halpin, editor of the *Star*, he wrote: 'Fight for me, I have no resources in myself; mind is gone, and body is hopeless. God knows my heart. I would do, but cannot. Memory, the first of goddesses, has forsaken me, and I am left without a hope but from those old resources that the public and myself are tired of. Damn, God damn ambition. The soul leaps, the body falls.'

Ambition, like a poison in his system, ebbed and flowed. He now prayed that if the public would only forgive him, he would attempt no more than he had already accomplished; he would fall back willingly on his old parts, hackneyed and threadbare though they were. If was an ordeal for him to face an audience again, but he did so, a week later, as Richard III. He need not have worried; his letter of apology had been sympathetically received. Even his old enemy, *The Times*, had agreed that it reflected great credit on him. At his first entrance, he was nervous and perspiring freely, but some friendly applause heartened him. When he cried, 'Richard's himself again!' the pit cheered him. The upper classes remained unmoved, as they now always did at Kean's performances, but down in the pit he was forgiven by those who loved the drama and remembered the glory he had brought to it.

He played intermittently until the end of May, but the strain had been too much for him and again he announced his retirement. During June and July he gave a farewell season at the Haymarket, Drury Lane being closed for the summer. He played Richard III, Othello, Shylock, Overreach and Lear. When, as Lear, he threw away his sword and cried, 'I am old now,' the pathos he gave to the line was doubly moving, as the audience applied the words to his own state. It was hard for them to realise that this actor, who had reached the end of his career, was only forty-two years old. On 19 July, he took his benefit at the King's Theatre, because the Haymarket was too small to hold the vast number of people who wanted to witness his final performance on the London stage. He gave highlights from five of his greatest parts: the fourth act of *Richard III*, the second act of *Macbeth*, the third act of *Othello*, the fourth act of *The Merchant of Venice* and the fifth act of *A New Way to Pay Old Debts*. It was a brilliant occasion; everything a farewell performance should be. The applause was warm and generous. In his final speech, he said that he hoped the English people would always select 'a proper person to fill the theatrical throne' and he wished them 'a long—a last—farewell'.

He planned to continue his farewells through the provinces and America, but again his health broke down. In Manchester, he had an attack of 'purulent ophthalmia'. His condition was so serious that he would not trust the local doctors, but sent for a specialist, George Douchez, from London. Douchez found him acting Richard III so blind that he could only distinguish the other characters by their voices. Kean had to abandon his plans for visiting America and, ironically, this forced him to change his mind about retiring. He had been hoping that an American tour would bring him a lot of money and the truth was that without this money he could not afford to retire. Although he must have made at least £150,000 since his Drury Lane début, he had not a penny to show for it. Over the years, he had squandered his money on drink and women, and on handouts to the toadies who surrounded him. Many of his cheques were signed under the influence of drink. Anyone who had helped him when he was poor had a special claim on his purse. His generosity in this respect was the wonder of the theatrical world. Mary, too, had made the money fly, with her fine house and servants, and her delight in playing Lady Bountiful to her numerous Irish relatives.

So, by January of the following year, 1831, he was back at Drury Lane, much to the amusement of the press, which made great fun of his second retirement. The theatre was under new management; Price had resigned, having found it impossible to make a profit. Kean had put in a bid, but the lease went to Alexander Lee. Kean had always wanted a theatre of his own and that spring he leased the King's Theatre at Richmond, a small country town, just outside London. He formed a company with himself as leading tragedian and from this time on he was to divide his time between Richmond, London, and the provinces. He accepted all the engagements he could get, for now that he was in the chancy business of theatre management he needed more money than ever.

He made his home at Richmond, in a cottage adjoining the theatre. Shortly after his arrival, he put himself in the care of the local doctor, James Smith. It was a strange experience for Smith when he first visited the slovenly cottage presided over by Ophelia. He could hardly believe that the feeble little man, who hobbled about the house, could be the great Edmund Kean who was still capable of rousing audiences by the passion of his acting. He learned that Kean did not take an ounce of solid food for weeks on end, but kept himself going on brandy. He visited Kean regularly and did all he could to make him cut down on his drinking, but no regimen could work where Ophelia was in charge.

All this changed when Aunt Tid came to visit Kean. She was now an old lady of seventy, but her character was as formidable as ever. She chased Ophelia from the house and moved in herself to nurse him. She nursed him so devotedly that at first Dr. Smith believed her to be his mother. When he eventually learned from her that this was not so, he asked her if she were related to Kean in some other way. She told him that she was not, but that she had known him from early childhood. She said that it was hard to see him fading away like this and she burst into tears.

Whenever the weather was fine, Kean and Aunt Tid went for a daily drive through Richmond Park, she erect and grey, he, beside her, huddled and bent. One day, the actress Helena Faucit, then a girl of fourteen, saw them walking together on the green. 'I was startled and frightened at what I saw,' she wrote; 'a small pale man in a fur cap, and wrapped in a fur coat. He looked to me as if come from the grave. A stray lock of very dark hair crossed his forehead, under which shone eyes which looked dark, and yet bright as lamps. So large were they, so piercing, so absorbing, I could see no other features. I shrank from them behind my sister, but she whispered to me that it would be unkind to show any fear, and so we approached and were kindly greeted by the pair. Oh, what a voice was that which spoke! It seemed to come from far away—a long, long way behind him.'

Despite his frailness, he was still acting. From August to October, 1831, in addition to playing at Richmond, he appeared twice a week at the Haymarket. In November, he was on the road again, playing, between lengthening bouts of illness, right through to May, 1832, when he was again in London, at Drury Lane and the Haymarket. His performances had become miserably tricky; he gabbled over some parts in his hurry to reach the 'points', but, occasionally the lightning would still flash and irradiate the theatre. At the best of times, he was hardly fit enough to stand upright on the stage; even Shylock, the least demanding of his roles, had become too much for him. At the end of his scene with Tubal, he was too exhausted to make his exit and so he changed the line 'Go, go, Tubal, and meet me at our synagogue,' to 'Lead me to our synagogue.' Then, supported by Tubal, he was able to make his way off the stage.

His Richard III was even more decrepit. He tottered across the stage with difficulty, using his sword as a stick. Doran, who saw him play the part at the Haymarket, in 1832, wrote: 'The sight was pitiable. Genius was not traceable in that bloated face; intellect was all but quenched in those once matchless eyes; and the power seemed gone, despite the will that would recall it. I noted in a diary, that night, the above facts, and, in addition, by bursts he was as grand as he had ever been . . . his old attitude of leaning at the side scene, as he contemplated Lady Anne, was as full of grace as ever,—save that the contemplator had now a swollen and unkingly face. . . . In the scene with the Mayor and Buckingham, he displayed talent unsurpassable . . . but he was exhausted before the fifth act, and when, after a short fight, Richmond gave him his death-wound in Bosworth Field, as he seemed to deal the blow, he grasped Kean by the hand, and let him gently down, lest he should be injured by a fall.'

The public were now tolerant of his shortcomings; he had become an institution, a battered relic, a picturesque ruin. Many came to see him out of curiosity, but there were those who were conscious of the aura of immortality about him, who sensed that in the years to come they would be proud to remember that they had seen Edmund Kean. They were wiser than they knew, for Kean founded no school; his interpretations were too personal to be reproduced by other actors. His imitators could only copy the externals of his art, without the unique power that made these meaningful. He had achieved much. He had shaken the hold of the classical school and had marvellously expressed on the stage the romantic spirit of the times, but romantic tragic acting was to develop not through Kean, but through Macready.

The past and present were closing in around him. In September, he had a letter from Nance Carey, asking to see him and telling him that she was sick and lonely. He brought her to live with him at Richmond and, as a result, Aunt Tid left. Nance's arrival was too much for her; she had hoped to nurse Kean until he died. She had always rejoiced that she had been the first to foster his genius as an actor; this was the source of her deep and fierce possessiveness towards him. Nance, on the other hand, had never done anything for him, deserting him in his infancy and living on his earnings as soon as he became useful to her. Yet now, in the end, it was obvious that he preferred her to Aunt Tid. As soon as Dr. Smith saw Nance, he had no doubt that she was Kean's mother; he had never seen so great a resemblance between mother and child. Kean was consoled by Nance's presence; she was low and dissipated, a superannuated whore, but she was his mother and he was happy to be with her.

All bitterness and hatred had left him. On 6 December, he sent Mary the first friendly letter since their separation. He wrote: 'Let us be no longer fools. Come home; forget and forgive. If I have erred, it was my head, not my heart, and most severely have I suffered for it. My future life shall be employed in contributing to your happiness; and you, I trust, will return that feeling by a total obliteration of the past.' But Mary could not bring herself to forget the harm he had done her; she did not go to him, but continued to live her own life.

Over the past two years, there had been great changes in the theatrical world. Elliston had died on 8 July 1831, and on 30 May 1832, Charles Mayne Young had retired from the stage. At the end of his farewell performance, he had told the audience that he was 'loath to remain before his patrons until he had nothing better to present to them than tarnished metal'. This was interpreted as a dig at Kean. Young was to enjoy a long and comfortable retirement; he was a cautious man, who had always saved his money. Urbane and equable, he was welcomed everywhere for his amusing reminiscences of the theatre. He would often speak pityingly of Kean and recall, as a boy, coming downstairs to his father's dinner party and noticing the little guttersnipe, with the astonishing black eyes, looking upwards at him from the hall.

With the departure of Young, Kean and Macready were the only tragedians of merit. Throughout their careers, they had never played together. On 5 November, 1832, Kean began his last season at Drury Lane. He had been given a contract on condition that he acted with Macready. This time he could not run away, because he badly needed the money. At long last he was to fight it out with Macready, but by this time he was half dead. On 26 November, he played Othello to the Iago of Macready. This was the play in which he had defeated both Booth and Young, and remembering these great contests, the public flocked to Drury Lane. Lewes wrote: 'I remember the last time I saw him as Othello, how puny he appeared beside Macready, until the third act, when roused by Iago's taunts and insinuations, he moved towards him with a gouty hobble, seized him by the throat, and, in a well-known explosion, "Villain, be sure thou prove my love a whore," seemed to swell into a stature which made Macready appear small.' But, considered as a whole, it was a patchy performance and he did not gain a victory over his younger rival.

The conjunction of Kean and Macready caused such interest that *Othello* was played twice a week throughout December. The play was billed again for 25 January 1833, but Kean was too ill to play. On 19 February, he acted at Brighton, but collapsed in the middle of the performance. He had missed so many engagements through illness that he was desperately short of money. He asked Captain Polhill, the new lessee of Drury Lane, for the loan of £500 against future earnings, but Polhill considered him too ill to take the risk. Kean was offended and went over to Covent Garden.

There, on Monday, 25 March, he played Othello to the Iago of Charles. This attracted a great crowd, as father and son had never played together in London. When Charles arrived at the theatre, he was told that his father wished to see him. He went to the dressing-room, where he found him weak and shivering. Kean said, 'I am very ill. I am afraid I shall not be able to act.' After drinking some brandy, he seemed better and he allowed himself to be dressed for the part. By the end of his first scene, he was already exhausted. He sat in the wings drinking brandy and again this seemed to revive him. He said to a fellow-actor, 'Charles is getting on well tonight—he's acting very well—I suppose that is because he is acting with me.'

Before the curtain rose on the third act, he said to his son, 'Mind, Charles, that you keep before me. Don't get behind me in this act. I don't know that I shall be able to kneel; but if I do, be sure to lift me up.' At first, all was well and he went off with Desdemona; but, at his next entrance, where Othello says, 'What! false to me?' he could hardly walk across the stage. He held up until the celebrated farewell, which had moved Hazlitt so profoundly in that first London season. He spoke the lines beginning,

O now, for ever,
Farewell the tranquil mind! Farewell content!

and ending with the words, 'Othello's occupation's gone'. His delivery of the Farewell had never altered throughout his career. George Vandenhoff, the actor, wrote: 'It ran on the same tones and semitones, had the same rests and breaks, the same *forte* and *piano*, the same *crescendo* and *diminuendo*, night after night, as if he spoke it from a musical score. And what beautiful, what thrilling music it was! the music of a broken heart—the cry of a despairing soul.' A drunken hoarseness had ruined his voice, but such was the desolation that sounded in his tones and expressed itself in gestures that the audience burst into applause.

Then a great silence fell as he moved towards his son. He attempted the speech, 'Villain, be sure thou prove my love a whore,' and at this very point, where a few weeks before he had dwarfed Macready, his head sank on his son's shoulder. He threw his arms around him and whispered, 'I am dying—speak to them for me.' But this time the audience did not demand the apology they had heard so often in the past; they watched quietly as he was carried from the stage.

He lay unconscious on the sofa in his dressing-room; he was as cold as ice and his pulse was scarcely beating. Several doctors from the audience tried unsuccessfully to revive him. He was carried to the nearby Wrekin Tavern, in Broad Court, and put to bed. He was so ill that no attempt was made until the next morning to wash the make-up from his face. He remained there until Saturday afternoon, when he was taken home to Richmond. For three weeks, he was critically ill, but by the end of April, he had recovered sufficiently to be driven as far as Chelsea to call on Aunt Tid. The excursion was too much for him and he had a relapse. Only now, when death was imminent, could Mary bring herself to visit him. He died on 15 May 1833, at twenty minutes past nine in the morning; he was forty-five years old.

BIBLIOGRAPHY

UNPUBLISHED SOURCES

Drury Lane Agreements Between Robert William Elliston and Edmund Kean as to Performances at the Theatre Royal Drury Lane. 20 July, 1824; 17 March, 1825. (Folger Shakespeare Library. Y.d. 387, 388)

PERIODICALS

Champion 1814, 1819.
Examiner 1814, 1815, 1817, 1825, 1828.
London Magazine 1820.
Morning Chronicle 1814, 1825.
Morning Herald 1819.
Morning Post 1814, 1817.
Tatler 1828.
Theatrical Inquisitor 1819.
Times 1814, 1818, 1825, 1830.

BOOKS AND ARTICLES

Archer, William. *William Charles Macready.* Kegan Paul, Trench, Trübner & Co., 1890.

Arnott, James Fullarton, *and* Robinson, John William. *English Theatrical Literature 1559–1900: a Bibliography Incorporating Robert W. Lowe's A Bibliographical Account of English Theatrical Literature, Published in 1888.* Society for Theatre Research, 1970.

Baker, Henry Barton. *The London Stage: its History and Traditions from 1576 to 1888.* 2 vols. W.H. Allen & Co., 1889.

Bingham, Madeleine. *Sheridan: the Track of a Comet.* George Allen & Unwin, 1972.

Boaden, James. *Memoirs of the Life of John Philip Kemble.* 2 vols. Longman, Hurst, Rees, Orme, Brown and Green, 1825.

Borgerhoff, J-L. *Le Théâtre Anglais à Paris sous la Restauration.* Paris, Hachette, 1912.

Broughton, Lord [John Cam Hobhouse]. *Recollections of a Long Life.* vols 1 and 2. John Murray, 1909.

Bucke, Charles. *The Italians . . . 5th Edition. With a Preface Containing the Correspondence of the Author with the Committee of Drury Lane Theatre; P. Moore, Esq. M.P.; and Mr. Kean.* G. and W.B. Whittaker, 1819.

Bunn, Alfred. *The Stage: both Before and Behind the Curtain.* 3 vols. Richard Bentley, 1840.

Clapp, William W. *A Record of the Boston Stage.* New York, Benjamin Blom, 1968. [Reissue of the 1853 Edition.]

[Cole, John]. *The Talents of Edmund Kean Delineated.* J. Johnston, 1817.

Cornwall, Barry. See under Procter, Bryan Waller.

Cole, John William. *The Life and Theatrical Times of Charles Kean, F.S.A.* 2 vols. Richard Bentley, 1860.

Cotton, William. *The Story of the Drama in Exeter During the Best Period 1787 to 1823. With Reminiscences of Edmund Kean.* Hamilton, Adams & Co., 1887.

Cowell, Joe. *Thirty Years Passed Among the Players of England and America.* New York, Harper & Brothers, 1844.

Creevey, Thomas. *The Creevey Papers.* Edited by Sir Herbert Maxwell. John Murray, 1905.

Dickens, Charles. *Memoirs of Joseph Grimaldi.* Edited by Richard Findlater, with new notes and introduction. MacGibbon & Kee, 1968.

Dictionary of National Biography.

Disher, Maurice Willson. *Mad Genius; a Biography of Edmund Kean, with Particular Reference to the Women who Made and Unmade Him.* Hutchinson, 1950.

Dobbs, Brian. *Drury Lane: Three Centuries of the Theatre Royal 1663–1971.* Cassell, 1972.

Donohue, Joseph W. Jr. *Dramatic Character in the English Romantic Age.* New Jersey, Princeton, Princeton University Press, 1970.

— *The Theatrical Manager in England and America.* New Jersey, Princeton, Princeton University Press, 1971.

Doran, John. *In and About Drury Lane.* 2 vols. Richard Bentley, 1881.

—*Their Majesties' Servants; Annals of the English Stage from Thomas Betterton to Edmund Kean.* 3 vols. John C. Nimmo, 1888.

Downer, Alan S. (editor). *Oxberry's 1822 Edition of King Richard III, with Descriptive Notes Recording Edmund Kean's Performance Made by James H. Hackett.* Facsimile Edition. Society for Theatre Research, 1959.

Farington, Joseph. *The Farington Diary.* Vols VII and VIII. Edited by James Greig. Hutchinson, 1922–1928.

Finlay, John. *Miscellanies.* Dublin, John Cumming, 1835.

Fitzgerald, Percy. *The Kembles.* 2 vols. Tinsley Brothers, 1871.

— *A New History of the English Stage from the Restoration to the Liberty of the Theatres . . .* 2 vols. Tinsley Brothers, 1882.

Fletcher, Ifan Kyrle. *The Life and Theatrical Career of Edmund Kean 1787–1833.* [Sale Catalogue] 1938.

Francis, John W. *Old New York, or, Reminiscences of the Past Sixty Years.* New York, Charles Roe, 1858.

Fulford, Roger. *Samuel Whitbread 1764–1815: a Study in Opposition.* Macmillan, 1967.

[Genest, John]. *Some Account of the English Stage, from the Restoration in 1660 to 1830.* 10 vols. Thomas Rodd, 1832.

Grattan, Thomas Colley. *Beaten Paths; and Those who Trod Them.* Chapman and Hall, 1865.

Hartnoll, Phyllis (editor). *The Oxford Companion to the Theatre.* Oxford University Press, 1965.

Hawkins, F.W. *The Life of Edmund Kean, from Published and Original Sources.* 2 vols. Tinsley Brothers, 1869.

Hazlitt, William. *A View of the English Stage, or a Series of Dramatic Criticisms.* Edited by W. Spencer Jackson. George Bell, 1906.

Hillebrand, Harold Newcomb. *Edmund Kean.* New York, Columbia University Press, 1933.

Hornblow, Arthur. *A History of the Theatre in America: from its Beginnings to the Present Time.* 2 vols. New York, Benjamin Blom, 1965.

Howard, Diana. *London Theatres and Music Halls, 1850–1950.* Library Association, 1970.

Howe, Percival Presland. *The Life of William Hazlitt.* Martin Secker, 1922.

[Hunt, Leigh]. *Critical Essays on the Performers of the London Theatres.* John Hunt, 1807.

Hunt, Leigh. *Dramatic Criticism 1808–1831.* Edited by Lawrence Huston Houtchens and Carolyn Washburn Houtchens. Oxford University Press, 1950.

Jerrold, William Blanchard. *The Life and Remains of Douglas Jerrold.* William Kent, 1858.

Johnson, Edgar. *Sir Walter Scott: the Great Unknown.* 2 vols. Hamish Hamilton, 1970.

Joseph, Bertram. *The Tragic Actor.* Routledge & Kegan Paul, 1959.

[Kelly, Michael]. *Reminiscences of Michael Kelly. . . .* ; edited by Theodore Hook. 2 vols. Henry Colburn, 1826.

Kemble, Frances Anne. *Record of a Girlhood.* Richard Bentley, 1878.

Kimmel, Stanley. *The Mad Booths of Maryland.* New York, The Bobbs-Merrill Company, 1940.

Lamb, Charles. *The Dramatic Essays of Charles Lamb.* Edited with an Introduction and Notes by Brander Matthews. Chatto & Windus, 1891.

Lewes, George Henry. *On Acting and the Art of Acting.* Smith, Elder & Co., 1875.

Maclean, Catherine Macdonald. *Born Under Saturn: a Biography of William Hazlitt.* Collins, 1943.

Macready, William Charles. *Reminiscences and Selections from His Diaries and Letters.* Edited by Sir Frederick Pollock, Bart. 2 vols. Macmillan, 1875.

Marchand, Leslie A. *Byron: a Biography.* 3 vols. John Murray, 1957.

Maude, Cyril (editor). *The Haymarket Theatre: some Records and Reminiscences.* Grant Richards, 1903.

Melville, Lewis. *The Beaux of the Regency.* 2 vols. Hutchinson, 1908.

Molloy, J. Fitzgerald. *The Life and Adventures of Edmund Kean, Tragedian 1787–1833.* 2 vols. Ward and Downey, 1888.

Nalbach, Daniel. *The King's Theatre 1704–1867: London's First Italian Opera House.* Society for Theatre Research, 1972.

Nelson, Alfred L. 'The Winston Diaries.' *Theatre Notebook.* Autumn 1970.

Nelson, Alfred L., *and* Cross, Gilbert B. *Drury Lane Journal: Selections from James Winston's Diaries 1819–1827.* Society for Theatre Research, 1974.

Nicoll, Allardyce. *A History of English Drama 1660–1900.* 5 vols. Cambridge University Press, 1955.

    Vol. III *Late Eighteenth Century Drama 1750–1800.*

    Vol. IV *Early Nineteenth Century Drama 1800–1850.*

Odell, George C.D. *Annals of the New York Stage.* 15 vols. New York, Columbia University Press, 1927.

    Vol. 2 [1798–1821].

    Vol. 3 [1821–1834].

    Shakespeare—from Betterton to Irving. 2 vols. Constable, 1963.

Partridge, Eric. *A Dictionary of Slang and Unconventional English.* 2 vols. Routledge & Kegan Paul, 1967.

Phippen, Francis. *Authentic Memoirs of Edmund Kean, of the Theatre Royal, Drury Lane.* J. Roach, 1814.

Playfair, Giles. *Kean: the Life and Paradox of the Great Actor.* Reinhardt & Evans, 1950.

— *Six Studies in Hypocrisy.* Secker and Warburg, 1969.

Pope, W.J. Macqueen. *Theatre Royal, Drury Lane.* W.H. Allen, 1945.

[Procter, Bryan Waller 'Barry Cornwall']. *The Life of Edmund Kean.* 2 vols. Edward Moxon, 1835.

Raymond, George. *The Life and Enterprises of Robert William Elliston, Comedian.* G. Routledge, 1857.

Reese, D. James. *Old Drury of Philadelphia: a History of the Philadelphia Stage.* Philadelphia, University of Pennsylvania, 1932.

Robinson, Henry Crabb. *Diary, Reminiscences, and Correspondence.* Selected and Edited by Thomas Sadler. 3 vols. Macmillan, 1869.

Rosenfeld, Sybil. *Strolling Players and Drama in the Provinces 1660–1765.* Cambridge, University Press, 1939.

Ruggles, Eleanor. *Prince of Players: Edwin Booth.* Peter Davies, 1953.

Scott, Sir Walter. *The Letters of Sir Walter Scott, 1817–19.* Centenary Edition vol. 5. Edited by H.J.C. Grierson. Constable & Co., 1933.

Sherwin, Oscar. *Uncorking Old Sherry: the Life and Times of Richard Brinsley Sheridan.* Vision, 1960.

Spencer, Hazelton. *Shakespeare Improved: the Restoration Versions in Quarto and on the Stage.* Cambridge, Harvard University Press, 1927.

Sprague, Arthur Colby. *Shakespeare and the Actors: the Stage Business in His Plays (1660–1905).* New York, Russell & Russell, 1963.

Vandenhoff, George. *Leaves from an Actor's Notebook.* New York, Appleton, 1860.

Young, Julian Charles. *A Memoir of Charles Mayne Young, Tragedian.* Macmillan, 1871.

INDEX

CG indicates Theatre Royal, Covent Garden
DL indicates Theatre Royal, Drury Lane